Free Video  # Free Video

MW00574448

Essential Test Tips Video from Trivium Test Prep

Dear Customer,

Thank you for purchasing from Trivium Test Prep! We're honored to help you prepare for your medical assistant exam.

To show our appreciation, we're offering a **FREE** *Medical Assistant Exam Essential Test Tips* **Video by Trivium Test Prep.*** Our video includes 35 test preparation strategies that will make you successful on the medical assistant exam. All we ask is that you email us your feedback and describe your experience with our product. Amazing, awful, or just so-so: we want to hear what you have to say!

To receive your **FREE** *Medical Assistant Exam Essential Test Tips* **Video**, please email us at 5star@triviumtestprep.com. Include "Free 5 Star" in the subject line and the following information in your email:

1. The title of the product you purchased.
2. Your rating from 1 – 5 (with 5 being the best).
3. Your feedback about the product, including how our materials helped you meet your goals and ways in which we can improve our products.
4. Your full name and shipping address so we can send your **FREE** *Medical Assistant Exam Essential Test Tips* **Video.**

If you have any questions or concerns please feel free to contact us directly at 5star@ triviumtestprep.com.

Thank you!

– Trivium Test Prep Team

*To get access to the free video please email us at 5star@triviumtestprep.com, and please follow the instructions above.

MEDICAL ASSISTANT EXAM PREP 2019-2020

Study Guide for the RMA (Registered Medical Assistant) & CMA Certification Exams with Comprehensive Practice Test Questions

TABLE OF CONTENTS

ONLINE RESOURCES

To help you fully prepare for your certified medical assistant examination, Ascencia includes online resources with the purchase of this study guide.

FLASH CARDS

A convenient supplement to this study guide, Ascencia's flash cards enable you to review important terms easily on your computer or smartphone.

CHEAT SHEETS

Review the core skills you need to master the exam with easy-to-read Cheat Sheets.

FROM STRESS TO SUCCESS

Watch "From Stress to Success," a brief but insightful YouTube video that offers the tips, tricks, and secrets experts use to score higher on the exam.

REVIEWS

Leave a review, send us helpful feedback, or sign up for Ascencia promotions—including free books!

Access these materials at:

http://ascenciatestprep.com/medical-assisting-online-resources

INTRODUCTION

Medical assistants support physicians in various medical settings, offices, and clinics. They perform in both administrative and clinical areas, with a focus on helping patients feel comfortable and informed.

What is the CMA and RMA?

The Certified Medical Assistant (CMA) title recognizes medical assistants who pass the CMA exam, which is certified through the American Association of Medical Assistants (AAMA). The Registered Medical Assistant (RMA) title recognizes medical assistants who pass the RMA exam, which is certified through American Medical Technologists (AMT).

These certifications are important for medical assistants to demonstrate they possess the knowledge and skills necessary to provide quality health care service. The exams both test on candidates' understanding of health care support in general, clinical, and organizational areas.

WHAT IS THE AAMA?

The American Association of Medical Assistants (AAMA) is an organization that aims to provide educational support for medical assistant certification. They provide many resources for CMAs, including professional networking and scope-of-practice protection. Other resources are listed on the AAMA website (http://aama-ntl.org).

The AAMA set of core values centers on delivering quality assistance in every aspect of patient health care and strongly encourages the practice of integrity and respect in handling confidential information.

WHAT IS THE AMT?

American Medical Technologists (AMT) is an international health care certification agency intent on maintaining standards in occupations such as medical assisting. Their exams assess practitioner competency and aim to ensure that medical assistants are trained and certified according to peak industry standards.

What's on the CMA and RMA?

The CMA exam is a computerized test consisting of 200 multiple-choice questions covering three broad areas of health care delivery: general, clinical, and administrative. Only 180 questions are scored; the remaining questions are used to plan future tests. You will have 160 minutes (two hours and 40 minutes) to answer all the exam questions, which are administered in four 40-minute sections.

Section	Concepts	Number of Questions	Percentage of the Exam
General	✦ Communication ✦ Medical Ethics ✦ Medical Law/Regulatory Guidelines ✦ Medical Terminology ✦ Psychology ✦ Professionalism ✦ Risk Management, Quality Assurance and Safety	50	28%
Clinical	✦ Anatomy and Physiology ✦ Emergency Management ✦ Diagnostic Testing ✦ Infection Control ✦ Nutrition ✦ Patient Intake and Documentation of Care ✦ Patient Preparation and Provider Assistance ✦ Pharmacology ✦ Specimen Collection/Processing	85	47%
Administrative	✦ Finances ✦ Medical Business Practices ✦ Medical Reception ✦ Patient Medical Records ✦ Patient Navigator/Advocate ✦ Scheduling Appointments	45	25%
Total		180 scored questions	3 hours & 15 minutes*

This includes breaks.

The RMA examination is available to take in either paper-and-pencil or computerized format. It consists of 200 – 210 multiple-choice questions with four answer choices each, testing on three broad areas of knowledge: general, clinical, and administrative. Candidates will have 180 minutes (three hours) to complete the exam.

Section	Concepts	Percentage of the Exam
General Medical Assisting Knowledge	✦ Anatomy and Physiology ✦ Medical Terminology ✦ Medical Law ✦ Medical Ethics ✦ Human Relations ✦ Patient Education	41%
Clinical Medical Assisting	✦ Asepsis ✦ Sterilization ✦ Instruments ✦ Vital Signs/Mensuration ✦ Physical Exams ✦ Clinical Pharmacology ✦ Minor Surgery ✦ Therapeutic Modalities ✦ Lab Procedures ✦ ECG ✦ First Aid/Emergency Response	35%
Administrative Medical Assisting	✦ Insurance ✦ Finance/Bookkeeping ✦ Medical Reception	24%
Total		3 hours

How are the CMA and RMA Administered?

CMA ADMINISTRATION

The CMA exam is a computerized test administered by Prometric. Before you take the test, make sure you meet the requirements listed on the AAMA website. To schedule an exam appointment, you can find a testing center near you at http://prometric.com. The testing fees and required forms of documentation vary depending on your eligibility. Special provisions must be requested through a special accommodations form.

On the day of the test you will have the option to complete a 15-minute tutorial (it will not count as part of the exam time). The exam will then be administered in four sections. You will have 40 minutes to complete each section, for a total of 160 minutes of test time. Twenty minutes total is allowed for breaks. The maximum allotted time to complete the exam, including breaks and the tutorial, is three hours and 15 minutes.

You will receive a pass/fail notification upon completion of the test, and exam scores will be sent by mail within three weeks of taking the CMA exam. If you do not pass, you may reapply immediately. Candidates are allowed a total of three exam attempts.

RMA Administration

The RMA exam is available to take in both paper-and-pencil and computerized formats. Before you take the test, you must be officially approved by the AMT and have received an "authorization to test" letter. Ensure you are eligible and apply on their website at https://www.americanmedtech.org/.

The computerized test is administered by Pearson VUE; testing locations may be found at www.pearsonvue.com, where you may also schedule an exam appointment. The paper-and-pencil tests are only administered at certain times as scheduled by the AMT.

Results are available immediately for the computerized exams. Paper-and-pencil exam results are sent out within eight weeks of taking the test. RMA candidates who do not pass can retake the exam three times.

Recertification

CMA candidates are required to recertify their credentials every five years, and the credential must remain current. RMA candidates must recertify their credentials every three years.

How are the CMA and RMA Scored?

CMA Scoring

The CMA exam consists of 200 questions, 20 of which are unscored. These are pretest questions being considered for future exams. However, you will not know which questions are unscored and there is no penalty for wrong answers, so you should answer every question to the best of your ability.

Your CMA exam scores are calculated based on the total number of correct responses and converted to a scaled score. The AAMA requires a minimum scaled score of 430 to pass the exam. Candidates who pass the exam will earn their official CMA credential, valid for five years after certification.

RMA Scoring

The minimum passing score for the RMA exam is a 70, on a scale from 1 – 100. Each question is weighted based on difficulty and converted to a scaled score. Your raw score is the total number of correct answers, which is then converted to a standard score.

Candidates who pass the exam will earn their official RMA credential, valid for three years after certification.

Ascencia Test Prep

With health care fields such as nursing, pharmacy, emergency care, and physical therapy becoming the fastest-growing industries in the United States, individuals looking to enter the health care industry or rise in their field need high-quality, reliable resources. Ascencia Test Prep's study guides and test preparation materials are developed by credentialed industry professionals with years of experience in their respective fields. Ascencia recognizes that health care professionals nurture bodies and spirits, and save lives. Ascencia Test Prep's mission is to help health care workers grow.

ONE: PSYCHOLOGY and COMMUNICATION

Psychology

Medical assistants often encounter patients who are experiencing emotional difficulties related to medical and health care issues. For this reason, it is important to understand basic psychological concepts like human growth and development, coping mechanisms, and responses to death and dying.

ERIKSON'S THEORY OF PSYCHOSOCIAL DEVELOPMENT

Erik Erikson's theory of psychosocial development maintains that the human life cycle has eight ego development stages spanning from birth to death. A psychosocial crisis occurs at each stage, and the objective of healthy development is to successfully resolve these crises and integrate the demands of physical growth, emotional maturation, and society. Certain psychosocial tasks must be accomplished during the life cycle in order to maintain wellness.

Table 1.1. Erikson's Stages of Psychosocial Development

Stage/Age	Psychosocial Crisis	Task	Successful Resolution	Unsuccessful Resolution
Infancy: birth to 18 months	trust vs. mistrust	attachment to the mother	trust in persons; faith in environment; hope for the future	difficulties relating to others; suspicion/fear of the future
Early childhood: 18 months to 3 years	autonomy vs. shame and doubt	gaining basic control over self and environment	sense of self-control and adequacy	independence-fear conflict; sense of self-doubt
Late childhood: 3 to 6 years	initiative vs. guilt	becoming purposeful and direct	ability to initiate own activities; sense of purpose	aggression-fear conflict; sense of inadequacy

Table 1.1. Erikson's Stages of Psychosocial Development (continued)

Stage/Age	Psychosocial Crisis	Task	Successful Resolution	Unsuccessful Resolution
School aged: 6 to 12 years	industry vs. inferiority	developing physical, social, and learning skills	competence; ability to learn and work	sense of inferiority; difficulty learning
Adolescence: 12 to 20 years	identity vs. role confusion	developing a sense of identity	sense of personal identity	confusion about self-identity; identity submerged in relationships or group attendance
Early adulthood: 20 to 35 years	intimacy vs. isolation	establishing intimate bonds and friendships	ability to love and commit	emotional isolation; egocentricity
Middle adulthood: 35 to 65 years	generativity vs. stagnation	fulfilling life goals related to career, family, and society	ability to give and care for others	self-absorption; inability to develop and grow
Late adulthood: 65 years to death	integrity vs. despair	looking back over life and accepting meaning	sense of integrity and fulfillment	dissatisfaction with life

PIAGET'S THEORY OF DEVELOPMENTAL LEARNING

Jean Piaget studied the basis for development of the mind, as well as learning and cognition. His theory holds that motor activity is stimulated by mental development and growth. Infants learn that motor activity can produce sound and that cognitive interaction is associated with the environment.

Table 1.2. Piaget's Stages of Development

Developmental Period	Age Group	Description
Sensorimotor	birth to 2 years	Children learn through motor skills and senses.
Preoperational	2 to 6 years	Children start to think symbolically and develop language skills, and thinking is self-centered.
Concrete Operational	7 to 11 years	Children understand differences and begin to reason.
Formal Operations	12 to adult	Children/adults grasp abstract concepts, set long-term goals, and relate new material to the past.

Maslow's Hierarchy of Needs

Abraham Maslow developed **Maslow's hierarchy of needs**, which he theorized to be the unconscious desires that motivate people to satisfy certain needs. According to Maslow, as each stage is achieved, a person is encouraged to move to the next stage. The stages are often depicted as a pyramid: a person must meet the needs at the bottom of the pyramid before they can address needs at higher levels.

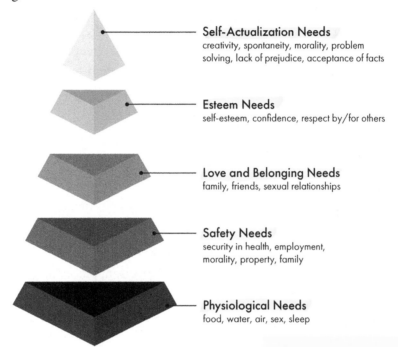

Self-Actualization Needs
creativity, spontaneity, morality, problem solving, lack of prejudice, acceptance of facts

Esteem Needs
self-esteem, confidence, respect by/for others

Love and Belonging Needs
family, friends, sexual relationships

Safety Needs
security in health, employment, morality, property, family

Physiological Needs
food, water, air, sex, sleep

Figure 1.1. Maslow's Hierarchy of Needs

Crisis and Patient Coping Mecha

For many patients, a serious illness and resulting ho
the overwhelming event or series of events that cre
unbearable. Crises often lead to disruption of norm

A situational crisis occurs when an unexpected
Examples of situational crises include an unwanted
of a loved one, onset or change in a disease process,
a violent act. Community situational crises are even
include terrorist attacks, floods, hurricanes, earthqu

The successful handling of a crisis includes fou

+ Phase 1. External precipitating event: A situation occurs, such as a death or a divorce.

+ Phase 2. Threat: A perceived or actual threat causes increased anxiety wherein the patient copes or fails to cope.

+ Phase 3. Failed coping: The patient fails to cope, which produces physical symptoms, relationship problems, and increased disorganization.
+ Phase 4. Resolution: There is mobilization of internal and external resources, and the patient returns to the precrisis level of function.

Many patients respond to crises using various coping skills they have learned over time. **Coping mechanisms** are learned external behaviors and internal thought processes used to decrease discomfort and pain. Coping behaviors can be emotion-focused or problem-focused. With **emotion-focused behaviors**, the patient alters a response to stress by thinking, saying, or doing something that makes him or her feel happier or normal. These behaviors include crying, screaming, and talking with others. **Problem-focused behaviors** are done to alter the stressor in some way, such as investigating the facts of a problem or devising a plan to overcome the situation.

DEFENSE MECHANISMS

A **defense mechanism** is an unconscious psychological process designed to protect a person from stress or emotional pain. Recognizing these defenses can help medical assistants work with distressed patients. Common defense mechanisms include:

+ denial: avoidance of a problem by refusing to recognize it or by outright ignoring it
+ displacement: transfer of feelings for a threatening person, place, or thing to a neutral person, place, or thing
+ intellectualization: expressive thinking and logic adoption to avoid uncomfortable thoughts and feelings
+ projection: assignment of personal feelings or motivation to another person, place, or thing
+ rationalization: giving logical and acceptable explanations to hide a feeling, concern, or motive that is not socially acceptable
+ regression: the demonstration of behavior characteristics from an earlier age

DEATH AND DYING STAGES

Loss is the absence of something wanted, available, and loved. With actual loss, others can identify the situation or event, whereas with perceived loss, the patient experiences something others cannot comprehend or verify. Anticipatory loss is when the patient expects and experiences the loss before it occurs.

Grief is a normal response to loss, and **mourning** is the public expression of grief. The three types of grief are acute (short-term), chronic (long-term), and anticipatory (grief before an impending loss). **Bereavement** is the time period of mourning after a loved one has died.

The medical assistant's role when handling patients' grief and loss is to provide a safe, emotionally supportive environment. When working with grieving patients and families, it is important to consider their religion, culture, and family dynamics. Medical assistants may also process patient referrals to mental health professionals.

Table 1.3. Stages of Grief and Loss Response

Stage 1: Shock and Disbelief	The survivor feels numb, has emotional outbursts, denies the situation or event, and isolates self.
Stage 2: Experiencing the Loss	The survivor feels angry regarding the loss/death, bargains regarding this event, and suffers from depression.
Stage 3: Reintegration	The survivor starts to reorganize his or her life, adapts to the situation/event, and accepts reality.

Communication

Communication is an essential part of a medical assistant's day-to-day work. Medical assistants will interact with patients and their families, other members of the health care team, and insurance companies. In order to communicate effectively with each of these groups, a medical assistant should know how to obtain and share information efficiently and accurately.

TYPES OF COMMUNICATION

Communication can be verbal or nonverbal. **Verbal communication** refers to words that are spoken or written. Verbal communication style should be appropriate for the situation. For example, words should be kept simple when working with patients and families. The medical assistant should avoid using abbreviated names, technical jargon, or medical terminology that is unfamiliar to the patient or family. On the other hand, accurate technical language is necessary when working with physicians or insurance companies.

Nonverbal communication includes all the physical aspects of communication, including posture, facial expression, and eye contact. These behaviors are an essential part of communication and have a significant impact on how the listener will interpret the message. Medical assistants should strive to keep their nonverbal communication professional and appropriate by

+ maintaining good posture (e.g., not slouching on a desk)
+ keeping a polite facial expression when dealing with patients and the health care team
+ respecting other people's personal boundaries (e.g., not hugging coworkers or touching patients without their consent)
+ maintaining eye contact when speaking with patients and the health care team
+ not using rude or inappropriate hand gestures

THE COMMUNICATION CYCLE

The communication cycle starts with the **sender**, who sends a verbal or nonverbal **message**. The message is sent through a **channel**, such as a phone call, email message, or in face-to-face conversation. The **receiver** receives the message and interprets it using their own context and knowledge. Finally, the receiver offers feedback to the sender, which allows the sender to decide if their message was interpreted correctly.

The receiver can help ensure they are interpreting the message correctly by being an active listener. **Active listening** simply means fully concentrating on the sender and the message. Nonverbal signals of active listening include making direct eye contact, smiling, and leaning toward the sender. The receiver can also provide verbal clues that they are listening closely to the message. These include:

+ reflection: repeating words or phrases back to the sender
+ restatement: paraphrasing the message back to the sender
+ clarification: asking questions to better understand the sender
+ feedback: responding to the content of the message

Barriers to Communication

The communication cycle can be disrupted by internal and environmental factors. The discomfort caused by pain, hunger, extreme temperatures, and loud noises can interfere with the sender's ability to compose a message and with the receiver's ability to interpret the message. Strong emotions such as anger and sadness can also lead to miscommunication. Medical assistants should take care to notice if any of these barriers are preventing clear communication with either patients or other members of the health care team.

Telephone Techniques

The telephone is the most-used technology for patient interaction with the medical office. For telephone communication to be effective, medical assistants should adhere to the guidelines in Table 1.4.

Table 1.4. Telephone Guidelines	
Speaking Voice	Enunciation: Speak clearly.
	Pronunciation: Speak words correctly.
	Speed: Speak at a normal rate.
	Volume: Use a normal voice.
	Inflection: Use correct pitch and tone.
	Courtesy: Speak politely.
	Attention: Focus on the caller.
Answering Calls	Answer before the fourth ring.
	Greet the caller with "Good morning" or "good afternoon."
	Provide the name of the facility, as well as your name.
	Use a standard closing phrase, such as "Thank you for calling."
	Allow the caller to hang up first.

Directing Multiple Incoming Calls	Ask the first caller if he or she minds being placed on hold. Be sure to explain that you have another call. Ask the second caller to wait and allow time for a response before placing him or her on hold. Attempt to respond within thirty seconds but provide options if the hold will be longer. Thank callers for waiting.
Screening Calls	Manage physicians' time by referring only necessary calls and taking messages for other calls. Refer patients to the appropriate source for assistance.
Routing Calls	Tell the caller whom you are forwarding the call to. Provide the forwarding number in case of disconnection. Inform the caller that if the party does not respond, the caller may leave a voicemail.
Dealing with Emergencies	Notify the physician of the emergency immediately. Activate the emergency medical system (EMS). Instruct the caller to hang up and call 911. Provide EMS with necessary information, including advance directives.
Managing Difficult Callers	Keep voice at a normal tone and remain calm when speaking with angry callers. Notify the appropriate staff member after determining the problem. Follow up with the patient to be sure the problem was addressed. Notify the office manager, administrator, or physician of irate callers or callers with unresolved issues. Obtain the identity of threatening callers and notify appropriate supervisor.
Telephone Confidentiality	*The following guidelines from the Health Insurance Portability and Accountability Act (HIPAA) should be observed when using the phone:* Verify that the caller is indeed the patient. Give information only to the patient. Be sure the conversation is not heard by other patients. Avoid discussing telephone conversations around patients. Do not leave information on a patient's voicemail.

Diverse Populations

All patients and their families deserve to be treated with compassion and respect. Medical assistants should strive to treat everyone they encounter in the office equally, without regard to race, religion, age, gender identity, sexual orientation, socioeconomic status, physical challenges, special needs, or lifestyle choices. To do this, medical assistants should be aware of their own stereotypes and biases. **Stereotypes** are widely held but oversimplified or incorrect assumptions about a group of people. **Bias** is a prejudice for or against a group of people. If stereotypes and biases are not examined and corrected, both can lead medical assistants to treat patients unfairly.

Medical assistants will often encounter members of diverse populations who may require specialized communication techniques. These groups are summarized in Table 1.5.

Table 1.5. Communicating with Diverse Populations

Population	Communication Techniques
Blind or low vision	Announce when you enter or leave the room. Address the patient by name. Describe the layout of the room. Narrate your actions.
Deaf or hard of hearing	Speak slowly and clearly. Allow the patient to see your face while you speak. Provide written materials. Use a sign language interpreter when needed.
Geriatric	Adjust language for confused or cognitively impaired patients. Rely on family members or caregivers as needed.
Pediatric	Move to patient's eye level. Use simple language. Explain exam procedures before you start. Allow patient to hold blunt, safe instruments.
Seriously or terminally ill	Respond promptly and allow patients any needed extra time. Be direct but kind. Do not offer false hope or make unfulfillable promises.
Intellectually disabled	Match the patient's level of vocabulary and sentence complexity. Speak directly to the patient.
Illiterate	Notice when patients do not read materials. Read or explain important documents.
Non-English speaking	Have materials available in multiple languages. Use an interpreter when needed.
Anxious, angry, or distraught	Stay calm and speak clearly. Wait for the patient to calm down before relaying complex information.
Socially, culturally, or ethnically diverse	Understand that many aspects of communication, including volume and eye contact, have a cultural component. Be respectful of the cultural needs of patients.

PROFESSIONALISM

A medical assistant must maintain a professional attitude and appearance at all times. The health care environment can be both stressful and enjoyable, but it is always necessary to maintain a professional appearance.

Being a professional means treating others with respect. Both patients and other members of the health care team should be listened to and treated courteously. Medical assistants should also strive to act responsibly in the office. The other members of the health care team need to know that medical assistants can be trusted to do their work correctly, and that they are being honest. Everyone makes mistakes in the office, so it is also important to take criticism well and work hard to fix problems.

To maintain a professional image, medical assistants should dress appropriately for the office and maintain good hygiene. Dress codes will vary among offices, so it is important to clarify at the beginning of a job what is expected in that particular environment. Using good grammar in both written and spoken communication is also an important part of professionalism.

PERFORMING AS A TEAM MEMBER

In addition to physicians, the medical assistant will work with a variety of health care team members, each of whom performs a specific set of duties. Medical assistants should be familiar with the roles and skills of other health care team members.

+ admissions clerk: An admissions clerk in a medical office has general administrative office skills. They obtain basic medical history and information from patients when they come into the facility.

+ certified nursing assistant (CNA): A CNA provides basic nursing skills and patient care to people in adult day care centers, nursing homes, office settings, and hospitals. CNAs are registered and/or licensed.

+ emergency medical technician (EMT): An EMT is trained in the administration of emergency care and transportation of patients to the medical facility.

+ laboratory technician: Often called a medical technologist, a laboratory technician works under the supervision of a pathologist or physician. These health care workers perform chemical, microscopic, and/or bacteriologic testing on blood and body tissues.

+ licensed practical nurse (LPN): An LPN is a one-year nurse trained in patient care and licensed by the state.

+ registered nurse (RN): An RN is a two- or four-year nurse trained in patient care and licensed by the state.

+ nurse practitioner (NP): An NP is an RN with advanced training to diagnose and treat patients in the health care environment.

+ phlebotomist: Also called an accessioning technician, a phlebotomist is trained in drawing blood.

- physician assistant (PA): A PA is trained to practice medicine under the supervision of a physician.
- radiologic technologist (RT): Also called an X-ray technician, an RT is trained to operate radiologic equipment under the supervision of a physician.

All the members of the health care team work together to ensure patients receive the care they need. To accomplish this goal, medical assistants should build good professional relationships with other health care team members by:

- being responsive to the needs of other team members
- communicating information promptly and clearly
- successfully completing their job responsibilities

TIME MANAGEMENT

Medical assistants will need to manage their time and balance their many responsibilities. The most important **time management** skill in the office is to prioritize tasks. Tasks should be ranked by whether they are urgent or important: **urgent** tasks require immediate attention, and **important** tasks have serious consequences. Urgent and important tasks should be done first, with other tasks ranked behind them.

High urgency	Do later	Do first
Low urgency	Do not do	Do next
	Low importance	**High importance**

Figure 1.2. Prioritizing Tasks

More guidelines for time management include the following:

- Do not procrastinate: completing tasks promptly will keep the office running smoothly.
- Do not multitask: work on a single task until it is completed and then move to the next task.
- Be self-aware: take breaks and ask for help when it is needed.
- Stay focused: do not get distracted by personal phone calls, coworkers, or other activities in the office.
- Maintain accurate records: keep track of completed and unfinished tasks.

TWO: LEGAL and ETHICAL RESPONSIBILITIES

Medical assistants encounter scenarios that involve potential legal and ethical issues on a daily basis. The **American Association of Medical Assistants (AAMA) Code of Ethics** establishes the guiding principles for the ethical standards of medical assisting, which are similar to those of any medical profession. Medical assistants are expected to maintain current knowledge of the profession, demonstrate respect for all patients and providers, and participate in activities that will improve the overall health of their communities. Although a medical assistant is an agent of the physician, their primary responsibility is protecting the dignity, confidentiality, and safety of the patient.

 Did You Know? Each state individually regulates the practice of medical assisting and may have a separate code of ethics.

Medical Assistant Scope of Practice

There is no nationally accepted scope of practice for medical assistants, although there are many commonalities among the states. All medical assistants must work under the supervision of a licensed health care professional who maintains ultimate responsibility for the actions of the medical assistant. Most states allow medical assistants to perform a wide variety of clinical tasks in the medical office as long as they have been properly trained and the tasks are not prohibited by state nursing or medical laws. For example, because they are not licensed health care professionals, medical assistants cannot:

+ triage, assess, evaluate, diagnose, or treat patients (although they can often provide education after the provider has diagnosed the patient)
+ interpret test results
+ administer IV medications or anesthetics intended to render the patient unconscious

+ prescribe or refill medications without an order from the licensed practitioner

+ perform physical therapy (other than assisting)

+ perform any other procedure, technique, or treatment that would be deemed practicing medicine

It is important for medical assistants to know the scope of practice laws, because if they do anything for which they are not qualified (whether the task was delegated by a licensed ... open to litigation. The AAMA's website contains links ... org/employers/state-scope-of-practice-laws) affecting the ... and provides a resource for direct inquiries about state

... and Regulatory

... ex set of laws and regulatory agency guidelines, many of ... ants, including laws that cover patient rights, confiden- ... y. The most important of these laws and regulations are

ADVANCE DIRECTIVES

Advance directives state the patient's wishes for medical decisions and are used if the patient becomes incapable of making decisions. These documents must be signed by the patient, witnessed by state policy, and notarized by a legal notary. Examples of advance directives include:

+ **Living will**: A document specifying means to sustain the patient in case of terminal conditions.

+ **Durable power of attorney**: A document identifying the person acting on the patient's behalf regarding necessary medical decisions if the patient is incapacitated.

+ **Organ donation**: A document specifying the patient's choice to donate organ(s) to a specified organization.

The federal **Patient Self-Determination Act of 1990 (PSDA)** requires that patients with Medicare and/or Medicaid be provided with information about their rights to make health care decisions. This legislation is intended to improve the use of advance directives and increase the appropriateness of care while ensuring the patient has the right to make various decisions. This act encourages patients to decide about the extent of medical care they want early in the care process.

Under the PSDA, the patient chooses which treatments and care activities they wish to accept or refuse. The act requires that all health care organizations recognize the advance directive(s) and explain the patient's rights under state law, including the right to make medical care decisions such as refusing or accepting treatment options. Additionally, the patient is entitled to information about their right to create an advance directive.

UNIFORM ANATOMICAL GIFT ACT

In 1968, the US government passed the **Uniform Anatomical Gift Act,** which specified that any person of sound mind and legal age could donate any part(s) of their body after death, whether to research or for transplantation purposes. Most states allow residents to sign the back of their driver's license to notify medical personnel of their donor status. No money can be exchanged for organs, and organs cannot be sold for profit.

FOOD AND DRUG ADMINISTRATION (FDA)

The **Food and Drug Administration (FDA)** is an agency within the Department of Health and Human Services. One of the core functions of the FDA is to oversee medical products and tobacco, including drugs, biologics, medical devices, tobacco products, and special medical programs. Within the Office of Medical Products and Tobacco Initiatives and Activities, there are several other centers of responsibility:

+ Center for Biologics Evaluation and Research: regulates biological products for human use

+ Center for Devices and Radiological Health: ensures safety, effectiveness, and quality of medical devices and safe radiation-emitting products

+ Center for Drug Evaluation and Research: ensures the safety and effectiveness of prescription and over-the-counter drugs as well as products that fall into the "drug" classification, such as sunscreen, fluoride toothpaste, antiperspirants, and dandruff shampoos

+ Center for Tobacco Products: ensures safety and effectiveness of new and modified-risk tobacco products, warning labels, and advertising restrictions; oversees Family Smoking Prevention and Tobacco Control Act

+ Office of Special Medical Programs: creates special programs and initiatives; coordinates review of pediatric science; handles safety, ethical, and international issues

+ Oncology Center of Excellence: helps expedite the development of oncology and hematology medical products; evaluates drugs, biologics, and devices for cancer treatment

CLINICAL LABORATORY IMPROVEMENT AMENDMENTS (CLIA '88)

The **Clinical Laboratory Improvement Amendments (CLIA)** statute was passed by Congress in 1988 and was developed to improve the quality of laboratory testing. Under this legislation, all laboratories must follow certain quality control and assurance standards, including employee training, written policies, documented maintenance of instruments, equipment, and procedures, and proficiency testing. Quality assurance does not apply to CLIA waived tests, but it does apply to moderate-complexity, high-complexity, and performed microscopy tests.

Quality control measures allow for testing accuracy through careful monitoring of various procedures. The laboratory must follow these procedures, which include control samples, calibration, reagent control, maintenance, and documentation. **Calibration** involves testing procedures in which the equipment generates a result set by a known value. **Control samples** are specimens with known values, used to check for testing accuracy. Reagents are chemicals that react in specific ways when exposed to known substances. A **reagent control log** documents the quality of reagents. Documentation of all quality control measures depends on facility policy, as well as CLIA standards and requirements.

CLIA WAIVED TESTS

+ urinalysis, dipstick
+ urinalysis, tablet reagent
+ fecal occult blood (guaiac)
+ urine pregnancy test
+ blood glucose
+ hemoglobin (Hgb)

+ hematocrit (Hct)
+ erythrocyte sedimentation rate (ESR)
+ strep A test
+ ovulation testing

MODERATE-COMPLEXITY TESTS

+ blood chemistry performed with automated analyzer
+ hematology performed with automated analyzer

+ pinworm preparation
+ gram staining
+ microscopic analysis of urine sediment

HIGH-COMPLEXITY TESTS

+ cytology testing
+ blood cross matching

+ blood typing
+ pap smears

AMERICANS WITH DISABILITIES ACT AMENDMENTS ACT (ADAAA)

The **Americans with Disabilities Act Amendments Act (ADAAA)** was originally passed in 1990 as the Americans with Disabilities Act (ADA). It prohibits employers with more than fifteen employees from discriminating against individuals with disabilities. This act provides protection through the job application process, hiring, training, promotion, compensation, and termination. It requires employers to make reasonable accommodations for employees with disabilities. For example, an employee with diabetes should be allowed to take additional breaks to eat or monitor their blood sugar levels.

The ADA also provides protection for those seeking medical services. Patients with disabilities must be given the same opportunities to receive the same level of care as those without disabilities. This could mean providing accessible exam rooms or equipment (e.g., exam tables, lifts), providing staff members to read forms to patients who are blind or have low vision, or providing access to a telephone relay system or a telecommunications device for the deaf (TDD). The ADAAA, which went into effect January 1, 2009, made substantial changes to and broadened the scope of the ADA's definition of a disability. These changes made it easier for individuals to demonstrate qualifying disabilities under the ADA guidelines.

HEALTH INSURANCE PORTABILITY AND ACCOUNTABILITY ACT (HIPAA)

In 1996, the US federal government enacted the **Health Insurance Portability and Accountability Act (HIPAA)**. A section of this act is concerned with the security and protection of electronic medical records (EMR) and electronic health records (EHR). HIPAA also specifies what is considered to be confidential information, including:

+ patient and family names
+ geographic areas
+ dates of birth, death, admission, and discharge
+ telephone and fax numbers
+ home and email addresses
+ social security numbers
+ health plan beneficiary members

+ vehicle, device, and equipment numbers
+ medical records and account numbers
+ photographs
+ biometric identifiers
+ any unique identifying number, code, or characteristic

One of HIPAA's primary purposes is to guarantee health insurance access, portability, and renewal. It limits the exclusion of some preexisting conditions and prohibits discrimination based on a person's health status. Under HIPAA guidelines, a preexisting condition is one for which the patient has received medical advice, diagnosis, or treatment within six months of the enrollment date. Pregnancy or treatment of a newborn is not considered a preexisting condition. HIPAA normally guarantees that a person's current coverage can be renewed regardless of health conditions.

> **Did You Know?** For employer plans, HIPAA provides protection from coverage denial due to preexisting conditions, whereas the Affordable Care Act (ACA) provides protection for plans not provided through an employer.

In most cases, an authorization form signed by the patient is required prior to the release of any **protected health information (PHI)**. Authorization forms vary by facility but usually include the name of the patient, the covered entity releasing the information, the effective dates of the authorization (if not open-ended), the extent of the authorization (the patient has the right to withhold records relating to mental health, communicable diseases, HIV or AIDS, and treatment of alcohol or drug abuse), and the patient's signature.

HIPAA allows for the disclosure of PHI without a signed authorization form when that information will be used for treatment, payment, or health care operations (e.g., case planning, customer service, medical review, or training purposes). This provision allows providers to consult each other regarding a patient's care, to provide referrals, and to coordinate care with third parties (e.g., long-term care facilities, medical equipment providers). HIPAA regulations can be very complex, so it is best to seek the advice of the office's HIPAA compliance or privacy officer with any questions.

HEALTH INFORMATION TECHNOLOGY FOR ECONOMIC AND CLINICAL HEALTH (HITECH) ACT

The **Health Information Technology for Economic and Clinical Health (HITECH) Act** was enacted under a section of the American Recovery and Reinvestment Act of 2009. The HITECH Act promotes the adoption of health information technology and EMR. The federal government created an incentive program to encourage medical practices to use EMR technology. Areas affected include medical billing, patient records, and employee communication. The goal is to make better use of technology for patient care and affordability.

Electronic health records provide patients with an increased ability to track and monitor their health, help them more effectively follow their treatment plans, allow them to find any errors in their health records, and give them the freedom to provide their information directly to researchers. The ability to access health records in real time empowers patients to actively participate in their health care decisions, leading to a more patient-centered health care system. The HIPAA Privacy Rule requires that covered entities (providers and health plans) allow patients to review and/or receive copies of their medical records upon request.

 Helpful Hint: The HITECH Act also provides financial incentives for medical providers to switch to EHR.

There are a few cases in which providers are not required to provide the patient with access to their records, most notably in the case of psychotherapy notes or records related to legal proceedings. The notice of privacy practices provided by each covered entity gives the patient information on how to request the records, whom to contact with questions, and how to file complaints. The request for medical records must be made in writing, and the provider generally has thirty days after receiving the request to provide the records. Most providers do charge a fee for making the copies.

Patients have the right to restrict certain items within their medical records to prevent them from being disclosed. For example, if a patient was embarrassed by having a previous sexually transmitted infection, she may request that part of her medical record not be shared with future providers. In most cases, the covered entity is not required to honor the patient's request, as it could affect future health care decisions. If the covered entity does agree to grant the patient's request, it must comply with the request at all times unless the patient needs emergency treatment and the disclosure of the information is necessary to provide treatment. The covered entity must then also request that the information not be disclosed in the future.

If patients discover errors in their medical records, they can file written requests detailing the proposed corrections. The covered entity must issue a response within sixty days (although an additional thirty days is acceptable if the patient is given an explanation of the delay and a new completion date in writing). If the request for correction is denied, the covered entity must explain the reason for the denial and how the patient can complain about the decision.

GENETIC INFORMATION NONDISCRIMINATION ACT OF 2008 (GINA)

The **Genetic Information Nondiscrimination Act of 2008 (GINA)** is a federal law prohibiting health insurers and employers from discriminating against a person based on genetic information. Genetic information includes family health history, the use of genetic services or counseling, or the results of genetic tests. This act allows patients to discuss family health history or genetic information with their health care providers with the assurance that the information cannot be used to discriminate against them. GINA prohibits health insurers from requiring or using genetic information to determine eligibility for insurance, establish preexisting conditions, or determine premiums.

PUBLIC HEALTH AND WELFARE DISCLOSURE

Public health activities focus on the health of a population group or entire population and are carried out primarily by governmental agencies at the local, state, and national levels. The goals of public health activities are to prevent the onset and spread of disease, diminish the likelihood of injury, offer outreach and health education, and provide culturally sensitive care and translation services. HIPAA recognizes the role that public health plays in the health and safety of the whole population and, consequently, allows certain PHI to be released without patient authorization. Covered entities can disclose information to public health agencies legally authorized to receive reports of certain incidents described below.

Communicable diseases: Information regarding those at risk of contracting or spreading a communicable disease may be released, and those who have potentially been exposed may be contacted to prevent or control further transmission of the disease. Currently, over 200 infectious diseases are listed in the American Public Health Association's *Control of Communicable Diseases Manual*. Some diseases are required to be reported by telephone within an hour of diagnosis, while others have up to seven calendar days.

Vital statistics: Information regarding births, deaths, marriages, divorces, and changes in civil status are collected to assess population trends and needs.

Abuse, neglect, or exploitation of a child or elder: There are laws to protect vulnerable populations unable to protect themselves or adequately meet their own essential needs. Covered entities are required to report known or suspected cases of child (under the age of eighteen) or elder (over the age of sixty) abuse or neglect to social services or another agency designated to receive this report. Most states also have laws protecting individuals between the ages of eighteen and fifty-nine with known disabilities that prevent them from caring for or protecting themselves. The offenses that must be reported include physical, emotional, psychological, financial, and sexual abuse or exploitation; neglect; and abandonment.

> 🔍 **Did You Know?** The **Child Abuse Prevention and Treatment Act** mandates the reporting of cases of child abuse. Failure to report suspected cases of child abuse could result in a misdemeanor.

Domestic abuse: The requirements for reporting domestic abuse vary from state to state. While it is mandatory for health care providers to report suspected cases of domestic abuse to the police, some states require that only providers of medical services for physical injuries report the abuse while excluding mental health professionals from the mandatory reporting requirements. Similarly, some states require only physical violence to be reported, while other states include emotional, psychological, or financial abuse. It is important to be aware of state laws regarding mandatory reporting of suspected domestic abuse.

Wounds of violence: The requirements for reporting "wounds of violence" vary from state to state, so it is important to be aware of what injuries are reportable according to state law. Some of the most commonly reportable injuries include:

+ bullet wounds, powder burns, or other apparent firearm-related injuries
+ injuries suspected to be caused by knife, axe, or other sharp instrument that appear to have been caused by a criminal act
+ injuries, illnesses (e.g., poisoning), or burns that appear to have been caused by a criminal act (e.g., fight, robbery, rape)

CONSUMER PROTECTION ACTS

A **Consumer Protection Act** incorporates both consumer law and commercial law to ensure the rights of all consumers and businesses, in addition to ensuring employment of ethical and legal practices. The **Federal Trade Commission's (FTC) Bureau of Consumer Protection** is responsible for collecting and investigating consumer complaints, protecting consumers' rights, regulating commercial affairs, and educating consumers and businesses about their rights and responsibilities. In addition to these federal protections, states also have their own consumer protection laws to stop unfair, deceptive, or fraudulent business practices.

The **Fair Debt Collection Practices Act (FDCPA)** protects consumers from improper debt collection activities related to personal, family, or household debts, but not business-related debts. It restricts the time of day during which consumers can be contacted and requires them to stop debt collection communications after receiving a written request (except in the case of legal action). It also allows consumers thirty days to request verification of the debt and/or dispute its validity.

The **Truth in Lending Act (TILA)**, also known as **Regulation Z**, promotes the informed use of consumer credit in an effort to protect consumers from deceptive business practices. TILA requires banks and other lenders to disclose the total cost of a loan (including interest, fees, and penalties) at the time the consumer signs the loan documents. This information must be provided in clear language to ensure the consumer understands the true cost of credit. Medical offices that provide financing for procedures such as cosmetic surgery must give patients a complete Truth in Lending disclosure statement detailing all fees and charges pertaining to the loan.

In addition to financial protections, there are federal product safety laws for items such as food, drugs, and cosmetics. The **Consumer Product Safety Act (CPSA)** and the **Federal Food, Drug, and Cosmetics Act (FD&C)** require these products to meet the safety standards outlined by agencies such as the US Consumer Product Safety Commission and the FDA.

Medical Regulatory Agencies

OCCUPATIONAL SAFETY AND HEALTH ADMINISTRATION (OSHA)

The **Occupational Safety and Health Administration (OSHA)** is part of the US Department of Labor and was created to set and enforce workplace standards, provide training and outreach, ensure compliance, prevent on-the-job injuries, and protect the well-being of American workers. OSHA guidelines for the medical office focus on minimizing incidents that could expose employees to communicable diseases or other hazards found specifically in medical offices. OSHA has five primary standards for the medical office:

1. Bloodborne Pathogens: all occupational exposure to blood or other potentially infectious materials
2. Hazard Communications: classification of chemicals and provision of hazard information on labels and safety data sheets
3. Ionizing Radiation: protection against occupational radiation exposure by radioactive materials or X-rays
4. Emergency Exit Routes: exit route identification, safety features, design, and construction requirements
5. Electrical: electrical hazards, grounding requirements, electrical requirements for equipment

A complete description of each standard can be found on the OSHA website.

DRUG ENFORCEMENT AGENCY (DEA)

The **Drug Enforcement Agency (DEA)** is responsible for enforcing the controlled substances laws as well as recommending and supporting programs to reduce the availability of illegal controlled substances. The DEA maintains the list of who is authorized to manufacture (drug companies), order, handle, prescribe (physicians, physician assistants, nurse practitioners, and some pharmacists), dispense (pharmacy), or store controlled substances. These individuals are responsible for maintaining logs that accurately reflect their inventory at any given time (usually at the end of a shift or end of the day). Medical assistants can only administer controlled substances under a physician's direct order and supervision (unless there is a state law prohibiting medical assistants from administering controlled substances).

The **Controlled Substances Act (CSA)** is the federal drug policy under which certain stimulants, anabolic steroids, narcotics, depressants, hallucinogens, and other chemicals are regulated. There are five schedules (I–V) used to classify drugs according to their potential for abuse, likelihood of causing dependence, accepted medical application, and safety.

CRITERIA					
	Abuse potential high	High	Low relative to CII	Low relative to CIII	Low relative to CIV
	No medical use	Medical Use			
		Psychological or Physiological Dependence			
	Lack of accepted safety under medical supervision	Severe psych or physical	High psych or moderate to low physical	Limited psych or physical relative to CIII	Limited psych or physical relative to CIV

SCHEDULES	Schedule I	Schedule II	Schedule III	Schedule IV	Schedule V
	Heroin	Opioids	Opioids (Codeine combinations, Buprenorphine)	Benzodiazepines and other depressants (Zaleplon, Zolpidem, Eszopiclone)	Opioids in limited quantities and in combinations (Codeine, Dihydrocodeine, Difenoxin)
	Hallucinogens	Barbiturates	Barbiturates (combinations and products)	Fenfluramine	Pregabalin
	Marijuana	Cocaine	Ketamine	Modafinil	Lacosamide
	Others	Amphetamine	GHB	Butorphanol	
		Methylphenidate	Marinol	Tramadol	
		Methamphetamine	Anabolic steroids		
		PCP			

Figure 2.1. Scheduled Drugs Under Controlled Substances Act

CENTERS FOR DISEASE CONTROL AND PREVENTION (CDC)

The **Centers for Disease Control and Prevention (CDC)** is an agency of the federal government within the Department of Health and Human Services. The main goals of the CDC are to protect and improve public health and safety by controlling and preventing disease, injury, and disability, as well as to research and provide information on noninfectious diseases (e.g., obesity, diabetes). The CDC collaborates with other agencies to provide expertise on health-related matters and to develop disease control and prevention policies.

The CDC focuses its attention on several key areas of public health:

+ infectious disease
+ foodborne pathogens
+ environmental health
+ occupational health and safety
+ health promotion
+ injury prevention
+ preparedness for new health threats
+ educational activities

The CDC publishes several resources to assist health care providers with assessing and reducing exposure to infectious disease in the workplace. These resources include but are not limited to the following publications:

+ Hand Hygiene in Health Care Settings
+ Guide to Infection Prevention for Outpatient Settings: Minimum Expectations for Safe Care
+ Guideline for Disinfection and Sterilization in Health Care Facilities
+ Guideline for Isolation Precautions: Preventing Transmission of Infectious Agents in Health Care Settings
+ Management of Multidrug-Resistant Organisms in Health Care Settings
+ Guidelines for Environmental Infection Control in Health Care Facilities
+ Guideline for Infection Control in Health Care Personnel

Confidentiality

All medical assistants are responsible for keeping patient records secure and confidential. The decision to disclose patient information is the patient's choice. The physician cannot refuse to release records if the patient requests disclosure to another party. However, each party to whom a physician discloses information requires new authorization. The patient has the right to rescind an authorization of record release, which is best done with a written and dated request. Physicians need permission to disclose records unless:

+ they are issued a court subpoena.
+ they are being sued by a patient.
+ they believe disclosure of the information will protect the welfare of the patient or a third party.

Because most medical assistants perform multiple duties in the office, the use of **electronic Protected Health Information (ePHI)** allows or even requires them to access many areas of a patient's record, not just the minimum information. However, availability of this information does not authorize them to access any areas of the medical record other than those necessary for patient care. Health care organizations must have security policies in place to hold staff accountable for the information they access. Security audits should be conducted periodically to ensure compliance with the facility's ePHI security policies or may be conducted on demand in response to a suspected or reported incident. Use of audit logs and audit trails can identify transactions such as what was accessed or modified. Audits can be useful for many purposes, including:

+ detecting unauthorized access or intrusion attempts to a patient's ePHI
+ tracking ePHI disclosures
+ reducing the risk of unauthorized employee access and creating accountability
+ responding to patient concerns about unauthorized access of their ePHI
+ addressing legal and/or accreditation compliance requirements

Health Care Rights and Responsibilities

PATIENT'S BILL OF RIGHTS AND THE PATIENT CARE PARTNERSHIP

The **American Hospital Association (AHA)** formulated the **Patient's Bill of Rights** in 1973. This document outlines a patient's right to:

+ receive respectful, considerate, and appropriate care.

+ expect privacy and confidentiality.

+ consult the physician of his or her choice.

+ make decisions regarding health care.

+ receive all information regarding diagnosis, treatment, and prognosis.

+ refuse treatment.

+ make informed decisions related to health care.

+ obtain copies of his or her medical record.

+ participate or refuse to participate in research.

+ receive continuity of care.

In 2003, the AHA replaced the Patient Bill of Rights with the **Patient Care Partnership**. This brochure explains to patients what to expect during their hospital stay and outlines the hospital's responsibilities. The Patient Care Partnership outlines six key rights for all patients:

+ high-quality hospital care

+ clean and safe environment

+ involvement in care

+ protection of privacy

+ help when leaving the hospital

+ help with billing claims

PROFESSIONAL LIABILITY

Although medical assistants work under the supervision of a licensed health care provider, they are not protected from liability. A medical assistant who makes a mistake while caring for a patient (e.g., hits a nerve while administering an injection) or oversteps the scope of practice boundaries (e.g., administers an intravenous medication) is potentially exposed to being sued. The result could be a civil fine of up to several thousand dollars, criminal charges, or other penalties in addition to legal fees.

The standard of care varies from state to state or region to region but is often considered "minimum safe professional conduct." The test for standard of care is determining if someone with equal training and experience would have acted the same under the same or similar circumstances. Failure to meet this standard of care is known as negligence, in which case the health care provider, the medical practice, and the medical assistant can all be sued.

> **Did You Know?** The most common reasons for lawsuits against medical assistants are **medication errors** (e.g., administering medication to the wrong patient), **lack of monitoring** (e.g., unwatched patients falling after receiving an IM injection), and **office administration errors** (e.g., failure to alert physician to patient symptoms).

Every employer should have a **code of conduct** detailing the professional behaviors expected from employees. This will provide guidance to all parties and will help to ensure that the practice is run in a lawful and ethical manner. While some situations will involve only a legal issue or only an ethical issue, most situations will involve both. The code of conduct should include such topics as how to deal with conflict of interest (e.g., caring for a family member); responsible marketing practices; how to handle potential cases of fraud or abuse; accounting policies and procedures; and, of course, confidentiality.

Malpractice or **professional liability insurance** gives the employee peace of mind knowing that if there is a claim or lawsuit, the risk will be transferred to the insurance company. Even if the facility has liability insurance that covers the employees, it is best for the medical assistant to have an individual policy as well. If a medical assistant is found liable for negligence, they would be responsible for all or part of the settlement with the patient and may also be responsible for reimbursing the employer's insurance company. The premiums for these policies are relatively inexpensive compared to the risk associated with not carrying insurance.

CONSENT TO TREAT

Consent for various medical services and health care involves verbal or written permission from the patient. Consent is a contract that can either be **expressed** in writing or verbally or **implied** by circumstances or actions. Implied consent is usually made in life-threatening circumstances and medical emergencies based on the assumption that the patient would consent to lifesaving care.

Expressed consent must be **informed**, which requires a trained health care worker explaining the necessary information to the patient so he or she can make an educated decision. Components of the consent involve the reason for and explanation of the test or procedure; the possible side effects, risks, and complications; alternative therapies and their side effects, risks, and complications; the prognosis with or without the test or procedure; and any additional information that assists in the decision-making process.

Only certain people can give consent for medical services and care:

+ patient
+ competent legal adult in charge of patient's care
+ emancipated minor
+ minors in the armed forces
+ minors seeking services for sexually transmitted infections (STIs)
+ minor parent with custody of his or her minor child

Categories of Law

Laws are rules that govern actions, regulate conduct, punish offenders, and remedy wrongs. Laws can generally be divided into two categories: statutory law and common law. The laws passed by legislatures are **statutory laws.** In a contract, **common laws** are derived from decisions made by the judicial branch. When using common law, previously established decisions by courts (called precedents) are referred to by judges to decide issues of law.

CRIMINAL LAW

Criminal law regulates behavior that is considered an offense against society, such as theft or assault. Charges are issued against a person by the government, and the outcome of the trial is usually decided by a jury. The most serious criminal violations are **felonies**, which are punishable by fines or prison sentences in excess of one year. Persons convicted of a felony may lose rights, such as the right to vote or own firearms. **Misdemeanors** are less serious crimes punishable by probation or short jail sentences.

CIVIL LAW

Civil law regulates behavior between individuals or individual entities. Cases are filed by or on behalf of the injured individual, and the trial outcome is usually decided by a judge. In civil cases, the plaintiff (who filed the suit) has the burden of proof, meaning they must prove that harm has been done to them by the defendant. Civil law includes contracts and torts.

Contract laws involve the rights and obligations of contracts, which are promises of obligation. A contract is an obligatory agreement between two or more parties. For a contract to be legal and binding, five things must occur: (1) an offer was made, (2) the offer was accepted, (3) there was an exchange of something of value (consideration), (4) all parties were legally capable to accept the terms (capacity), and (5) the intent was legal. Once a physician establishes the physician-patient relationship, there are certain legal obligations that must be met throughout that relationship.

+ The physician has a responsibility to communicate with patients in a timely manner regarding their diagnoses, medications, procedures, and potential side effects or dangers.

+ Physicians must provide competent care to all patients without discrimination based on race, gender, sexual orientation, or religion.

+ The physician is obligated to continue treating the patient until the patient no longer needs the physician's services, the patient fires the physician, or there is a mutual agreement to terminate the relationship.

Despite the physician's best efforts, some patients are **noncompliant** and will not follow their treatment plans or take prescribed medications. Noncompliance is a risk not only for the patient but also for the physician. A patient's lack of improvement or worsening health might be blamed on the physician not meeting the standard of care, even though the patient is noncompliant. If a patient continually refuses to comply with the treatment plan or fails to keep appointments, the physician may consider terminating the relationship.

> **Helpful Hint:** To avoid accusations of abandonment, it is important for the physician (and the medical assistant) to keep a record of missed appointments, refusal of care, noncompliance, or failure to pay for services.

If the physician decides to terminate the physician-patient relationship, the patient must be given sufficient time to find a new physician. The decision to terminate medical care could be based on several factors including patient noncompliance, failure to pay for services, or a disagreement with a patient that cannot be resolved. When terminating care, the physician should

+ notify the patient in writing of the decision to terminate care.
+ provide documentation supporting the decision (if appropriate).
+ specify the date on which the physician-patient relationship will end.
+ advise the patient of the need for further care.
+ offer to provide records to the new physician.

A **tort** is a wrongful civil act. Tort laws involve the accidental or intentional harm to a person or property that results from the wrongdoing of a person or persons. **Negligence** is a type of tort, defined as failure to offer an acceptable standard of care that is comparable to what a competent medical assistant, nurse, or other health care worker would provide in a similar situation. There are four types of negligence:

+ Nonfeasance: a willful failure to act when required.
+ Misfeasance: the incorrect or improper performance of a lawful action.
+ Malfeasance: a willful and intentional action that causes harm.
+ Malpractice: a professional's failure to properly execute their duties.

Malpractice is the most serious form of negligence. To prove malpractice, four legal points must be shown: the patient-physician relationship was established (duty), the professional neglected to act or acted improperly (dereliction), a negative outcome occurred from an action or lack of an action (direct cause), and the patient sustained harm (damages).

Invasion of privacy is the violation of tort law that involves the intrusion into the personal life of another without just cause.

Intentional torts are committed when a person purposefully causes harm to another. Some examples are listed below:

+ (a) battery: harmful or offensive contact with another person
+ (b) assault: an attempted battery in which there was threat of injury, but no injury occurred
+ (c) slander: saying something false about someone that causes damage to their reputation
+ (d) libel: writing something false about someone that causes damage to their reputation

Medical Ethics

Ethics are moral principles, values, and duties. Whereas laws are enforceable regulations set by the government, ethics are moral guidelines set and formally or informally enforced by peers, the community, and professional organizations. Ethics include norms and duties. A **norm** is short for "normal," a behavior or conduct that is valued and usually expected. **Duties** are commitments or obligations to act in an ethical and moral manner.

The code of ethics is a statement of the expected behaviors of its members. This code also sets standards and disciplinary actions for violations, including suspension, censure, fines, or expulsion. The **American Medical Association (AMA)** code of ethics was written in 1847 and has been continually revised since then. The AMA specifies the physician's ethical duty to the patient.

The **American Association of Medical Assistants (AAMA)** sets forth principles of moral and ethical conduct for the practice of medical assisting. Medical assistants pledge to:

+ uphold the honor and principles of the profession.

+ accept the profession's disciplines.

+ render service with full respect for human dignity.

+ respect confidential information.

+ participate in additional service activities for the improvement of community health.

Risk Management, Quality Assurance, and Safety

Safety Signs, Symbols, Labels

Danger signs indicate an immediate hazard that could result in death or serious injury.

Warning signs indicate a hazardous situation that could result in death or serious injury.

Caution signs identify potentially hazardous situations that could result in minor or moderate injury or equipment damage, or to caution against unsafe practices.

Biological hazard signs identify the potential presence of a biohazard.

Notice signs provide general information.

General safety signs provide notices of general office practices and safety measures.

Fire safety signs indicate the location of emergency firefighting equipment.

 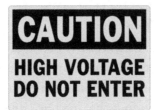

Figure 2.2. Examples of Safety Signs

ENVIRONMENTAL SAFETY

Although rare, **fires** in physician offices do occur. The medical assistant should be aware of certain fire safety measures:

+ Keeping open spaces free of clutter.
+ Marking fire exits.
+ Knowing the locations of fire exits, alarms, and extinguishers.
+ Knowing the fire drill and evacuation plan of the health care facility.
+ Not using the elevator when a fire occurs.
+ Turning off oxygen in the vicinity of a fire.

Before use, **electrical equipment** should be inspected for defects and safety by checking three-pronged outlets and reading warning labels. Any electrical cords that are exposed, damaged, or frayed should be discarded, and circuits should not be overloaded. Safety measures include:

+ Never running electrical wiring under carpets.
+ Not pulling a plug by yanking the cord.
+ Never using electrical appliances near bathtubs, sinks, or other water sources.
+ Disconnecting plugs from the outlet before cleaning appliances or equipment.
+ Never operating unfamiliar equipment.

Radiation safety involves the use of various protocols and guidelines of the health care facility. Radiation exposure is monitored with a film badge. Safety measures include:

+ Labelling potentially radioactive material.
+ Limiting time spent near the source.
+ Using a shielding device to protect vital organs.
+ Placing the patient with radiation implants in a private room.

A **poison** is any substance that destroys or impairs health or life when inhaled, ingested, or otherwise absorbed by the body. The reversibility of the poison effect is determined by the capacity of the body tissue to recover from the poison. Poisonous substances can alter various body systems, including the respiratory, central nervous, circulatory, hepatic, renal, and gastrointestinal systems. Safety measures include:

+ Keeping the Poison Control Center phone number visible.
+ Removing obvious substances/materials from patient's mouth, eyes, or body area.
+ If the patient vomits, saving the vomitus for examination.
+ Never inducing vomiting unless specified in poison control policies.
+ Never inducing vomiting in an unconscious patient.

COMPLIANCE REPORTING

A medical assistant's primary responsibility is protecting the dignity, confidentiality, and safety of the patient. Unfortunately, there may be a time when the medical assistant observes the unsafe or unethical behaviors of a coworker or even a physician. In most cases, the most appropriate course of action is to report these behaviors to a supervisor. It is important to document the conversation in writing and to establish a time line for resolution of the problem. If the situation is not resolved, the next step is to report the problem to the appropriate government agency (e.g., nursing board, medical board).

Most health care providers will make a mistake at some point in their careers. In some cases, there will be no adverse effects for the patient, while in others there could be extensive damage or even fatality. No matter how minor a mistake may seem at the time of occurrence, it is important to report it quickly and accurately. The physician should be notified of the mistake so that he or she can determine the best course of action.

Did You Know? The medical assistant should not notify the patient of an error—that is the responsibility of the physician unless it is delegated to someone else, such as the office manager.

Health care fraud is an intentional act of deceit, deception, or misrepresentation of services. Examples of fraud are changing claims forms for higher payments or billing for procedures that were not performed. **Health care abuse** is reckless conduct inconsistent with acceptable practices that result in unnecessary charges to the patient or insurance company. An example of abuse would be a physician performing unnecessary tests just to receive additional payment. The primary difference between fraud and abuse is the ability to prove the physician's intent to deceive the insurer. If a medical assistant suspects fraud or abuse, it is important to document and report it to a supervisor or government agency, depending on the circumstances.

A **conflict of interest** may arise in a medical office when a health care provider's professional responsibilities to a patient have been or could be compromised by other outside factors. A physician referring a patient to a lab in which he or she has a financial interest could be a conflict of interest. A conflict of interest could also arise if a physician is treating his or her own family members because the relationship may alter the way care is provided. An arrangement between a physician and a pharmaceutical company that would alter how prescriptions were written could also be a conflict of interest. If there is a question about whether a conflict exists, the medical assistant should discuss it with a supervisor and not get involved in the potential conflict.

Most facilities require **incident reports** to be completed when there has been a problem with the care provided to the patient or a deviation from policies or procedures. Examples of reportable incidents include medication errors, patient falls, or failure of a medical device. The purpose of the report is to identify what problem occurred as well as any consequences of the incident. Incident reports provide the facility with the opportunity to identify, correct, and prevent future incidents. An incident report is not intended to place blame but rather to document the event and track the occurrence of similar events. It is important to word the documentation as objectively and honestly as possible because these reports can be used in court if the incident turns into a lawsuit.

Medicolegal Terms

arbitration: a formal alternative to traditional litigation in which a neutral third party tries to resolve the dispute; the arbitrator's decision is final and binding

defendant: an individual who is required to answer the complaint of the plaintiff (civil law) or is accused of committing a crime (criminal law)

deposition: testimony or sworn evidence given before trial, usually in an attorney's office

Good Samaritan laws: a compilation of laws that offer legal protection for individuals who give emergency medical care to those believed to be injured, ill, in danger, or incapacitated

locum tenens: a person who temporarily fills in for another person; Latin for "to hold a place"

mediation: an informal alternative to traditional litigation in which a neutral third party tries to resolve the dispute by facilitating negotiations; does not impose a solution and is nonbinding unless both sides reach and sign a settlement

plaintiff: the party who initiates the civil action or lawsuit (civil law) or the prosecution (criminal law)

res ipsa loquitur: a person presumed to be negligent, in the absence of direct evidence, based on the fact that he or she had direct control of the circumstance causing the accident or injury; Latin for "the thing speaks for itself"

respondeat superior: a legal doctrine that holds an employer responsible for the wrongful actions of an employee; Latin for "let the master answer"

subpoena: a formal document, or writ, issued by a court or government agency requiring a person to appear in court to provide testimony or produce documents (e.g., medical records) or other items for the court

subpoena ad testificandum: a court order requiring a person to appear in court to provide testimony

subpoena duces tecum: a court order requiring the production of documents (e.g., medical records) or other items for the court; sometimes known as a "subpoena for the production of evidence"

THREE: RECEPTION

Reception is about more than letting patients into the waiting room: it is a patient's first impression of the physician and the practice. The medical assistant plays a key role in making it a positive impression and serves as the interface between the patient and the practice. The medical assistant's attitude and demeanor set the tone for the patient's experience and can mean the difference between calm, cooperative patients and anxious, fearful patients who are resistant to health care interactions.

> **Did You Know?** *White coat syndrome* is the term used to describe the anxiety some patients experience in medical environments, usually evidenced by an atypically high blood pressure reading. Medical assistants who are calm, confident, respectful, and empathetic can help reduce patients' anxiety and, hopefully, hypertension.

Medical Reception
PREPARING FOR PATIENTS

Preparing the patient's chart is one of the medical assistant's first administrative responsibilities. Most offices keep digital records, so the medical assistant may need to access and print relevant sections per office protocols. Organization of medical record hard copies is up to the physician.

> **Helpful Hint:** Medical assistants may call patients to confirm their appointment a day before it is scheduled, which helps reduce patient no-shows. When confirming appointments, new patients should be asked to arrive fifteen minutes early to complete the necessary paperwork.

As part of establishing the patient-physician relationship, the patient must receive a practice information packet. This packet should be prepared before the patient arrives and will include the following important policies and notifications as well as forms for the patient to complete:

- patient demographic information
- patient consent for evaluation and treatment
- practice policies for patients
- insurance assignment/information
- notice and written acknowledgment of receipt of patient privacy practice
- Medicare Part B signature authorization
- advance directives
- patient history
- family history
- medication list

If the medical office uses a **sign-in sheet**, the medical assistant should keep a blank sheet accessible to patients with clear directions for how to use the sign-in sheet. Throughout the day, the medical assistant should update the sign-in sheet by crossing off the names of patients who have been seen and adding blank sheets as needed.

DEMOGRAPHIC DATA REVIEW

When current patients check in, the medical assistant should perform a **demographic data review** to ensure that the patient's information is up to date. The patient should be asked to verify demographic information (in person or on a form), and the medical assistant should make any necessary updates to the patient record. Patient demographics are the starting line of the patient health record and include:

- name
- date of birth
- gender
- marital status
- address, phone number, and email address
- physician referral information
- insurance information and responsible party
- emergency contact information

Depending on office procedures, the medical assistant may also ask the patient to provide a specific piece of demographic data to verify their identity. Identity theft prevention is a priority in all medical practices. Diverted medical records are in demand because stolen records are used to obtain prescription medication, commit insurance fraud, and obtain health care via Medicare and Medicaid.

For new patients, the medical assistant should ask for identification and insurance information, and will need to scan both for the patient's file. **Insurance eligibility verification** should occur before services are provided. This information is usually collected when the appointment is made and is verified before the patient's arrival. If no insurance information is on file, the medical assistant should follow office procedures to verify the insurance before the patient is seen by the medical provider.

RECEPTION ROOM ENVIRONMENT

The reception room requires attention to maintain safety, comfort, and sanitation. The medical assistant is responsible for:

- ✦ arranging furniture to promote patient safety, movement, and accessibility
- ✦ providing lighting that allows for safety and reading
- ✦ ensuring that the temperature is an average of 72°F
- ✦ providing comfortable chairs and adequate reading materials to relax patients
- ✦ monitoring and cleaning the reception room (e.g., throwing away coffee cups, rearranging furniture and magazines, and wiping down surfaces)

HANDLING VENDORS AND BUSINESS ASSOCIATES

Under the Health Insurance Portability and Accountability Act (HIPAA; see chapter 2 for details), any business that encounters protected health information (PHI) while performing contracted work for a medical provider is a **business associate**. Examples of business associates include:

- ✦ third-party claims processors
- ✦ medical transcriptionists
- ✦ case managers
- ✦ pharmacy benefits managers

- ✦ answering services
- ✦ document storage or disposal companies
- ✦ accounting and legal firms

 Did You Know? Releasing PHI to a business associate who has not signed a HIPAA agreement can result in lost payments, financial penalties, and practice restrictions.

HIPAA requires that business associates review and sign a contract with the medical provider regarding use of PHI. The contract should specify what information will be shared and require the business associate to properly safeguard PHI.

As a representative of the medical office, the medical assistant will interact with business associates as well as **vendors** who provide non-medical-related services (e.g., janitors or maintenance personnel). The medical assistant needs to know with whom PHI can be shared and should ensure that vendors do not have access to patient medical information. In order to protect patient and physician practice privacy, no discussions or transactions should be held in the reception area, and information should be given only on an as-needed basis.

Patient Medical Records

TYPES OF RECORDS

Medical records contain all the information relevant to a patient's health care, including demographic information, medical history, diagnoses, diagnostic tests, treatment plans, and outcomes. While some offices may keep hard copies of these records, most medical providers store medical records digitally. Digital medical records come in two forms: electronic medical records and electronic health records.

Electronic medical records (EMRs) are digital copies of a patient's chart for a single medical practice. They contain information about the patient's medical history with only that provider. They are easily accessible within the practice but usually cannot be accessed by anyone outside the practice.

Electronic health records (EHRs) include the patient's medical history with multiple providers, including primary care physicians, specialists, and diagnostic facilities. Ideally, when a patient interacts with a medical provider of any kind, their information is included in the EHR, making it available to all medical providers treating them. In practice, however, the IT infrastructure to support EHRs is still being developed, and EHRs are often incomplete or duplicated.

Both hard copy and digital medical records are categorized as active, inactive, or closed based on the last date the patient was seen in the office. These guidelines are set by individual practices, but general guidelines are below:

+ **Active**: Patient has been seen within three to five years.

+ **Inactive**: Patient has not been seen within the past three to five years.

+ **Closed**: Patient is deceased, has moved, or has reached legal age limit (pediatrics).

OWNERSHIP AND STORAGE OF MEDICAL RECORDS

Ownership of medical records is viewed differently from state to state, but as a general rule patients own the information in their medical record. However, whether paper or electronic, the record itself belongs to the physician or facility. Patients can get copies of their medical records, but the facility is required by law to maintain the original record. The facility is responsible for protecting the medical record from loss, alteration, or unauthorized use. The original medical record is a legal document that cannot be removed from the facility without a court order.

Retention (how long records are kept) and destruction of closed medical records is covered by state law. For hard copy medical record retention, the typical guidelines are seven to ten years after the last date of treatment. When that time period has passed, the files should be **destroyed**, usually by shredding. This process is often handled by an outside contractor.

Retention and destruction of EMRs are less clearly regulated, but most states follow a similar policy as with hard copy records. Destruction of EMRs can be complicated, as the goal is not only to delete the digital file but also to ensure that no PHI can later be retrieved. This goal is usually accomplished by deleting and writing over the file. This process can be especially important when disposing of office equipment (such as computers or printers) that may contain PHI.

MEDICAL RECORD TASKS

medical assistants are responsible for a variety of tasks related to medical records. The process for each task will depend on medical office systems and policies. Described generally, these tasks include:

+ Assembling: Constructing files in the correct order.

+ Filing: Keeping medical records in a secure storage area.

+ Maintaining: Adding and updating all medical record documentation.

- ✦ Retrieving: Recovering medical records from storage when needed.
- ✦ Transferring: Sending medical records to another physician's office.
- ✦ Protecting: Keeping medical records secure at all times.
- ✦ Retaining: Keeping medical records for a specified length of time.
- ✦ Purging: Removing medical records kept past the statute of limitations.
- ✦ Destroying: Shredding medical records.

READING MEDICAL RECORDS

Recognizing and understanding the data in medical records is a crucial aspect of medical assistant responsibility that helps assist the physician and promotes safe patient care. This data is outlined below:

- ✦ The **history** and **physical** give concise, up-to-date information about the patient's medical history and the findings of their physical exam.
- ✦ The **discharge summary** summarizes the following efforts and outcomes of patient treatment:
  - ✧ reason for the visit
  - ✧ significant findings
  - ✧ treatment and procedures provided
  - ✧ patient's condition at the end of the visit
  - ✧ patient and family instructions, if any
- ✦ **Operative notes** discuss the details of operations the patient has undergone, as well as procedures the patient may have in the future.
- ✦ **Diagnostic tests** and **lab reports** show the results of tests such as CT scans.
- ✦ **Clinic progress notes** are made by health care practitioners to sequentially describe the patient's condition and the interventions provided or planned.
- ✦ **Consultation reports** are provided by practitioners other than the patient's primary care physician.
- ✦ **Correspondence** includes any patient-specific data received from or sent to the practitioner, health organization, or patient.
- ✦ **Charts**, **graphs**, and **tables** are the visual documents and summaries of patient data.
- ✦ The **flow sheet** is a graphic or checklist record of ongoing data collection such as vital signs or medications.

CHARTING SYSTEMS

Documentation is often referred to as **charting**. This is any information health care providers enter into the record, such as reports, test results, and consultation notes. Charting can be done by one of three methods: SOMR, POMR, or SOAP.

- ✦ **Source-oriented medical record (SOMR):** This file is divided into two sections: one for progress notes and one for diagnostic reports.

- + **Problem-oriented medical record (POMR):** This file lists the patient's problems at the front of the chart, with the number and problem noted after each encounter.
- + **Subjective/Objective/Assessment/Plan (SOAP):** This file documents the chief complaint along with symptoms (subjective), the physician's findings (objective), the diagnosis (assessment), treatment, tests, education, and follow-up (plan).

Scheduling Appointments

TYPES OF SCHEDULES

The flow of patients can be managed using several different scheduling styles. Most primary care physician offices use **stream scheduling**, in which patients are scheduled at regular intervals throughout the day. Typically, appointments are scheduled at ten-, fifteen-, twenty-, or thirty-minute intervals, although this will depend on the provider and the purpose of the visit. New patient appointments take longer than those for established patients, so extra time should be built into the schedule. The schedule should be flexible to accommodate established patient requests for urgent or emergency appointments.

Some offices may use a **wave schedule**, in which several patients are booked at the same time at regular intervals throughout the day (e.g., three patients at 9:00 a.m., three patients at 10:00 a.m., and so on). Patients are usually seen on first-come, first-serve basis, although more urgent patients may be seen first. This system is often used when there are enough rooms and personnel to quickly move people out of the waiting room. A wave schedule is also useful for practices that often have no-shows.

Specialists often use **cluster scheduling** to group similar appointments together during the day or week. For example, pediatricians may schedule all well-baby checks between 9:00 and 11:00 a.m., or a cardiac clinic may book appointments for patients with dysrhythmias only on Tuesdays and Thursdays. This practice can help streamline care by spending less time setting up specialized equipment. Cluster schedules may be necessary when specialized staff or equipment have limited availability.

Urgent care clinics and emergency rooms use **open hours scheduling** in which patients are seen on a first-come, first-serve basis. Patients may also be triaged by a medical professional when they arrive in order to attend to the most urgent patients first. Community clinics and other medical offices that see underserved populations may also use this system.

SCHEDULING GUIDELINES

When scheduling appointments, it is important to provide the patient's full name, use correct spelling, list the patient's date of birth, and obtain both home and work telephone numbers. Depending on office policy, the purpose of the visit should be recorded as well.

Appointments are usually scheduled on a computer with scheduling software. An **appointment matrix** is any kind of scheduling software or desktop chart that shows the date and time of physician availability, usually in color-coded grids or sections. Patient name and the appointment date and time are entered into the matrix.

Scheduling of two or more patients for the same appointment slot is called **double-booking** and is often done to accommodate patients with specific needs who cannot wait for another day. **Advanced scheduling** involves scheduling patients weeks or months in advance. **Under-booking** occurs when there are too many gaps between appointments and can be costly to the practice.

Patient flow refers to the round-turn traffic in and out of a physician's practice. The medical assistant must effectively balance patient needs (e.g., their work schedule) with the physician's schedule and preferences. The medical assistant is also responsible for coordinating patient activities that require limited equipment or other facilities, such as electrocardiogram (ECG) machines and ultrasonography rooms.

 Helpful Hint: Tracking arrival time, wait time, and departure time for each patient can help the medical office set realistic guidelines for scheduling patients.

Making appointments for patients to obtain outside services such as X-rays, outpatient procedures, and hospital admissions requires the medical assistant to work with both sides, since outside facilities usually have their own schedules and limited equipment.

The medical office should have systems in place to help patients remember their appointment times. Reminders/recall systems may include appointment cards, telephone calls, and mailed reminders. **Appointment cards** are given to the patient at the end of their visit when they schedule new appointments. Phone calls can be made in person or through automated messaging systems. A **tickler file** is a manual or automated system that alerts office staff to send out reminders for patient appointments in chronological order.

APPOINTMENT PROTOCOLS

When scheduling appointments, the medical assistant may be asked to **screen calls** to evaluate the urgency of the appointment. When screening calls, the medical assistant must work within their scope of practice: medical assistants cannot triage, treat, or diagnose patients, nor can they interpret test results or give medical advice to patients. However, the medical assistant should be able to question the patient about their complaint and place them accordingly in the schedule. In offices where urgent calls are frequent, such as a pediatrician's office, screening calls may be handled by a nurse.

Did You Know? The phrases *screening calls* and *phone triage* are often used interchangeably in the practice office. Regardless of the term, medical assistants can follow strict clinical protocols when screening calls, but they may not make triage decisions independently.

Physician referrals should be prioritized. When making appointments for referrals, the medical assistant will usually call the patient using the information provided by the referring physician's office. If a patient calls about a referral that has not yet been received, the medical assistant should let the patient know that the office will call them as soon as their referral information is available.

If the patient cancels their appointment, the missed appointment must be removed from the schedule before another one is made. If the cancellation is made by the physician, the patient must be notified of the reason for the cancellation and offered an alternative appointment. The cancellation then needs to be documented in the chart.

For no-show patients, the patient should be contacted to determine why the appointment was missed and to schedule another appointment. A note must be made in the patient's chart documenting the no-show and any attempts to contact the patient.

> **Helpful Hint:** A patient appointment with the physician is a kind of contract. The reason for delay and cancellation must always be entered in the chart to prevent the liability of patient abandonment.

Physician delay is often unavoidable. If the physician is late getting to the office, call scheduled patients to notify them and ask if they can come in later or reschedule. If the physician is delayed seeing patients who have already arrived at the office, the patients should be notified and given a reason for the delay. The delay needs to be charted in the patient's medical record.

Advocating and Navigating for Patients

Advocates represent or plead the cause of those who cannot speak for themselves. medical assistants are often considered patient advocates because they serve in this role for patients, but they cannot be forced to act as a patient advocate if there are conflicts between value systems.

One of the most important ways that medical assistants can assist patients is to help them navigate their health care experience. Medical assistants can provide information on available community resources and help them access those resources by providing necessary contact information.

Medical assistants also help patients with **referrals**. When the physician refers a patient to a specialty practice, the medical assistant usually initiates the process. The physician may request a particular practice, or the patient may specify a preference. Patients with HMO or PPO insurance plans must be referred to physicians associated with that plan. A referral form must be completed and sent to the insurance agency per protocol, with one copy for the specialist and one for the patient's record.

FOUR: THE BUSINESS ENVIRONMENT

Medical assistants play a vital role in medical offices, hospitals, and other medical facilities. The medical assistant will often be the first person the patient sees when entering the medical office and will be responsible for managing the non-medical aspects of the patient's experience. The responsibilities of the medical assistant may include:

+ check-in
+ check-out
+ scheduling appointments
+ insurance verifications

+ authorizations
+ billing claims
+ receiving payments
+ posting payments.

Administrative medical assistants will also have clerical responsibilities that keep the office running smoothly. As the person who manages client medical records, the medical assistant ensures that medical offices are compliant with legal privacy standards (see chapter 2 for details).

Written Communication
LETTERS

The medical assistant will be responsible for writing business **letters** on behalf of the physician and the medical facility. Each letter should be tailored to fit the situation and formally composed, as if the physician had written it him- or herself. However, the letter should not include medical terminology or jargon that may confuse the patient. When necessary, terms should be clearly explained. Other guidelines for professional letters are below.

+ Compose business letters of no more than one page.
+ Write clearly using correct grammar and punctuation.
+ Try to anticipate questions the reader may have and answer them in the letter.
+ Proofread the letter to catch typos and other errors.

There are four main parts of a letter:

FRIENDLY COLLECTION LETTER

_____
_____
_____

_____

Dear _____

This is just a friendly reminder that your account with us appears as past due. Our records indicate that you have a total outstanding balance of $_____ with the following invoice(s) overdue:

Invoice #	Invoice Date	Due Date	Amount

TOTAL DUE: _____

We would much appreciate if you would let us know the status of your payment. Please do not hesitate to call us if you have any questions about the balance due on your account. If you have already sent us your payment, please disregard this reminder.

Thank you very much for your attention to this matter and your continued business.

Sincerely,

_____
_____
_____

Figure 4.1. Block Style Collections Letter

1. **Heading**: The heading should have the office address, subject, date, and sender's name. Printed letterhead can be used, but the office address appear at the top of the page. The date may be fully written out, abbreviated, or written with numbers (e.g., 9-30-15, Sept. 30, 2015, or September 30, 2015).

2. **Opening**: The opening should have the recipient's address. Always address the person as *Mr.*, *Ms.*, or *Mrs.* If you are writing to a doctor, the abbreviation *M.D.* should always follow the doctor's name.

3. **Body**: The body includes subject lines, salutations, and the text of the letter. **Subject lines**, if used, should be included immediately after the opening. They consist of one line informing the recipient of the reason for the letter (e.g., "balance due," "reminder," etc.). The **salutation** is found on the next line following the subject line. Most salutations begin with *Dear....* If addressing a patient, use the patient's name, followed by a comma ("Dear Mr. Garcia,"). The text of the body should be aligned along the left side of the page.

4. **Closing**: The letter should end with either a typed signature, a written signature, or initials.

Most business letters are written in block style. Text is aligned at the left and single spaced; paragraphs are separated by a blank line.

 Helpful Hint: Keep a list of common medical terminology that is used in the office to ensure accurate spelling and usage.

MEMOS AND INTEROFFICE COMMUNICATIONS

Memos are written communications that record events or alert recipients to changes or problems at the office. A medical office memo may inform staff about issues such as meeting schedules or changes to policies and procedures. Memos should always start with the following information:

+ recipient(s)
+ sender
+ date
+ subject

MEMO   Company Name

To: _____

From: _____

cc: _____

Date: _____

Re: _____

This is what a memo looks like.

Figure 4.2. Memo

Emails are used for daily communication with staff or other medical professionals. A medical assistant can also email patients advising them of a no-show or cancelled appointment. Copies of such emails should always be placed in the patient's chart or filed electronically. The medical assistant should always remember that they are representing the physician and the office. While an email may seem more casual than a letter or memo, it is still a professional correspondence and should be treated as such.

REPORTS

Physicians use or run a variety of monthly **reports**. An important one is the **profit and loss (P&L)** report, which shows total revenues and expenses on a monthly and/or quarterly basis.

Accounts receivable (AR) reports show outstanding patient account balances. The report will show any issues with insurance payments for medical services or procedures. This report can help determine if changes should be made in accepting certain insurance coverage.

 Did You Know? At the end of the year, physician offices may "write off" unpaid balances that patients or insurance companies have disputed.

Explanation of benefits (EOB) reports show medical service payments, denial of claims, and verification of patient's benefits or insurance payments. It will also explain any denials of claim pertaining to CPT codes or ICD-10 diagnoses codes.

Business Equipment and Inventory

Medical assistants should be comfortable using a wide range of office equipment, including computers, fax machines, printers, credit card readers, tablets, and office telephones. Medical assistants may also be asked to schedule routine maintenance or other services for office equipment. When using business equipment, medical assistants should always be aware of HIPAA rules and be on the lookout for potential privacy violations. For example, unlocked computers should never be left unattended, and confidential information should not be discussed on the phone in front of other patients.

The medical assistant will be responsible for recording inventory levels of office and exam room supplies and may also be asked to order supplies as needed. These items include copier paper, forms, office supplies, and medical supplies for exam rooms. Medical assistants may also be responsible for recording the distribution of controlled substances that are kept in a secured location. Most inventory is tracked using signed log and journal entries.

Electronic Applications and Patient Confidentiality

Electronic health records (EHR) contain information on the patient's demographics, medical history, immunization dates, allergies, diagnoses, medications, imaging, treatment plans, and laboratory and test results. The office's patient database can be used to search for patients by name, diagnosis, and CPT codes; reports can be printed based on these criteria.

The use of EHR is governed by **meaningful use regulations**, which set standards for exchanging patient health information between all providers and insurers involved in the patient's care. The program is run by the Centers for Medicare and Medicaid Services (CMS), and health care providers that adhere to these regulations are eligible for incentive payments. According to meaningful use, information from EHR can be shared when it:

+ is meaningful (i.e., it serves a purpose for the patient).

+ contributes to improvements in quality of care.

+ is being sent to the Department of Health and Human Services as part of the incentive program.

Security is a central concern when using electronic applications. Medical assistants have access to patients' protected health information (PHI), which should be safeguarded at all times. Below are guidelines for maintaining a secure environment when using electronic applications.

+ Use a secure password or ID card to log in to any office computer.

+ Log off the computer any time it is not being used.

+ Use encryption software when appropriate to send PHI.

+ Equip all computers with up-to-date firewalls and antivirus software.

+ Never leave medical documents unattended on printers, copiers, or fax machines.

+ Double check the name, address, and/or fax number when sending documents containing PHI.

Patients may be able to access parts of their EHR through a **patient portal**. These websites allow patients to schedule appointments, see test results, and send messages to health care providers. As with other electronic applications, the patient portal process should be carefully monitored to ensure patient privacy. Medical assistants may need to provide patients with passwords or access codes, and they should always ensure that this information is given only to the patient.

Lastly, medical assistants may be asked to monitor or manage their office's **social media accounts** on platforms such as LinkedIn, Facebook, Twitter, and Instagram. Typical posts may include informational articles on health topics, updates on office hours and policy, or advertisements designed to attract patients. Medical assistants who manage social media accounts should not post information about patients, even if it is anonymized. Similarly, medical assistants should not post patient information to their personal social media accounts.

FIVE: FINANCES

Financial Procedures

BILLING PROCEDURES

Itemized statements are monthly bills summarizing invoices and are a request for payment. These statements should reflect the service rendered on each date, the date the claim was submitted to the insurance company, the date of payment from the insurance company, and how much the insurance company covered, as well as the balance due from the patient. Time limits for payment and payment due must also be stated along with the balance due. Typically, patients are expected to pay bills within a thirty-day period, called a **billing cycle**.

Offices should establish a regular system of mailing statements, and larger physician practices or facilities may spread out the monthly billing of patients over the thirty-day period. For example, invoices can be sent to patients whose last names begin with A – E on one day, and then to those whose names begin with F – G on another day, and so on, to minimize the time spent each day on this process.

In addition to monthly patient invoicing, invoices for supplies need to be checked and processed as supplies arrive. For all supplies sent to the office, whether administrative or medical supplies, invoices and contents of the order should be checked against the packing slip to make sure the full order was received. The invoice should then be marked and placed in a special folder according to the payment due date until paid. When paid, the check number, date, and payment amount should be recorded on the invoice, and the invoice placed in the paid folder. Disbursements may be entered into the accounting records in several ways, depending on the accounting software. Copies of all bills and order forms for supplies should be kept on file for ten years in case the IRS audits the practice.

COLLECTION PROCEDURES

Accounts payable is the money due to utilities or for lease payments for office space. Also included on the medical office's balance sheet are the amounts due for the goods purchased from suppliers by the medical office, such as medical and office supplies needed for daily operations. Accounts payable is considered a **liability** because it is money owed to creditors. When suppliers are paid for goods purchased, the accounts payable is reduced, which in turn reduces the company's liability.

Accounts receivable is the money that companies are owed for services provided to a customer. In the medical field, these services may include the nursing and/or physician's assessment, any medications administered during the office visit, and the amount of billable time of the office visit (e.g., thirty versus sixty minutes). Accounts receivable is considered an **asset** because when payments are received for services rendered, they can be **debited**, or deducted, from the company's balance sheet and converted into cash on a future date.

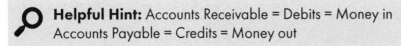

Helpful Hint: Accounts Receivable = Debits = Money in
Accounts Payable = Credits = Money out

Accounts with overdue payments fall into the delinquent account category. Payment on overdue accounts is the most difficult to collect from patients who are going through hardship or who have moved and may not have received an invoice. However, physicians must be paid in order to pay company expenses and to continue to treat patients.

Aging of accounts is the process of classifying and reviewing delinquent accounts by age from the first date of billing. Usually credits are classified as one to thirty days past due, thirty-one to sixty days past due, and so on. Most accounting software has an age analysis tool to help identify and classify delinquent accounts. Delinquent accounts should list all patient account balances, when these charges were incurred, the most recent payment date, and any notes regarding attempts to contact patients for payment or conversations with patients regarding payment due.

Collection techniques may include telephone calls and letters or statements. Letters including statements should be sent when the account is thirty days past due, again at sixty days, ninety days, and 120 days. Calls to the patient should be made in private and during business hours. Being respectful and willing to help the patient meet their financial obligation assists in collecting past-due debts on delinquent accounts.

Did You Know? It is illegal to harass a creditor by making threatening calls or calls late at night (after 9:00 p.m.). It is also illegal to threaten legal action that is not intended to be taken.

Preplanned payment options, or a payment plan agreement, may be another option offered by the practice. It is based on an estimate of cost for a procedure provided by the patient's insurance carrier and physician, not a guarantee of what will be owed, and includes what the patient is expected to owe after any co-payments, coinsurance, or deductibles have been billed and paid. This option allows for a predetermined monthly payment to be billed to the patient's bank card or credit card on a certain date so that payment can be secured on a monthly basis and the patient can spread out the cost over a predetermined amount of time.

If a patient is not able to make the full payment at the time services are rendered, the practice may make a **credit arrangement** or extension of credit so that a procedure can be performed without the cost paid up front. This option carries more risk to the physician and also requires the establishment of a payment schedule to satisfy the amount due.

Collection agencies are used when internal follow-up has been exhausted on an outstanding account and payment has not been received. If a patient has failed to respond to the final letter sent when the account is 120 days past due, or has failed to fulfill a promise on payment, the account should be sent to a collection agency. Once an account has been handed over to a collection agency, the patient can no longer make payments to the physician's office but must be referred to the collection agency to resolve the account.

HANDLING PAYMENTS

Processing patient payments will depend on the forms of payment accepted by the practice (e.g., credit cards, checks, or cash). Co-pay amounts depend on the patient's insurance plan and are determined by the insurance company. Co-pays for services are generally due in full at the time of the office visit.

For extenuating circumstances, such as procedures and services involving large fees, patients may be able to set up a payment plan or extensions of credit if the practice has provisions in place. Patients setting up payment plans should be informed of what the charges will be, what services these charges will cover, credit policies of the practice, when payment is due, circumstances that require payment at the time of services, insurance benefits that may be accepted, and whether the office staff or the patient will be responsible for completing insurance forms for submission. In addition, collection procedures, including circumstances in which accounts will be sent to a collection agency, should be discussed.

> **Helpful Hint:** When an account is overpaid by a patient or their insurance company, this overpayment is termed a **credit**, which is money owed to the patient or insurance company. This will show on the patient's account as the most current balance with brackets indicating a credit.

After payments are collected, a receipt is printed and given to the patient stating payment in full. A record of the money received should be included in the general journal (book of original entry), often called the day sheet, where all transactions are first recorded.

MANAGING THE PETTY CASH ACCOUNT

Petty cash is a small amount of money kept on hand to be used for expenses instead of writing a check. It is considered a current asset and is listed as a debit on the company balance sheet. To fund the account, the office manager or business manager writes a check made out to "petty cash" in the range of seventy-five to one hundred dollars, and cashes the check at the practice's bank.

The person responsible for managing the petty cash account disburses it from the fund in exchange for a receipt for the expense. Examples of petty cash disbursement may include employee expenditures for postage, office supplies, and so on, and is meant for small expenses that generally do not exceed twenty-five dollars. To ensure the expenses are entered in the proper accounting period, petty cash accounts are typically replenished at the end of each accounting period or as needed.

 Helpful Hint: Petty cash should be kept separate from patient cash payments in a secure, locked area.

FINANCIAL CALCULATIONS

Some of the medical assistant's daily financial duties include handling co-payments, which involves making change for patients paying with cash, data entry, daily balancing of petty cash (if included in job responsibilities), and reconciliation of bank statements for the practice.

The medical assistant may also have to make financial calculations to determine the best deal when ordering office or medical supplies in order to save the practice money without sacrificing quality. On large orders suppliers will often discount the price for items commonly used, such as gloves. The medical assistant must be able to balance the demand for supply against the discount offered.

For example, a case of twenty packs of gloves costs fifty dollars, but if four cases or more of gloves are ordered at a time, the price is reduced to forty dollars per case. The practice generally uses eighty packs of gloves per month, so ordering four cases of gloves reduces the unit cost from $2.50 to $2 per box. The practice will use approximately eighty gloves per month, so ordering enough gloves to get the discount will work in the practice's favor.

Diagnostic and Procedural Coding Applications

A universal set of codes is used to simplify health care communication, particularly for reimbursement. These medical codes define diagnoses, procedures, equipment, and services for health care professionals, insurance companies, and government health programs.

INTERNATIONAL CLASSIFICATION OF DISEASES

The **International Classification of Diseases (ICD)** is a coding system used to classify diseases. It was created by the International Statistical Institute and entrusted to the World Health Organization (WHO) in 1948. The most current version is the ICD-10. Each ICD code corresponds to a different medical diagnosis. The codes are used to help identify and group diseases for billing, disease monitoring, and other research or public health purposes. There are multiple coding reference books with the complete list of ICD-10 codes available for purchase, but the ICD-10 reference book can be ordered or accessed for free through a search application on the WHO website.

The ICD-10 codes are alphanumeric. The first character is always a letter, and the second character is always a number. The rest of the code could contain between one and five more characters, which could be letters or numbers, and there is always a decimal after the first three characters. For example, the ICD-10 code for "fatty changes of the liver" is K76.0, and "nonalcoholic fatty liver inflammation" is K75.81.

WHO released the ICD-11 in June 2018, but it will not go into effect until January 1, 2022.

CURRENT PROCEDURAL TERMINOLOGY

Current Procedural Terminology (CPT) uses a set of standardized five-digit codes to identify medical, surgical, or diagnostic services. CPT codes refer only to medical procedures and are used with ICD codes (which give the diagnosis for the underlying medical condition). The CPT coding system was developed by the American Medical Association (AMA), which releases updated codes every October.

Medical assistants who handle billing and patients' records need to be familiar with CPT/ICD codes and know how to read bills and reports containing these codes. For example, the medical assistant may be asked to use codes to create client bills or submit claims to insurance companies.

CPT is divided into three categories of codes:

+ Category I is for common medical procedures that are widely used. This category includes evaluation and management, medicine, surgery, anesthesiology, radiology, pathology, and laboratory codes.

+ Category II codes are optional and are used for tracking and performance monitoring. For example, they document an assessment of tobacco use or blood pressure measurement.

+ Category III codes are temporary codes for new procedures or technology that is involved in research.

Sometimes a simple CPT code is not enough, and a **CPT code modifier** (CM) is needed to give extra information to the insurance company. For example, a modifier may describe why a procedure was necessary, where on the body a procedure was performed, if multiple procedures were performed, or if multiple physicians were present.

 Helpful Hint: Examples of using a modifier include 24156-12; code-modifier; 24156-12-18; code-functional-informational

CPT modifiers are always two characters; they may be numeric or alphanumeric. The modifier is added to the end of a CPT code with a hyphen. If more than one modifier is needed, the functional modifier is coded first and the informational modifier second.

Sometimes the unexpected happens during an office visit or procedure, and more time or more resources are needed to care for a patient. For example, an office visit that was supposed to take thirty minutes turns into sixty minutes based on information obtained during a physical assessment, or an in-office procedure needs to happen on the same day.

CPT codes must be adjusted to account for the additional time or procedure, and proper documentation made in the patient's chart to explain the reason for the code change. The physician may need to provide a new ICD-CM if a new medical condition is diagnosed as a result of an assessment or test findings.

 Did You Know? Upcoding, whether intentional or an oversight, is a serious compliance risk and is considered health care fraud with grave legal ramifications for all involved.

This documented explanation for code changes is extremely important so the physician and/or practice will not be accused of upcoding. **Upcoding** is the act of using a CPT code in a claim to insurance companies that indicates a higher level of service or a more complex diagnosis not supported by medical necessity, medical facts, or the medical provider's documentation.

LINKING PROCEDURE AND DIAGNOSIS CODES

Every CPT code must be linked to a corresponding ICD-10-CM code to support medical necessity for the service or procedure performed. For example, "chest pain" (786.50) would be linked to a corresponding 93000 or 93010 CPT code to establish the medical necessity of the electrocardiogram. For patients with more than one diagnostic code the physician must identify the relevant diagnosis related to the service or procedure and list it in Column E of the CMS-1500 form after the CPT code, thereby linking the diagnosis to the procedure. (CMS stands for "the Centers for Medicare and Medicaid Services"; these services are discussed later in the chapter.)

DIAGNOSIS-RELATED GROUP

To simplify reimbursement and reduce costs, Medicare pays a predetermined amount for a given diagnosis while a patient is hospitalized, a system called the **Inpatient Prospective Payment System (IPPS)**. The **Diagnosis-Related Group (DRG)** is a classification system used to determine payments in the IPPS.

Medicare uses **Medicare Severity Diagnosis Related Groups (MS-DRGs)** to classify patients. The DRG is assigned to the patient based on:

+ the primary diagnosis
+ any secondary diagnoses
+ surgical procedures performed during the hospital stay
+ complications and comorbidities (CC) or major complications and comorbidities (MCC)

Each DRG is a three-digit number describing a specific diagnosis (e.g., 176: "pulmonary embolism without MCC"). Medicare then determines the cost of the average resources used to treat patients in that DRG and pays the hospital a flat rate for each patient assigned that DRG. This process ensures that the hospital is paid the same amount for every patient hospitalized with the same DRG. Medicare's use of DRGs is designed to incentivize hospitals to provide only necessary care.

Other organizations have developed more complex DRG systems that incorporate factors such as the severity of the illness, the age and sex of the patient, and the patient's status at discharge. Some hospitals use these for billing outside the Medicare program. These systems include:

+ All Patient DRGs (AP-DRGs)
+ All Patient Refined DRGs (APR-DRGs)
+ International Refined DRGs (IR-DRGs)

DIAGNOSTIC AND STATISTICAL MANUAL OF MENTAL DISORDERS

The **Diagnostic and Statistical Manual of Mental Disorders (DSM)** is published by the American Psychiatric Association. It lists the symptoms of psychiatric disorders and their related states and provides guidelines regarding differential diagnosis of mental disorders and how to determine the severity of a diagnosis (e.g., length of time symptoms have been present, number of symptoms present). The *DSM-5*, published in 2013, is the most recent version. Clinicians and researchers use the *DSM* as a diagnostic tool. Like medical diagnoses, the diagnoses in the *DSM* have corresponding ICD-10 codes, so clinicians can use them to bill for services.

Basic Insurance Principles

Health insurance companies act as the financial "middleman" between patients and medical providers. The consumer pays the insurance company a **premium**—a regular, predetermined amount of money. In return, the insurer covers some amount of the financial costs of the consumer's medical care. The types of services covered and the amount the insurance company will pay is determined by each person's individual health insurance plan.

Every patient who pays premiums to the insurance company is a risk and has the potential to cost the company money in the form of payouts for medical services. The premiums collected from multiple consumers are expected to offset these payout amounts and allow the insurance company to earn a profit. The insurance company may also earn investment returns on the premiums collected.

> **Did You Know?** Many medical assistants will work closely with insurance companies. Medical assistants may be asked to submit insurance claims, send referrals, and acquire pre-authorization for tests and procedures.

Federal health insurance programs are available to some individuals, including people with disabilities or low incomes, veterans, and people over sixty-five. These programs do not require a premium, or require only a small premium, and are largely funded through taxes. The services covered under these programs are defined by federal and state laws and regulations.

Managed Care Organizations

Most health care in the United States is provided through **managed care organizations (MCOs)**, which seek to control quality and costs by managing patients' use of medical services.

MCOs use a variety of techniques to meet these goals. They contract with providers so their members can access their services at a discounted rate, and they may require patients to use only specific providers. MCOs may also require referrals or preapproval for specialized medical care while easing access to lower-cost preventive care. They may also limit the amount paid for specific services or deny payment for services they feel are not medically necessary.

MCOs also minimize the money they pay out for a patient's medical care by sharing the cost of care with the patient.

In addition to the cost of their premium, patients also share the cost of their medical expenses through payments referred to as co-pays, deductibles, and coinsurance. **Co-pays** are set payments that patients pay every time they seek medical care. For example, their insurance requires them to pay a fifteen-dollar co-pay every time they see their medical provider.

A **deductible** is a set amount that patients must pay before the insurance company will cover any of their medical care. Typically, a deductible is much higher than a co-pay, but the patient only has to pay it once a year. A patient could also have both a co-pay and a deductible. In that instance, if a patient has a deductible of $1,000 a year and a $250 co-pay for emergency room care, she will have to pay $1,000 of her emergency room care even if it only costs $1,001. If she needs additional emergency room care at any time during the remainder of the covered year, she would only have to pay the $250 co-pay no matter the total cost of the additional emergency room care.

Another way insurance companies share the cost of medical care with the patient is through coinsurance. **Coinsurance** is the total percentage an insurance company will pay for a patient's medical care. If a patient has an insurance policy with an 80 percent coinsurance, that means the insurance company will only pay 80 percent of the cost of the care regardless of the total amount. This is not a set amount; the amount the patient ends up paying depends on the total cost of care.

It is possible for a patient to have a coinsurance, a deductible, and a co-pay in one insurance policy. Fortunately, insurance policies usually come with a maximum out-of-pocket limit. For example, a patient might have a maximum out-of-pocket limit of $5,000 per year, an 80/20 coinsurance, and a deductible of $1,500 for hospital care. If the patient experiences a costly medical problem and is admitted to the hospital, they will have to pay the $1,500 deductible and 20 percent of the cost of his care until he has paid an additional $3,500. If his care costs more than that or he ends up back in the hospital, the insurance company is responsible for paying the rest.

There are four main types of MCOs available to patients:

+ preferred provider organization (PPO)
+ exclusive provider organization (EPO)
+ health maintenance organization (HMO)
+ point-of-service (POS) plans

These plans exist on a spectrum that balances flexibility and cost. PPO health care plans offer the most flexibility but are also the most expensive. HMO plans offer the least flexibility but generally will be cheaper for the consumer.

Preferred Provider Organizations

In a **preferred provider organization (PPO)**, providers contract with the insurance company to create a **network**. If the plan member sees medical professionals included in this network, the member receives the PPO's negotiated rate, which is usually substantially lower than the provider's cash rate. The insurer will then cover some portion of the cost (depending on the plan), and the member pays the specified coinsurance.

In a PPO, pre-authorization for medically necessary services may be required. In addition, the insurance company might not pay for a service a physician requests if it does not feel the service is medically necessary. For example, a PPO plan might not authorize payment for an expensive brand-name prescription if a cheaper generic version is available.

 Helpful Hint: In a PPO, providers are usually compensated using a fee-for-service arrangement by which they bill the insurance company for each separate service provided.

PPO plans allow members to go directly to a specialist without a referral from a primary care physician. However, prior authorization from the insurance company may be needed to ensure coverage.

Members in a PPO may use the services of health care providers outside the network but will have to pay higher rates and will have a higher coinsurance and maximum out-of-pocket amount (which may not be limited for out-of-network services).

PPO plans typically have higher premiums than other health plans. Once members have met their annual deductible, the insurance company will pay a larger portion of the cost. If members meet their out-of-pocket maximum, the insurer will cover all approved health care costs. Deductibles and max out-of-pocket costs are usually lower for in-network care and much higher for out-of-network care.

Exclusive Provider Organizations

An **exclusive provider organization (EPO)** also contracts with providers to form a network. The EPO will cover in-network health care services in the same manner as a PPO. However, out-of-network services are not covered except in cases of medical emergencies (once the patient is stable, the insurance plan may request to transfer to an alternative hospital within the network). Because the plan member is responsible for all out-of-network costs, the premiums for an EPO plan are usually lower than those for a PPO.

A referral to a primary care physician (PCP) is not needed for specialist services, but the patient is responsible for ensuring that all providers are in-network. Pre-authorization is usually required to have services approved for reimbursement.

Health Maintenance Organizations

A **health maintenance organization (HMO)** requires the member to have a primary care physician who coordinates all care. Members may choose their own PCP from a list of in-network providers. If a PCP is not chosen, the insurance company will assign one.

Referrals from the PCP are needed for any type of medical service, including specialist visits, diagnostic tests, and medical equipment. The primary care provider in an HMO contract is often referred to as a **gatekeeper**. They oversee all primary and preventive care. The gatekeeper authorizes referrals, lab studies, diagnostic testing, and hospitalization.

All medical providers must be in-network for the insurance company to pay for their services. If the gatekeeper refers the patient to a specialist, and the patient attempts to see a different specialist, services will not be covered. Because HMOs can control costs by excluding out-of-network providers, their premiums are lower than those for a PPO or an EPO.

Providers are reimbursed by the HMO through an arrangement called **capitation**, in which providers are payed a fixed amount per member, per month. If a patient sees his HMO primary care physician several times in one month, the primary care physician is only paid the amount provided in the contract.

HMOs may have some services, called **carve-outs**, that are excluded from the capitation rate and are usually handled by a designated provider. Common carve-outs include mental health and addiction services, cancer treatments, and ambulance services. The insurance company's payment and pre-authorization policies may be different for carve-outs than for other covered specialist services.

Point-of-Service Plans

Point-of-service (POS) health plans combine characteristics of HMO and PPO plans. As in an HMO plan, the member must designate a PCP to act as gatekeeper for medical services. The insurer will cover authorized, in-network services much like an HMO. However, the patient may choose to go out of network and pay higher out-of-pocket expenses. Typically, a POS plan will have a high deductible and coinsurance to encourage members to use in-network services. This type of health plan is designed for individuals who want the lower premiums and PCP-centered care of an HMO but also want some coverage for out-of-network costs.

Indemnity Insurance

Indemnity insurance does not use a network and instead allows members to use the services of any medical provider, including specialists. Indemnity plans provide a flat fee for services based on the **usual, customary, and reasonable rate (UCR)** for a specific location (and thus are sometimes called fee-for-service plans). For example, if an indemnity plan includes $5,000 in coverage for hospitalization costs, the plan will pay up to $5,000 for hospitalization at any location. However, the patient will be responsible for any additional costs. The patient may also be asked to pay medical costs up front and then be reimbursed by the insurer. In addition, most indemnity plans will include a deductible.

 Helpful Hint: Some types of indemnity insurance can be used to cover nonmedical expenses or make up for missed income due to illness or injury.

Indemnity plans used to be the main type of health insurance available but today are very rarely used as primary insurance. Instead, they are used as a supplemental policy to help cover co-pays, deductibles, and coinsurance fees accumulated from a primary managed care insurance plan. Some plans will cover only hospital-surgical costs, and others may cover other medical services.

Private Benefit Programs

Consumers can purchase insurance plans through their employer as part of a group plan or through the health insurance marketplace established under the Affordable Care Act (ACA).

EMPLOYER-SPONSORED HEALTH COVERAGE

Companies may choose to offer health coverage through **employer-sponsored health coverage**. These plans are also called **group plans** because the same insurance coverage is offered to all members of the group (in this case, the employees). The employer picks the insurance policy and pays for part of the premiums. All employees and their dependents are offered the insurance.

Employer-sponsored plans tend to have more comprehensive coverage and cost less than individually purchased plans. As a group, businesses can negotiate better rates for their members, and businesses will often offer high-quality benefit plans to recruit and retain employees.

The **Consolidated Omnibus Budget Reconciliation Act of 1985 (COBRA)** requires employers with twenty or more employees to offer employees and their dependents continued coverage if they have a qualifying event. These events include:

+ employee is laid off
+ divorce that ends spouse's eligibility for benefits
+ death of the employee
+ dependant child reaches the age at which benefits end

COBRA coverage is offered for up to eighteen months. During this time, the insured person must pay the entire premium as well as an administration fee (usually 2 percent). This added expense can make COBRA coverage unaffordable for many people. Some states have passed legislation that extends COBRA coverage by applying regulations to smaller businesses or adding qualifying events.

INDIVIDUALLY PURCHASED INSURANCE

Consumers can purchase individual health care plans through the **health care marketplace** (also called **health exchanges**). The **Patient Protection and Affordable Care Act (PPACA)**, colloquially referred to as "Obamacare," regulates the type of insurance available through the marketplace. All plans available to consumers must meet the following requirements:

+ Plans must cover **essential health benefits**: ambulatory care, emergency services, hospitalization, maternity and newborn care, mental health and substance abuse services, prescription drugs, rehabilitative and habilitative services, laboratory services, preventive and wellness services, and pediatric services.

+ Plans cannot include an annual spending cap on essential health benefits spending.

+ No insurer may exclude patients or vary rates based on a patient's preexisting conditions.

Individually purchased plans are managed care plans with the same structure as employer-based plans. They can be PPOs, HMOs, EPOs, or POS plans and can carry highly variable premiums, deductibles, coinsurance, and max out-of-pocket amounts. Plans are categorized as bronze, silver, gold, or platinum based on the level of insurance provided.

 Did You Know? Government subsidies for purchasing health care plans on the marketplace are available to individuals and families with low incomes.

Health care exchanges have an **open enrollment period** (typically from November 1 to December 15) during which individuals can purchase insurance. Consumers can also purchase insurance from the exchange if they have a qualifying event (e.g., losing employer coverage).

Public Benefit Programs
MEDICARE

The US federal government provides insurance for certain individuals through the **Medicare** program, which is administered through the Centers for Medicare and Medicaid Services (CMS). People eligible for Medicare include those who:

+ are sixty-five or older and have paid payroll taxes

+ are younger than sixty-five and have a disability

+ have end-stage renal failure

+ have amyotrophic lateral sclerosis (ALS)

Medicare includes four parts. **Medicare Part A (hospital/hospice)** covers inpatient services, including hospitalization, rehabilitation or nursing services at a skilled nursing facility, and hospice care. Hospitalization is covered for up to ninety days, with coinsurance required after sixty days. Stays at a skilled nursing facility are covered for one hundred days with co-pays required after twenty days. Patients will only be covered after hospitalization and must receive medically necessary care or therapy; inpatient services solely for activities of daily living are not covered. Hospice services will be covered for patients with less than six months to live.

Medicare Part B (medical) covers outpatient services, including preventive services, diagnostic tests, outpatient procedures, emergency care treatment, home nursing and therapy visits, and some ambulance services. Part B also covers **durable medical equipment (DME)**, which is equipment that provides medical benefit to patients in their day-to-day life. DME must:

+ have a primarily medical purpose

+ be prescribed by a physician

+ be used at home

+ be for repeated use (durable)

Helpful Hint: Healthcare Common Procedure Coding System, or **HCPCS**, are medical codes used when filing Medicare claims. HCPCS Level I codes are the numeric CPT codes. The Level II codes are alphanumeric and are usually for non-physician services (e.g., ambulance transport).

Medicare Part C (**Medicare Advantage plans**) is administered through a private insurer that contracts with the government. These plans must include coverage for all services covered in both Medicare Part A and Part B. They are usually HMO-style plans with a network and a PCP who acts as a gatekeeper; however, a small number are PPOs.

Medicare Part D (**prescription drug plans**) is administered by private insurers or pharmacy benefits managers who provide prescription drug coverage. The insurer may choose which drugs to cover, but the CMS requires that insurers cover drugs from specific classes. In addition, the CMS also provides a list of drugs that it does not allow Part D plans to cover. Part D plans can be stand-alone prescription drug plans (PDPs) or can be bundled with Medicare Advantage (Part C) plans.

Medicare has a system of premiums, deductibles, and coinsurance that is similar to private insurance plans. These costs vary by part.

+ Medicare Part A has no premiums if the person or their spouse has paid Medicare taxes for ten years (forty quarters). People over sixty-five who do not meet the tax requirement may buy into Medicare by paying premiums. There is also a standard deductible and coinsurance amount set by the CMS.

+ Medicare Part B requires a monthly premium that is based on income. It also has a standard deductible set by the CMS. After meeting the deductible, patients will usually pay 20 percent of the cost of treatment (as set by Medicare).

+ The premiums, deductibles, and coinsurance for Medicare Parts C and D are set by the individual insurance plan purchased.

+ Neither Medicare Part A nor Part B has an annual maximum out-of-pocket amount. Purchased plans for Parts C and D may set a maximum out-of-pocket amount.

MEDICAID

Medicaid is a joint federal-state program that provides health coverage for individuals with low incomes. Because Medicaid is partially funded and regulated by states, eligibility and coverage vary widely. Generally, Medicaid will cover individuals with low incomes and has special provisions for coverage of pregnant people, children, the elderly, and people with disabilities.

 Did You Know? Medicaid also provides nursing home coverage that is not covered by Medicare.

The ACA expanded Medicaid coverage in 2014 to cover all individuals whose household income is below 133 percent of the federal poverty line. However, the Supreme Court ruled that states could refuse to participate in the expansion, creating a division in Medicaid coverage between states that chose to expand and those that did not. In addition, some states have implemented cost-sharing measures such as premiums, coinsurance, and deductibles (these costs cannot be imposed for pregnancy-related services, emergency care, or preventive care for children).

Depending on state requirements, some people may qualify for both Medicare and Medicaid. For those with **dual eligibility**, Medicare must be billed first, with Medicaid billed second for services Medicare does not cover.

SOCIAL SECURITY DISABILITY INSURANCE

Social Security Disability Insurance (SSDI) is a benefit program for people who are blind or disabled and cannot work. It is paid for out of the federal disability trust fund. To be eligible, recipients must have been employed for at least ten years or be the dependant of someone who has been employed for at least ten years. Recipients must also be blind or fit the Social Security Administration's definition of permanently disabled. The amount of SSDI recipients receive depends solely on what they earned during their working years. If they are a dependant, the amount is based on their provider's earnings. After two years of being on SSDI, a patient is also eligible to receive federal health insurance through Medicare.

SUPPLEMENTAL SECURITY INCOME

Unlike SSDI, **Supplemental Security Income (SSI)** is a cash benefit for those who are disabled and have a limited income. It is paid for through tax revenues. Eligibility does not have any requirements regarding former employment. A recipient must meet the federal government's definition of disabled or blind, or they must be older than sixty-five and have a limited income. Typically, because of their limited income, SSI beneficiaries are also immediately eligible for their state's Medicaid health insurance program.

Military Benefit Programs
TRICARE

TRICARE is a health care program for military personnel, including active-duty US armed forces, those in the National Guard or military reserve, and military family members. Dependents and surviving spouses are also covered if the veteran was killed in active duty. The Defense Health Agency manages the program, but health benefits are provided by a civilian provider network.

> **Helpful Hint:** TRICARE was formerly known as CHAMPUS (Civilian Health and Medical Program of the Uniformed Services). In 1997, CHAMPUS became TRICARE (a managed care plan) to help cut costs and streamline administration.

TRICARE offers many different options. Costs vary and are based on the plan selected, whether the service member enlisted before or after January 1, 2018, and whether the member is currently on active duty, retired, or medically retired. Survivors are also eligible to enroll and pay the same rates as medically retired members. Premiums for TRICARE are referred to as *enrollment fees* and can be a one-time fee or a monthly fee, depending on the plan. Active-duty members typically do not pay an enrollment fee. Active-duty TRICARE Prime members pay nothing for deductibles, premiums, and max out-of-pocket rates, but TRICARE For Life medically retired members pay a $300 premium, a $3,500 deductible, and a coinsurance of 20 percent for all in-network care and 25 percent for all out-of-network care with no cap.

+ **TRICARE Prime** is a managed care plan and the least expensive plan available. It is for active-duty members who live within Prime service areas in the United States. Eligible enrollees include active-duty military and their families, retired military and their families, National Guard reserve members who have been on active duty for more than thirty-one consecutive days, nonactivated Guard/reserve members and their families who qualify for Transitional Assistance benefits, retired Guard/reserve members age sixty and older and their families, surviving family members, Medal of Honor awardees and their families, and qualified ex-spouses of non-active military members and their families who live and receive their medical care within the United States.

+ **TRICARE Prime Remote**, **TRICARE Prime Overseas**, and **TRICARE Prime Remote Overseas** are all managed care policies for active-duty service members, including National Guard/reserve members who are ordered to active-duty service for thirty-one or more consecutive days and family members who live with enrolled service members. Plan eligibility depends on where the member lives in relation to a military health care facility. **TRICARE Select** is a fee-for-service plan. The same members who are eligible for a Prime plan and receive their medical care within the United States are eligible for the Select plan.

+ **TRICARE Select Overseas** is a fee-for-service plan that has more options but is more expensive than the Prime Overseas plans. Membership eligibility is the same as above.

+ **TRICARE For Life** is accepted worldwide, but a beneficiary must have Medicare A and B to be eligible. It is the secondary insurance for those on Medicare but acts as the primary insurance when Medicare is not accepted. It has no annual premium. There is a deductible of $150 for an individual and no more than $300 for a family whose members are medically retired or for a surviving family member.

+ **TRICARE Reserve Select** is a managed care plan for reserve members that may be used with any TRICARE authorized provider, but services may require pre-authorization.

+ **TRICARE Retired Reserve** is a PPO plan for qualified retired reserve members and surviving family members.

+ **TRICARE Young Adult** plans are open to eligible adult children of service members between the ages of twenty-one and twenty-six. Prime, Prime Overseas, and Prime Remote managed care options are available for the young adult policies as well as a Select PPO option similar to the general TRICARE policies with the same names.

✦ **US Family Health Plan (USFHP)** and **TRICARE Young Adult** are managed care plans that require the service member to choose a provider for care, but the member cannot receive care from providers who are eligible for reimbursement through TRICARE or Medicare, or from a military medical provider.

TRICARE also offers other benefits, such as pharmacy and dental programs.

VETERANS HEALTH ADMINISTRATION

Once military service members retire or otherwise separate themselves from military service, the **Veterans Health Administration** will provide them and their dependents with medical care at **Veterans Administration (VA)** medical facilities all over the United States. Veterans are automatically eligible for services if they received an honorable discharge and served a minimum of twenty-four months in active duty or, for reserve members, the full length of their call-up to active duty during wartime. The minimum service requirement can be waived depending on the reason for discharge. Care is free for veterans who meet certain military service conditions or income guidelines. Veterans who make more than the income limit will have a co-pay.

Veterans who received an *other than honorable* (OTH) discharge can apply for a discharge upgrade or a VA character review in order to get benefits. These can sometimes take up to a year to process. Veterans with an OTH discharge who have trauma or another mental illness related to their service, including sexual trauma, are immediately eligible for benefits regardless of their discharge status.

Health care provided by the VA includes primary and specialty care services like mental health services, prescription coverage, surgeries, emergency room, and inpatient hospital care. Under certain conditions, the VA will also cover vision and dental care. The VA also provides reimbursement for travel to a VA medical center, covers home health or long-term care, and offers support services for caregivers.

To apply for VA health benefits, a veteran can submit the required forms online, in person, over the phone, or by mail. An eligibility letter should arrive in the mail one week after submission of the application. A short time later the veteran will receive a "welcome phone call" during which their benefits will be reviewed and their first appointment with a medical provider will be scheduled.

CHAMPVA

CHAMPVA (Civilian Health and Medical Program of the Department of Veterans Affairs) is another military health coverage benefit. CHAMPVA provides comprehensive health coverage for a spouse or dependant of a veteran who is permanently disabled due to military service, or a spouse or dependant of a veteran who was totally and permanently disabled due to a service-related injury at the time of death. The family members are also eligible for CHAMPVA if the military member died in the line of duty and the death was not caused by misconduct. Typically, those beneficiaries are eligible for TRICARE rather than CHAMPVA.

Pharmacy Benefits Management

A **pharmacy benefits manager (PBM)** is a third-party administrator who handles prescription medication claims for insurance companies and federal benefits programs. The goal of pharmacy benefits management is to reduce the amount patients and insurers spend on prescription medications. PBMs accomplish this goal through a variety of techniques:

+ processing prescription claims
+ maintaining a network of participating pharmacies
+ negotiating drug costs
+ managing patients' access to specialty medications
+ obtaining rebates from drug manufacturers
+ operating mail order pharmacies

Another major PBM duty is maintaining the **formulary**, a list of medications that are approved for reimbursement. Most formularies use a **tiered system** designed to encourage physicians and patients to choose lower-cost drugs. Tier 1 drugs are usually generic and available to the patients at little to no cost. Higher-tier drugs are specialty or brand-name medications; the patient usually pays an escalating co-pay or coinsurance for drugs in each tier. Medications not on the formulary are not covered by the insurance or benefits providers, meaning the patient must pay the full price out of pocket.

 Helpful Hint: The three largest PBMs—Express Scripts, CVS Health (Caremark), and OptumRx (UnitedHealth)—handle 70 percent of all prescriptions filled in the United States.

Workers' Compensation

Workers' compensation (sometimes known as *workman's compensation*) is an insurance benefit that most employers are required to carry in the United States. The only exception is the state of Texas. States determine which businesses must carry worker's compensation and the type of insurance carrier that can carry it. Worker's compensation provides medical benefits and a replacement income while an employee recovers from a work-related injury. If the injury results in a permanent disability, worker's compensation benefits would provide the employee with an income for a predetermined length of time or a lump sum compensation payment, medical benefits, and job retraining. If an employee is killed on the job, some states require a predetermined minimum benefit to be paid to the employee's dependents.

The Occupational Safety and Health Administration (OSHA) has defined a "work-related" injury as an injury occurring while the employee was performing a work-related task. When an employee is injured on the job, the employer is required to mail or give the employee a claim form and directions on how to file a workers' compensation claim within one business day of the injury being reported. Once the employee files the claim, the insurance company will then instruct the employee to see a physician who will evaluate the injury. This physician then reports back to the insurance company on the severity of the injury and confirms if it is work related. If it is determined that the employee's injury qualifies for workers' compensation, the employee can choose to claim these benefits. However, by claiming workers' compensation benefits, employees give up their right to sue their employer for any negligence regarding their injury.

Reimbursement and Payment Methodologies

With a **fee-for-service** reimbursement, each item involved in patient care is billed separately. If an insurance policy is not a managed care policy, it is typically a fee-for-service policy. Even a policy that uses a PPO can be a fee-for-service policy. If, for example, a patient is to have a hip replacement, medical supplies, hospital room, fees for surgeons and all other medical professionals involved, and anesthesia would be individually charged. By contrast, **bundled payments** are reimbursed as one fee for all medical care provided. In the example of the hip replacement, all items would be reimbursed in one lump sum.

Bundled payments for health care were created to encourage quality medical care and reduce health care costs. Many Medicaid insurance companies use bundled payments. The expected costs for all provider services are predetermined prior to the services being rendered. In order to make money, or at least to not lose money, providers need to minimize complications and provide effective and efficient services to their patients. **Case rates** are a type of bundled payment. They are a flat fee typically paid by the day for a specific diagnosis, such as myocardial infarction. Bundled payments can also take the form of capitated payments. The payment made to the provider is based on a specific length of time and a specific number of patients. For example, an Accountable Care Organization (ACO) may pay a primary care organization $3,500 per patient per month to manage all care for their patients.

> **Helpful Hint:** Medicare payments are based on relative value units (RVUs), a cost formula that includes the physician and practice expense of a procedure multiplied by a geographic practice cost index that accounts for differences among regions.

Medicare is a type of **prospective payment system**. The payments for patient services are determined according to the average cost of the services provided and the severity of the patient's diagnoses prior to treatment. The facility uses these predetermined rates to cover all services needed for a specific patient. The payment amounts for the same services will differ among patients depending on their diagnoses. If the care is inefficient or the patient suffers a preventable complication, like a hospital-acquired infection, or if the patient is readmitted to the hospital within a certain time frame, it will negatively impact the hospital's reimbursement for that patient. Hospitals that have multiple readmissions will be subject to decreased payments for all Medicare patients.

SIX: ANATOMY and PHYSIOLOGY

Medical Terminology

Many medical terms can be broken down into three main parts to help determine their meaning:

prefix – root – suffix

Prefixes are added to the beginning of a word, and **suffixes** are added to the end of the word. They carry assigned meanings and can be attached to a word to modify the word's meaning. **Roots** are the building blocks of all words: they are what is left when prefixes and suffixes are removed from the word. Roots are not always easily recognizable words because they often come from Latin or Greek words. The table below shows how medical terms can be built from these word parts.

Table 6.1. Breaking Down Medical Terminology			
Prefix	**Root**	**Suffix**	**Meaning of Word**
pre *before*	natal *born*		**prenatal**: before birth
	arthro *joint*	scope *viewing instrument*	**arthroscope**: instrument for viewing joints
leuko *white*	cyto *cell*	penia *decreased*	**leukocytopenia**: decrease in white blood cells

When preparing for your medical assistant exam, it's better to learn these word parts than to try to memorize a long list of medical diagnoses, procedures, and specialties. The tables below give the most common prefixes, roots, and suffixes found in medical terms.

Table 6.2. The Most Common Word Roots in Medical Terminology

Word Root	Definition	Example
acous/o	hearing	acoustic
acusis	hearing	hyperacusis
aden/o	gland	adenoid
adip/o	fat	adipose
alb	white	albumin
ambul/o	walk	ambulatory
andr/o	male	androgen
angi/o	vessel	angiogram
arthr/o	joint	arthritis
bucc/o	cheek	buccal
canc	crab	cancerous
carcin/o	cancer	carcinogen
cardi	heart	cardiology
cereb	brain	cerebellum
chem/o	chemistry	chemotherapy
chol	bile	cholesterol
cyan	blue	cyanosis
cyst/o	bladder	cystitis
cyt/o	cell	cytology
dactyl	finger	syndactylism
derm/a	skin	dermatitis
duoden/o	duodenum	duodenostomy
enter/o	intestine	enteralgia
erythr/o	red	erythrocyte
esophag/o	esophagus	esophageal
fibr/o	fibrous tissue	fibromyalgia
gastr/o	stomach	gastritis
gluc/o	sugar	glucose
glyc/o	sugar	glycogen
gynec/o	woman	gynecology

Word Root	Definition	Example
hemat/o, hem/o	blood	hemoglobin
hepat/o	liver	hepatic
hist/o	body tissue	histamine
hyster/o	uterus	hysterectomy
lact/o	milk	lactating
lapar/o	abdomen	laparotomy
leuk/o	white	leukemia
lipid	fat	sphingolipid
lymph/o	lymphoid tissue	lymphocyte
mamm/o, mast/o	breast tissue	mammogram
melan/o	black	melanoma
myel/o, my/o	muscle	myalgia
nas/o	nose	nasal
necr/o	dead	necrosis
nephr/o	kidney	nephrology
neur/o	nerve	neuralgia
ocul/o	eye	ocular
ophthalm/o	eye	ophthalmologist
orchid/o	testes	orchidectomy
oste/o	bone	osteoarthritis
ot/o	ear	otalgia
ox, oxy	oxygen	oxyhemoglobin
pancreat/o	pancreas	pancreatitis
path	disease	pathogen
pector/o	chest	pectoral
ped/o	foot	bipedal
pelv/o	pelvis	pelvic
phleb/o	vein	phlebotomist
pneum/o	lungs	pneumonia
proct/o	rectum	proctologist
prostat/o	prostate	prostatic

Table 6.2. The Most Common Word Roots in Medical Terminology (continued)

Word Root	Definition	Example
psych/o	mind	psychology
pulm/o	lungs	pulmonary
ren/o	kidney	renal
retin/o	retina	retinal
rhin/o	nose	rhinoplasty
somat/o	body	somatotonia
spir/o	breathing	spirometer
spondyl/o	spine	spondylosis
stenosis	narrowing	spinal stenosis
thromb/o	blood clot	thrombolysis
thym/o	thymus gland	thymogenic
tox/o	poisonous	toxoplasmosis
tympan/o	ear drum	tympanoplasty
urethr/o	urethra	urethroplasty
uria	excess	glycosuria
uro, ur	urine	urology
uter/o	uterus	intrauterine
vas, vascul/o	blood vessel	vasoconstriction
ven/o	vein	ventostasis
vesic, vesicul/o	vesicle, bladder	vesicular
xanth/o	yellow	xanthine

Table 6.3. Common Medical Prefixes

Prefix	Definition	Example
a–	without, not, no	aphasia
ab–	away from	abnormal
ad–	toward	adduct
ambi–	both	ambidextrous
an–	not, without	anorexia
ante–	before	anteroom

Prefix	Definition	Example
anti–	against	antivenin
auto–	self	autograft
bi–	two	bilateral
bio–	life	biochemical
brady–	slow	bradycardia
chlor–	green	chlorosis
circum–	around	circumcision
cirrh–	yellow	cirrhosis
con–	together	congenital
contra–	against	contradiction
cyan–	blue	cyanide
dia–	completely	diagnosis
dys–	bad, painful, abnormal	dysfunction
ec–	out of	ecbolic
ecto–	out, outside	ectopic
endo–	within, inner	endometriosis
epi–	upon, above	epidermis
eryth–	red	erythrocyte
eu–	good, normal	euphoria
ex–, exo–	out, away from	exoskeleton
extra–	outside	extracellular
hemi–	half	hemisphere
hyper–	over, above	hyperglycemia
hypo–	below, under	hypoallergenic
im–	not, without	imperfect
immun–	having immunity	immunosuppressant
in–	not, without	incorrect
infra–	below, under	infracostal
inter–	between, among	intervertebral
intra–	within, inside	intradermal
iso–	equal	isochromatic

Table 6.3. Common Medical Prefixes (continued)

Prefix	Definition	Example
leuk–	white	leukemia
macro–	large	macrocephaly
mal–	poor	malnutrition
medi–	middle	medicine
melan–	black	melanoma
meso–	middle	mesothelioma
meta–	after, beyond	metamorphic
micro–	small	microscopic
mid–	middle	midsection
mono–	one	monochromatic
multi–	many	multicellular
neo–	new	neonatal
pan–	all	pandemic
para–	near, alongside, abnormal	parathyroid
per–	through	percutaneous
peri–	around	pericardial
poly–	many, excessive	polycystic
post–	after	postsurgical
pre–	before	prenatal
pro–	to go forth	procreation
pseudo–	false	pseudonym
purpur–	purple	purpuriferous
quadri–	four	quadriplegic
re–	again	regenerate
retro–	behind, backward	retroactive
rube–	red	rubella
semi–	half	semicircle
sub–	below, under	sublingual
super–	above, excess	supernumerary
supra–	above	suprarenal

Prefix	Definition	Example
sym–, syn–	together	synthetic
tachy–	fast	tachycardia
trans–	across	transverse
tri–	three	triangle
ultra–	beyond, excessive	ultrasound
uni–	one	unilateral
xanth–	yellow	xanthine
xer–	dry	xerodermatic

Table 6.4. Common Medical Suffixes

Suffix	Definition	Example
–ac	pertaining to	cardiac
–al	pertaining to	buccal
–algia	pain	neuralgia
–ar, –ary	pertaining to	urinary
–asthenia	weakness	myasthenia
–cele	hernia, bulging	hydrocele
–centesis	surgical puncture for removal of fluid	amniocentesis
–cyte	cell	leukocyte
–dipsia	thirst	polydipsia
–dynia	pain	encephalodynia
–eal	pertaining to	esophageal
–ectasis	dilation or distension of an organ	lymphangiectasis
–ectomy	surgical removal	hysterectomy
–emia	blood condition	leukemia
–genic	producing, forming	carcinogenic
–gram	record, picture	electrocardiogram
–graphy, –graph	instrument for recording	electrocardiograph
–ia	disease, abnormal condition	anorexia
–iasis	pathological condition	elephantiasis

Table 6.4. Common Medical Suffixes (continued)

Suffix	Definition	Example
–iatry	treatment	psychiatry
–ic	pertaining to	anorexic
–icle	small	ventricle
–ism	state, condition	alcoholism
–itis	inflammation of	arthritis
–ium	metallic element	barium
–lepsy	seizure	epilepsy
–lith	stone	tonsillolith
–logy	study of	biology
–lysis	breaking down	thrombolysis
–lytic	destroy, reduce	hemolytic
–malacia	softening	osteomalacia
–megaly	enlarged	osteomegaly
–meter	measuring instrument	cytometer
–metry	process of measuring	optometry
–oid	resembling, like	carcinoid
–oma	tumor	hematoma
–opia, –opsia	vision	presbyopia
–osis	abnormal condition	cyanosis
–osmia	odor, smell	dysosmia
–ous	processing, full of	ferrous
–paresis	incomplete, partial	hemiparesis
–path, –pathy	disease	osteopath
–penia	deficiency, decreased number	leukocytopenia
–pepsia	digestion	dyspepsia
–phagia	eating, swallowing	dysphagia
–philia	attraction to	hemophilia
–phobia	fear of	agoraphobia
–plasia	formation	dysplasia
–plasty	surgical repair	rhinoplasty

Suffix	Definition	Example
–plegia	paralysis, stroke	paraplegia
–rrhage	blood bursting forth	hemorrhage
–rrhea	flow, discharge	amenorrhea
–sclerosis	hardening	arteriosclerosis
–scope	instrument to view	microscope
–scopy	process of viewing	endoscopy
–spasm	twitching, involuntary contraction	neurospasm
–stasis	control, stop	homeostasis
–stenosis	narrowing	tracheostenosis
–stomy	artificial opening	colostomy
–therapy	treatment	hydrotherapy
–tic	pertaining to	paralytic
–tocia	conditions of labor	tomotocia
–tomy	incision, cut	cystotomy
–toxic	poison	cardiotoxic
–tripsy	rubbing, crushing	lithotripsy
–trophy	nourishment, development	atrophy
–tropic, –tropia	turning	exotropia
–ula, –ule	small	globule
–uria	urine, urination	nocturia

The Biological Hierarchy

The biological hierarchy is a systematic breakdown of the structures of the human body organized from smallest to largest (or largest to smallest). The human body is made up of small units called **cells**. A cell is a microscopic, self-replicating, structural, and functional unit of the body that performs many different jobs. The cell is made up of many smaller units that are sometimes considered as part of the biological hierarchy, including cytoplasm, organelles, nuclei, and a membrane that separates the cell contents from its surroundings.

Tissues comprise the next largest group of structures in the body; they are a collection of cells that all perform a similar function. To simplify, the human body has four basic types of tissue:

+ **Connective** tissues—which include bones, ligaments, and cartilage—support, separate, or connect the body's various organs and tissues.

+ **Epithelial** tissues are found in the skin, blood vessels, and many organs.

+ **Muscular** tissues contain contractile units that pull on connective tissues to create movement.

+ **Nervous** tissue makes up the peripheral nervous systems that transmit impulses throughout the body.

After tissues, **organs** are the next largest structure on the biological hierarchy. Organs are a collection of tissues within the body that share a similar function. For instance, the esophagus is an organ whose primary function is carrying food and liquids from the mouth to the stomach.

The esophagus is part of the digestive **organ system**. Organ systems, a group of organs that work together to perform a similar function, rank above organs as the next largest structure on the biological hierarchy. The digestive organ system is the entire group of organs in the body that processes food from start to finish.

Finally, an **organism** is the total collection of all the parts of the biological hierarchy working together to form a living being; it is the largest structure in the biological hierarchy.

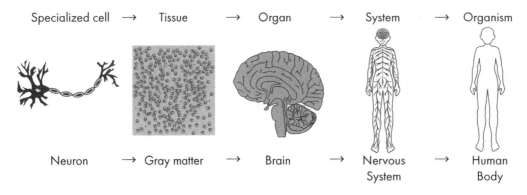

Figure 6.1. Biological Hierarchy and Levels of Organization

Directional Terminology

When discussing anatomy and physiology, specific terms are used to refer to directions. Directional terms include the following:

+ **inferior**: away from the head

+ **superior**: closer to the head

+ **anterior**: toward the front

+ **posterior**: toward the back

+ **dorsal**: toward the back

+ **ventral**: toward the front

+ **medial**: toward the midline of the body

+ **lateral**: further from the midline of the body

+ **proximal**: closer to the trunk

+ **distal**: away from the trunk

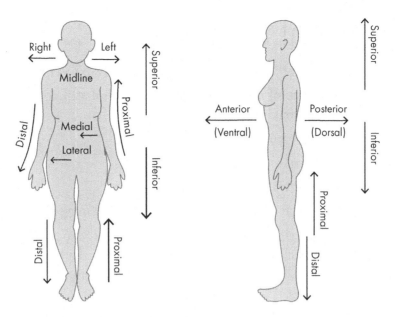

Figure 6.2. Directional Terminology

Body Cavities

The internal structure of the human body is organized into compartments called **cavities**, which are separated by membranes. There are two main cavities in the human body: the dorsal cavity and the ventral cavity (both named for their relative positions).

The **dorsal cavity** is further divided into the **cranial cavity**, which holds the brain, and the **spinal cavity**, which surrounds the spine. The two sections of the dorsal cavity are continuous. Both sections are lined by the **meninges**, a three-layered membrane that protects the brain and spinal cord.

The **ventral cavity** houses most of the body's organs. It also can be further divided into smaller cavities. The **thoracic cavity** holds the heart and lungs, the **abdominal cavity** holds the digestive organs and kidneys, and the **pelvic cavity** holds the bladder and reproductive organs. Both the abdominal and pelvic cavities are enclosed by a membrane called the **peritoneum**.

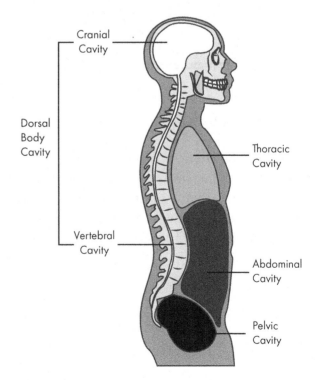

Figure 6.3. Body Cavities

The Skeletal System
STRUCTURE AND FUNCTION OF THE SKELETAL SYSTEM

The skeletal system is made up of over 200 different **bones**, a stiff connective tissue in the human body with many functions, including:

+ protecting internal organs
+ synthesizing blood cells
+ storing necessary minerals
+ providing the muscular system with leverage to create movement

Bones are covered with a thin layer of vascular connective tissue called the **periosteum**, which serves as a point of muscle attachment, supplies blood to the bone, and contains nerve endings. **Osseous tissue** is the primary tissue that makes up bone. There are two types of osseous tissue: cortical (compact) bone and cancellous (spongy) bone. **Cortical bone** is the dense, solid material that surrounds the bone and gives it hardness and strength. It is usually concentrated in the middle part of the bone.

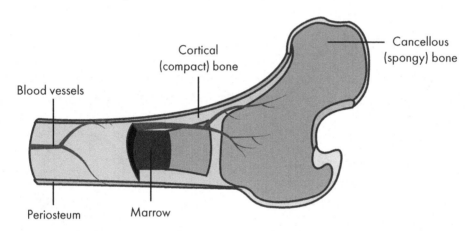

Figure 6.4. Structure of Bone

Cancellous bone is less dense, more porous, and softer. It is located at the ends of long bones, where it does not bear a structural load. Instead it is a site of the bone's blood production and metabolic activity, as it stores both blood vessels and **bone marrow. Red bone marrow** is responsible for producing red blood cells, platelets, and white blood cells. **Yellow bone marrow** is composed mostly of fat tissue and can be converted to red bone marrow in response to extreme blood loss in the body.

Table 6.5. Types of Bones		
Name	**Shape**	**Example**
Long bones	Longer than they are wide	Femur, humerus
Short bones	Wider than they are long	Clavicle, carpals
Flat bones	Wide and flat	Skull, pelvis
Irregular bones	Irregularly shaped	Vertebrae, jaw

The hundreds of bones in the body make up the human **skeleton**. The **axial skeleton** contains eighty bones and has three major subdivisions: the skull, which contains the cranium and facial bones; the thorax, which includes the sternum and twelve pairs of ribs; and the vertebral column, which contains the body's thirty-three vertebrae. These eighty bones function together to support and protect many of the body's vital organs, including the brain, lungs, heart, and spinal cord. The **appendicular skeleton**'s 126 bones make up the body's appendages. The main function of the appendicular skeleton is locomotion.

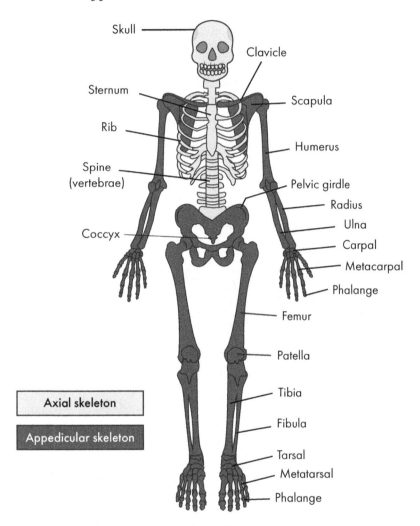

Figure 6.5. The Axial and Appendicular Skeletons

Various connective tissues join the parts of the skeleton together to other systems, as shown in the table below.

Table 6.6. Connective Tissue in the Skeletal System

Tissue	Function
Ligament	Joins bone to bone.
Tendon	Joins bones to muscles.

Table 6.6. Connective Tissue in the Skeletal System (continued)

Tissue	Function
Cartilage	Cushions bones in joints. Provides structural integrity for many body parts (e.g., the ear and nose), maintains open pathways (e.g., the trachea and bronchi).

Joints

The point at which a bone is attached to another bone is called a **joint**. There are three basic types of joints:

+ **Fibrous joints** connect bones that do not move.

+ **Cartilaginous joints** connect bones with cartilage and allow limited movement.

+ **Synovial joints** allow for a range of motion and are covered by articular cartilage that protects the bones.

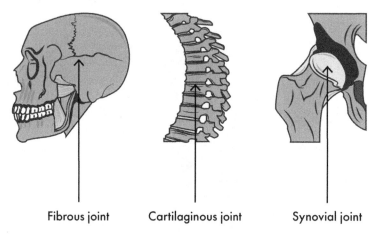

Fibrous joint   Cartilaginous joint   Synovial joint

Figure 6.6. Types of Joints

Synovial joints are classified based on their structure and the type of movement they allow. There are many types of synovial joints; the most important are discussed in Table 6.7.

Table 6.7. Types of Synovial Joints

Name	Movement	Found In
Hinge joint	movement through one plane of motion as flexion/extension	elbows, knees, fingers
Ball-and-socket joint	range of motion through multiple planes and rotation about an axis	hips, shoulders
Saddle joint	movement through multiple planes, but cannot rotate about an axis	thumbs
Gliding joint	sliding movement in the plane of the bones' surfaces	vertebrae, small bones in the wrists and ankles

Name	Movement	Found In
Condyloid joint	movement through two planes as flexion/extension and abduction/adduction, but cannot rotate about an axis	wrists
Pivot joint	only movement is rotation about an axis	elbows, neck

PATHOLOGIES OF THE SKELETAL SYSTEM

Arthritis is inflammation in joints that leads to swelling, pain, and reduced range of motion. There are many different kinds of arthritis. The most common is **osteoarthritis**, which is caused by the wearing down of cartilage in the joints due to age or injury. **Rheumatoid arthritis** and **psoriatic arthritis** are both types of inflammation at the joint caused by chronic autoimmune disorder, which can lead to excessive joint degradation.

Osteoporosis refers to poor bone mineral density due to the loss or lack of the production of calcium content and bone cells, which leads to bone brittleness. It is most common in post-menopausal women.

Postural deviations that cause excessive curvatures of the spine can have painful ramifications for the human body. These include **lordosis** (an excessive anterior curvature of the natural S-shape of the spine), **kyphosis** (an excessive posterior curvature of the natural S-shape of the spine), and **scoliosis** (an excessive lateral curvature of the spine).

Bone cancers include **Ewing sarcoma** and **osteosarcoma**. In addition, white blood cell cancers, such as myeloma and leukemia, start in bone marrow.

The Muscular System

The primary function of the muscular system is movement. Muscles contract and relax, resulting in motion. This includes both voluntary motion, such as walking, as well as involuntary motion that keeps the body systems, such as circulation, respiration, and digestion, running. Other functions of the muscular system include overall stability and protection of the spine as well as posture.

MUSCLE CELL STRUCTURE

The main structural unit of a muscle is the **sarcomere**. Sarcomeres are composed of a series of **muscle fibers**, which are elongated individual cells that stretch from one end of the muscle to the other. Within each fiber are hundreds of **myofibrils**, long strands within the cells that contain alternating layers of thin filaments made of the protein **actin** and thick filaments made of the protein **myosin**. Each of these proteins plays a role in muscle contraction and relaxation.

Muscle contraction is explained by the **sliding filament theory**. When the sarcomere is at rest, the thin filaments containing actin are found at both ends of the muscle, while the thick filaments containing myosin are found at the center. Myosin filaments contain "heads," which can attach and detach from actin filaments. The myosin attaches to actin and pulls the thin filaments to the center of the sarcomere, forcing the thin filaments to slide inward and causing the entire sarcomere to shorten, or contract, creating movement. The sarcomere can be broken down into zones that contain certain filaments.

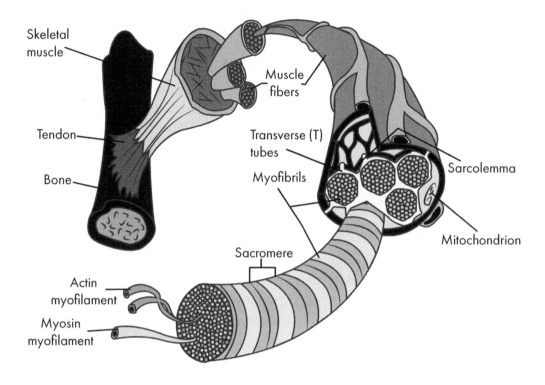

Figure 6.7. Structure of Skeletal Muscle

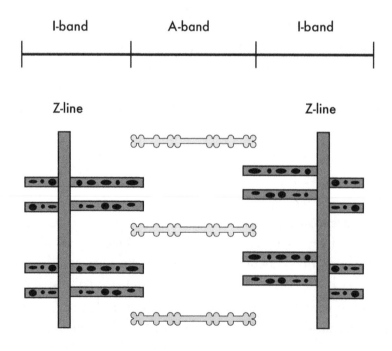

Figure 6.8. Sliding Filament Theory

- The **Z-line** separates the sarcomeres: a single sarcomere is the distance between two Z-lines.
- The **A-band** is the area of the sarcomere in which thick myosin filaments are found and does not shorten during muscular contraction.
- The **I-band** is the area in the sarcomere between the thick myosin filaments in which only thin actin filament is found.
- The **H-zone** is found between the actin filaments and contains only thick myosin filament.

MUSCLES AND THE NERVOUS SYSTEM

Skeletal muscles are activated by special neurons called **motor neurons**. Together, a motor neuron and its associated skeletal muscle fibers are called a **motor unit**. These motor neurons are located within the spinal cord and branch out to the muscles to send the nervous impulses for muscular contraction. The **neuromuscular junction** is the site at which the motor neuron and muscle fibers join to form a chemical synapse for nervous transmission to muscle.

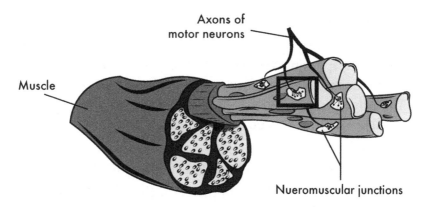

Figure 6.9. Neuromuscular Junctions

Muscles have unique mechanisms that provide the body with feedback based on the stimuli received. To achieve this, **proprioceptors**, such as **muscle spindle fibers** and **Golgi tendon organs**, provide sensory information to the nervous system. Proprioceptors are sensory receptors that provide the body with kinesthetic awareness of its surroundings via stimuli. The mechanisms behind these proprioceptors help protect the body from injury and provide a sense of coordination in space.

TYPES OF MUSCLES

The muscular system consists of three types of muscle: cardiac, visceral, and skeletal. **Cardiac muscle** is only found in the heart. It is a **striated** muscle, with alternating segments of thick and thin filaments, that contracts involuntarily, creating the heartbeat and pumping blood. **Visceral**, or **smooth, muscle** tissue is found in many of the body's essential organs, including the stomach and intestines. It slowly contracts and relaxes to move nutrients, blood, and other substances throughout the body. It is known as smooth muscle because, unlike cardiac and skeletal muscle, this tissue is not composed of sarcomeres with alternating thick and thin filaments. Visceral muscle movement is involuntary.

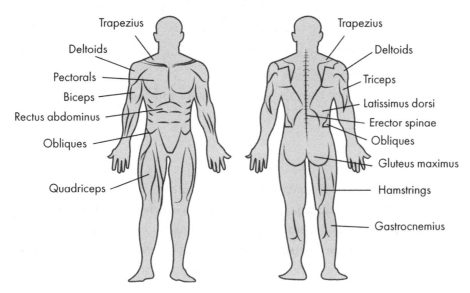

Figure 6.10. Major Muscles of the Body

Skeletal muscle is responsible for voluntary movement, and, as the name suggests, is inextricably linked to the skeletal system. There are two basic types of skeletal muscles: **slow-twitch**, or type I, which move more slowly but hold contractions for long periods of time and do not tire easily, and **fast-twitch**, or type II, which allow for powerful, quick motion for short periods of time.

Skeletal muscles can engage in several different types of muscle actions:

+ **concentric**: muscular contraction in which the length of the muscle is shortening to lift the resistance (upward curl of bicep)

+ **eccentric**: muscular contraction in which the muscle is resisting a force as it lengthens (downward curl of bicep)

+ **isometric**: muscular contraction in which the resistance and force are even and no movement is taking place (holding an object)

PATHOLOGIES OF THE MUSCULAR SYSTEM

Injuries to muscle can impede movement and cause pain. When muscle fibers are overstretched, the resulting **muscle strain** can cause pain, stiffness, and bruising. Muscle fibers can also be weakened by diseases, as with **muscular dystrophy** (MD). MD is a genetically inherited condition that results in progressive muscle wasting, which limits movement and can cause respiratory and cardiovascular difficulties.

The Respiratory System

STRUCTURE AND FUNCTION OF THE RESPIRATORY SYSTEM

The **respiratory system** is responsible for the exchange of gases between the human body and the environment. Oxygen is brought into the body for use in glucose metabolism, and the carbon dioxide created by glucose metabolism is expelled. Gas exchange takes place in the **lungs**. Humans have two lungs, a right and a left, and the right lung is slightly larger than the left. The right lung has three **lobes**, and the left has two. The lungs are surrounded by a thick membrane called the **pleura**.

 Helpful Hint: In anatomy, the terms *right* and *left* are used with the respect to the subject, not the observer.

Respiration begins with pulmonary ventilation, or **breathing**. The first stage of breathing is **inhalation**. During this process, the thoracic cavity expands and the diaphragm muscle contracts, which decreases the pressure in the lungs, pulling in air from the atmosphere. Air is drawn in through the **nose** and **mouth**, then into the throat, where cilia and mucus filter out particles before the air enters the **trachea**.

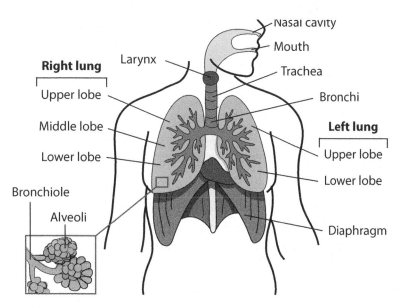

Figure 6.11. The Respiratory System

Once it passes through the trachea, the air passes through either the left or right **bronchi**, which are divisions of the trachea that direct air into the left or right lung. These bronchi are further divided into smaller **bronchioles**, which branch throughout the lungs and become increasingly small.

Eventually, air enters the **alveoli**—tiny air sacs located at the ends of the smallest bronchioles. The alveoli have very thin membranes, only one cell thick, and are the location of gas exchange with the blood: oxygen diffuses into the blood while carbon dioxide is diffused out.

Carbon dioxide is then expelled from the lungs during **exhalation**, the second stage of breathing. During exhalation, the diaphragm relaxes and the thoracic cavity contracts, causing air to leave the body as the lung pressure is now greater than the atmospheric pressure.

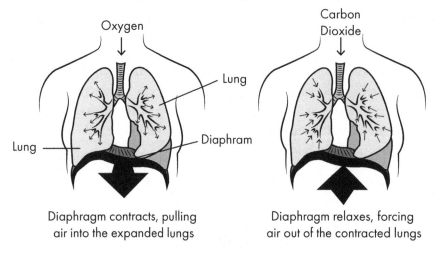

Figure 6.12. The Breathing Process

PATHOLOGIES OF THE RESPIRATORY SYSTEM

Lung diseases that result in the continual restriction of airflow are known as **chronic obstructive pulmonary disease (COPD)**. These include **emphysema**, which is the destruction of lung tissues, and **asthma**, in which the airways are compromised due to a dysfunctional immune response. The main causes of COPD are smoking and air pollution, and genetic factors can also influence the severity of the disease.

The respiratory system is also prone to **respiratory tract infections**, with upper respiratory tract infections affecting air inputs in the nose and throat and lower respiratory tract infections affecting the lungs and their immediate pulmonary inputs. Viral infections of the respiratory system include influenza and the common cold; bacterial infections include tuberculosis and pertussis (whooping cough). **Pneumonia**, the inflammation of the lungs that affects alveoli, can be caused by bacteria, viruses, fungi, or parasites. It is often seen in people whose respiratory system has been weakened by other conditions.

Lung cancer is the second most common type of cancer diagnosed in the United States. (Breast cancer is the most common.) Symptoms of lung cancer include cough, chest pain, and wheezing. Lung cancer is most often caused by smoking, but can develop in non-smokers as well.

The Cardiovascular System
STRUCTURE AND FORM OF THE CARDIOVASCULAR SYSTEM

The cardiovascular system circulates blood, which carries nutrients, wastes, hormones, and other important substances dissolved or suspended in liquid **plasma**. Two of the most important components of blood are **white blood cells**, which fight infections, and **red blood cells**, which transport oxygen. Red blood cells contain **hemoglobin**, a large molecule that includes iron atoms, which binds to oxygen.

Blood is circulated by a muscular organ called the **heart**. The pumping action of the heart is regulated primarily by two neurological nodes, the **sinoatrial** and **atrioventricular nodes**, whose electrical activity sets the rhythm of the heart. The heart includes several layers of tissue:

+ **pericardium**: the outermost protective layer of the heart that contains a lubricative liquid
+ **epicardium**: the deepest layer of the pericardium that envelops the heart muscle
+ **myocardium**: the heart muscle
+ **endocardium**: the innermost, smooth layer of the heart walls

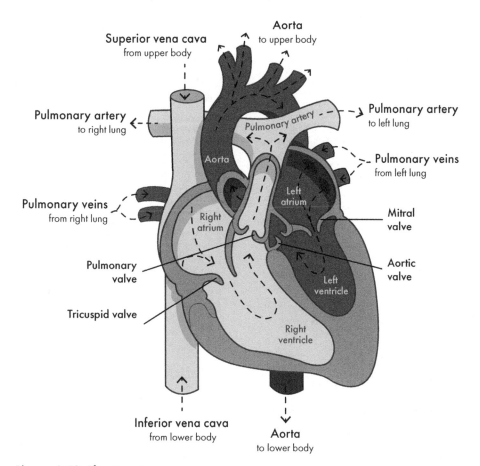

Figure 6.13. The Heart

The human heart has four chambers, the right and left atria and the right and left ventricles, as shown in Figure 6.13. Each chamber is isolated by valves that prevent the backflow of blood once it has passed through. The **tricuspid** and **mitral valves** separate atria from ventricles, and the **pulmonary** and **aortic valves** regulate the movement of blood out of the heart into the arteries.

Blood leaves the heart and travels throughout the body in blood vessels, which decrease in diameter as they move away from the heart and toward the tissues and organs. Blood exits the heart through **arteries**, which become **arterioles** and then **capillaries**, the smallest branch of the circulatory system in which gas exchange from blood to tissues occurs. Deoxygenated blood travels back to the heart through **veins**.

The circulatory system includes two closed loops. In the **pulmonary loop**, deoxygenated blood leaves the heart and travels to the lungs, where it loses carbon dioxide and becomes rich in oxygen. The oxygenated blood then returns to the heart, which pumps it through the **systemic loop**. The systemic loop delivers oxygen to the rest of the body and returns deoxygenated blood to the heart.

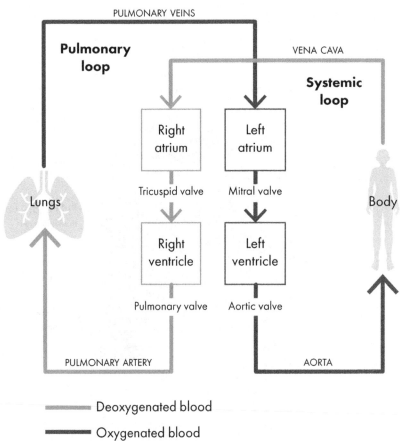

Figure 6.14. Path of Blood Flow Through the Cardiovascular System

PATHOLOGIES OF THE CARDIOVASCULAR SYSTEM

Heart disease is the most common cause of death in the United States. This umbrella term includes a number of different pathologies that cause the heart to weaken or stop:

- **atherosclerosis**: hardening or narrowing of the arteries due to plaque deposits
- **arrhythmia**: abnormal heart rhythm
- **congenital heart defect**: a problem with the physical structure of the heart present from birth
- **myocardial infarction (heart attack)**: death of heart tissue, typically caused by a lack of blood flow from blockage

A heart attack is a life-threatening emergency that requires immediate treatment. Symptoms of a heart attack include tightness in the chest, back, and arms, shortness of breath, nausea, and vomiting.

Hypertension is increased blood pressure, usually above 140/80 mmHg. Hypertension usually has no symptoms, but has been linked to heart disease and stroke. **Hypotension** is decreased blood pressure, usually below 90/60 mmHg.

A **stroke**, or **cardiovascular accident (CVA)**, occurs when a blood vessel in the brain ruptures or is blocked. The resulting lack of oxygen to the brain can result in significant brain damage or death. Symptoms of a stroke include trouble walking or speaking and paralysis on one side of the body.

An **embolus** is a mass, such as a blood clot or fat globule, that travels through the blood stream. An embolus can occlude (block) blood flow to a region of the body. For example, a **pulmonary embolism** is a blood clot (usually originating in the legs) that travels to the lungs, causing chest pain, shortness of breath, and low blood oxygen levels.

The Nervous System
STRUCTURE AND FORM OF THE NERVOUS SYSTEM

The **nervous system** coordinates the processes and actions of the human body. **Nerve cells**, or **neurons**, communicate through electrical impulses and allow the body to process and respond to stimuli. Neurons have a nucleus and transmit electrical impulses through their **axons** and **dendrites**. The **axon** is the stem-like structure, often covered in a fatty insulating substance called **myelin**, that carries information to other neurons throughout the body. Myelin is produced by **Schwann cells**, which also play an important role in nerve regeneration. **Dendrites** receive information from other neurons.

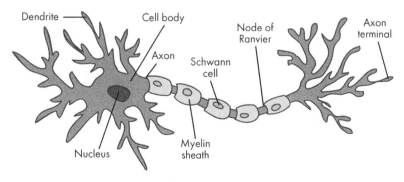

Figure 6.15. The Structure of a Neuron

The nervous system is broken down into two parts: the **central nervous system (CNS)** and the **peripheral nervous system (PNS)**. The CNS is made up of the **brain** and **spinal cord**.

The brain acts as the control center for the body and is responsible for nearly all the body's processes and actions. The spinal cord relays information between the brain and the peripheral nervous system; it also coordinates many reflexes. The spinal cord is protected by the vertebral column, a structure of bones that enclose the delicate nervous tissue. The PNS is the collection of nerves that connect the central nervous system to the rest of the body.

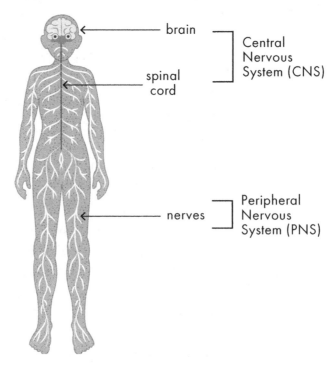

Figure 6.16. The Nervous System

The functions of the nervous system are broken down into the **autonomic nervous system** and the **somatic nervous system**. The autonomic nervous system controls involuntary actions that occur in the body, such as respiration, heartbeat, digestive processes, and more. The somatic nervous system is responsible for the body's ability to control skeletal muscles and voluntary movement as well as the involuntary reflexes associated with skeletal muscles.

The autonomic nervous system is further broken down into the **sympathetic nervous system** and **parasympathetic nervous system**. The sympathetic nervous system is responsible for the body's reaction to stress and induces a "fight-or-flight" response to stimuli. For instance, if an individual is frightened, the sympathetic nervous system increases in the person's heart rate and blood pressure to prepare them to either fight or flee.

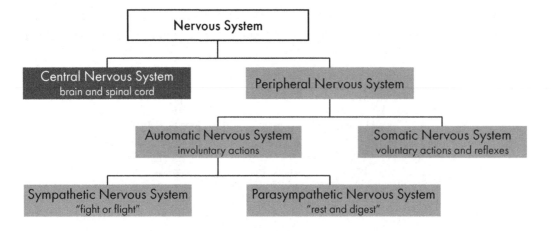

Figure 6.17. Divisions of the Nervous System

In contrast, the parasympathetic nervous system is stimulated by the body's need for rest or recovery. The parasympathetic nervous system responds by decreasing heart rate, blood pressure, and muscular activation when a person is getting ready for activities such as sleeping or digesting food. For example, the body activates the parasympathetic nervous system after eating a large meal, which is why people then feel sluggish.

PATHOLOGIES OF THE NERVOUS SYSTEM

Epilepsy is a chronic disease involving episodic seizures due to disruption of the CNS. There are a number of different kinds of epileptic diseases that are defined by the type of seizure, age of the person, and other factors, like the location of the brain that is affected. The diagnosis is usually given when the person suffers more than one seizure separated by at least a day.

Alzheimer's disease is characterized by the loss of memory and deteriorating cognitive function, usually later in life, due to the degeneration of neurons in the brain. The disease is a form of dementia that progresses gradually and has no known cure. Onset usually occurs past age sixty but can also occur as early as age forty. Individuals with Alzheimer's disease have trouble retaining newly acquired information to the point where life is negatively affected. Significant details, such as people, places, and more, are forgotten.

Multiple sclerosis (MS) involves the gradual breakdown and scarring of the myelin sheaths on axons, causing disruption of nervous transmission of impulses. The nerve damage associated with MS causes vision trouble, difficulty walking, fatigue, pain, involuntary spasms, and numerous other symptoms. This disease is thought to be genetic, and there is no known cure. However, treatments are available to slow the disease's progression.

The Digestive System
STRUCTURE AND FORM OF THE DIGESTIVE SYSTEM

The digestive system is responsible for the breakdown and absorption of food necessary to power the body. The digestive system starts at the **mouth**, which allows for the consumption and mastication of nutrients via an opening in the face. It contains the muscular **tongue** to move food and uses the liquid **saliva** to assist in the breakdown of food.

The chewed and lubricated food travels from the mouth through the **esophagus** via **peristalsis**, the contraction of smooth muscles. The esophagus leads to the **stomach**, the organ of the digestive tract found in the abdominal cavity that mixes food with powerful acidic liquid for further digestion. Once the stomach has created an acidic bolus of digested food known as *chyme*, it travels to the **small intestine**, where a significant amount of nutrient absorption takes place. The tube-like small intestine contains millions of finger-like projections known as villi and microvilli to increase the surface area available for the absorption of nutrients found in food.

The small intestine then transports food to the **large intestine**. The large intestine is similarly tube-like but larger in diameter than the small intestine. It assists in water absorption, further nutrient absorption, waste collection, and the production of feces for excretion. At the end of the large intestine are the **rectum** and **anus**, which are responsible for the storage of feces and removal of feces, respectively. The anus is the opening at the opposite end of the digestive tract as the mouth.

Along the digestive tract are several muscular rings, known as **sphincters**, which regulate the movement of food through the tract and prevent reflux of material into the previous cavity. These include:

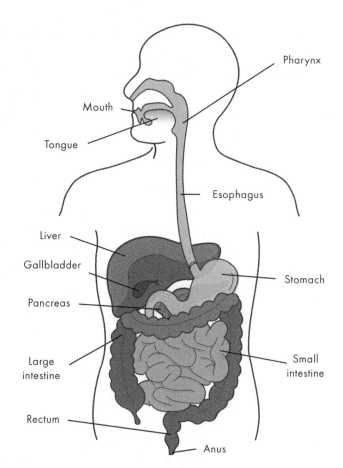

Figure 6.18. The Digestive System

+ upper esophageal sphincter: between the pharynx and esophagus

+ lower esophageal sphincter: between the esophagus and stomach

+ pyloric sphincter: between the stomach and small intestine

+ ileocecal sphincter: between the small intestine and large intestine

+ anus: between the rectum and the outside of the body

The digestive system also includes accessory organs that aid in digestion:

+ salivary glands: produce saliva, which begins the process of breaking down starches and fats

+ liver: produces bile, which helps break down fat in the small intestine

+ gallbladder: stores bile

+ pancreas: produces digestive enzymes and pancreatic juice, which neutralizes the acidity of chyme

PATHOLOGIES OF THE DIGESTIVE SYSTEM

The digestive system is prone to several illnesses of varying severity. Commonly, gastrointestinal distress is caused by an acute infection (bacterial or viral) affecting the lining of the digestive system. A resulting immune response triggers the body, as an adaptive measure, to void the contents of the digestive system in order to purge the infection.

Chronic gastrointestinal disorders include **irritable bowel syndrome** (the causes of which are largely unknown) and **Crohn's disease**, an inflammatory bowel disorder that occurs when the immune system attacks the digestive system.

A number of different cancers can arise in the digestive system, including colon and rectal cancer, liver cancer, pancreatic cancer, esophageal cancer, and stomach cancer. Of these, colon cancer is the most common. People over fifty are recommended to get regular **colonoscopies** to screen for colon cancer, which has few symptoms in its early stages.

The Immune System
Structure and Function of the Immune System

The human immune system protects the body against bacteria and viruses that cause disease. The system is composed of two parts, the innate and adaptive systems. The **innate immune system** includes nonspecific defenses that work against a wide range of infectious agents. This system includes both physical barriers that keep out foreign particles and organisms along with cells that attack invaders. The second part of the immune system is the **adaptive immune system**, which "learns" to respond only to specific invaders.

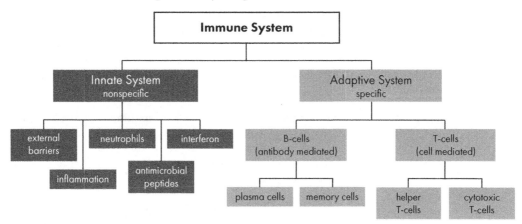

Figure 6.19 Divisions of the Immune System

Barriers to entry are the first line of defense in the immune system:

+ The **skin** leaves few openings for an infection-causing agent to enter.
+ **Native bacteria** outcompete invaders in openings.
+ The **urethra** flushes out invaders with the outflow of urine.
+ **Mucus** and **earwax** trap pathogens before they can replicate and cause infection.

However, pathogens can breach these barriers and enter the body, where they attempt to replicate and cause an infection. When this occurs, the body mounts a number of nonspecific responses. The body's initial response is **inflammation**, which increases blood flow to the infected area. This increase in blood flow increases the presence of **white blood cells**, also called **leukocytes**. (The types of white blood cells are discussed in Table 6.8.) Other innate responses include **antimicrobial peptides**, which destroy bacteria by interfering with the functions of their membranes or DNA, and **interferon**, which causes nearby cells to increase their defenses.

> 🔍 **Helpful Hint:** Memory B-cells are the underlying mechanisms behind vaccines, which introduce a harmless version of a pathogen into the body to activate the body's adaptive immune response.

The adaptive immune system relies on molecules called **antigens** that appear on the surface of pathogens to which the system has previously been exposed. Antigens are displayed on the surface of cells by the **major histocompatibility complex** (MHC).

In the cell-mediated response, **T-cells** destroy any cell that displays an antigen. In the antibody-mediated response, **B-cells** are activated by antigens. These B-cells produce **plasma cells**, which in turn release **antibodies**. Antibodies will bind only to specific antigens and destroy the infected cell. **Memory B-cells** are created during infection, allowing the immune system to respond more quickly if the infection appears again.

Table 6.8. Types of White Blood Cells

Type of Cell	Name of Cell	Role	Innate or Adaptive	Prevalence
Granulocytes	Neutrophil	First responders that quickly migrate to the site of infections to destroy bacterial invaders	Innate	Very common
	Eosinophil	Attack multicellular parasites	Innate	Rare
	Basophil	Large cell responsible for inflammatory reactions, including allergies	Innate	Very rare
Lymphocyte	B-cells	Respond to antigens by releasing antibodies	Adaptive	Common
	T-cells	Respond to antigens by destroying invaders and infected cells	Adaptive	
	Natural killer cells	Destroy virus-infected cells and tumor cells	Innate and adaptive	
Monocyte	Macrophage	Engulf and destroy microbes, foreign substances, and cancer cells	Innate and adaptive	Rare

PATHOLOGIES OF THE IMMUNE SYSTEM

The immune system of individuals with an **autoimmune disease** will attack healthy tissues. Autoimmune diseases (and the tissues they attack) include:

+ psoriasis (skin)
+ rheumatoid arthritis (joints)
+ multiple sclerosis (nerve cells)
+ lupus (kidneys, lungs, and skin)

The immune system may also overreact to harmless particles, a condition known as an **allergy**. Allergic reactions can be mild, resulting in watery eyes and a runny nose, but they can also include life-threatening swelling and respiratory obstruction.

Some infections will attack the immune system itself. **Human immunodeficiency virus (HIV)** attacks helper T-cells, eventually causing **acquired immunodeficiency syndrome (AIDS)**, which allows opportunistic infections to overrun the body. The immune system can also be weakened by previous infections or lifestyle factors such as smoking and alcohol consumption.

Cancers of the immune system include **lymphoma** and **leukemia**, which are caused by irregular growth of cells in lymph and bone marrow. Both white and red blood cells can become cancerous, but it is more common for the cancer to occur in white blood cells. Leukemia is the most common type of cancer to occur in children.

The Endocrine System
STRUCTURE AND FORM OF THE ENDOCRINE SYSTEM

The endocrine system is made up of **glands** that regulate numerous processes throughout the body by secreting chemical messengers called **hormones**. These hormones regulate a wide variety of bodily processes, including metabolism, growth and development, sexual reproduction, the sleep-wake cycle, and hunger.

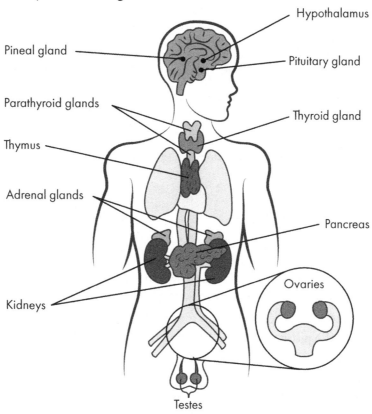

Figure 6.20. The Location of Endocrine Glands

The **hypothalamus** is a gland that plays a central role in the endocrine system by connecting it to the nervous system. Input from the nervous system reaches the hypothalamus, causing it to release hormones from the **pituitary gland**. These hormones in turn regulate the release of hormones from many of the other endocrine glands.

Table 6.9. Endocrine Glands and Their Functions

Gland	Regulates	Hormones Produced
Hypothalamus	Pituitary function and metabolic processes including body temperature, hunger, thirst, and circadian rhythms	Thyrotropin-releasing hormone (TRH), dopamine, growth-hormone-releasing hormone (GHRH), gonadotropin-releasing hormone (GnRH), oxytocin, vasopressin
Pituitary gland	Growth, blood pressure, reabsorption of water by the kidneys, temperature, pain relief, and some reproductive functions related to pregnancy and childbirth	Human growth hormone (HGH), thyroid-stimulating hormone (TSH), prolactin (PRL), luteinizing hormone (LH), follicle-stimulating hormone (FSH), oxytocin, antidiuretic hormone (ADH)
Pineal gland	Circadian rhythms (the sleep-wake cycle)	Melatonin
Thyroid gland	Energy use and protein synthesis	Thyroxine (T_4), triiodothyronine (T_3), calcitonin
Parathyroid	Calcium and phosphate levels	Parathyroid hormone (PTH)
Adrenal glands	*Fight-or-flight* response and regulation of salt and blood volume	Epinephrine, norepinephrine, cortisol, androgens
Pancreas	Blood sugar levels and metabolism	Insulin, glucagon, somatostatin
Testes	Maturation of sex organs, and secondary sex characteristics	Androgens (e.g., testosterone)
Ovaries	Maturation of sex organs, secondary sex characteristics, pregnancy, childbirth, and lactation	Progesterone, estrogens
Placenta	Gestation and childbirth	Progesterone, estrogens, human chorionic gonadotropin, human placental lactogen (hPL)

Many important hormones can be broken down into either anabolic hormones or catabolic hormones. **Anabolic hormones** are associated with the regulation of growth and development; these include testosterone, estrogen, insulin, and human growth hormone. **Human growth hormone** is released by the pituitary gland and regulates muscle and bone development. Another example of an anabolic hormone is an **insulin-like growth factor** (**IGF**), which is synthesized in the liver and aids in tissue growth and many other functions. **Catabolic hormones** help regulate the breakdown of substances into smaller molecules. For example, the breakdown of muscle glycogen for energy via the release of **glucagon** is a catabolic process.

PATHOLOGIES OF THE ENDOCRINE SYSTEM

Disruption of hormone production in specific endocrine glands can lead to disease. An inability to produce insulin results in uncontrolled blood glucose levels, a condition called **diabetes**. Over- or underactive glands can lead to conditions like **hypothyroidism**, which is characterized by a slow metabolism, and **hyperparathyroidism**, which can lead to osteoporosis.

Thyroid cancer is relatively common, but has few or no symptoms. In addition, benign (non-cancerous) tumors on the thyroid and other endocrine glands can damage the functioning of a wide variety of bodily systems.

The Reproductive System
THE MALE REPRODUCTIVE SYSTEM

The male reproductive system produces **sperm**, or male gametes, and passes them to the female reproductive system. Sperm are produced during **spermatogenesis** in the **testes** (also called testicles), which are housed in a sac-like external structure called the **scrotum**. The scrotum contracts and relaxes to move the testes closer or farther from the body. This process keeps the testes at the appropriate temperature for sperm production, which is slightly lower than regular body temperature.

Mature sperm are stored in the **epididymis**. During sexual stimulation, sperm travel from the epididymis through a long, thin tube called the **vas deferens**. Along the way, the sperm are joined by fluids from three glands:

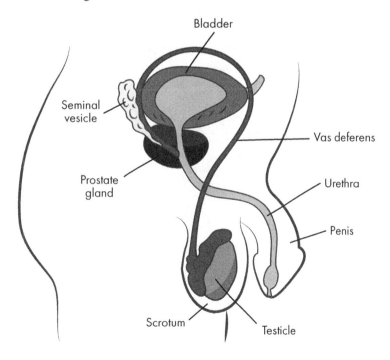

Figure 6.21. The Male Reproductive System

+ The **seminal vesicles** secrete a fluid composed of various proteins, sugars, and enzymes.

+ The **prostate** contributes an alkaline fluid that counteracts the acidity of the vaginal tract.

+ The **Cowper's gland** secretes a protein-rich fluid that acts as a lubricant.

The mix of fluids and sperm, called **semen**, travels through the **urethra** and exits the body through the **penis**, which becomes rigid during sexual arousal.

The main hormone associated with the male reproductive system is **testosterone**, which is released by the testes (and in the adrenal glands in much smaller amounts). Testosterone is responsible for the development of the male reproductive system and male secondary sexual characteristics, including muscle development and facial hair growth.

THE FEMALE REPRODUCTIVE SYSTEM

The female reproductive system produces **eggs**, or female gametes, and gestates the fetus during pregnancy. Eggs are produced in the **ovaries** and travel through the **fallopian tubes** to the **uterus**, which is a muscular organ that houses the fetus during pregnancy. The uterine cavity is lined with a layer of blood-rich tissue called the **endometrium**. If no pregnancy occurs, the endometrium is shed monthly during **menstruation**.

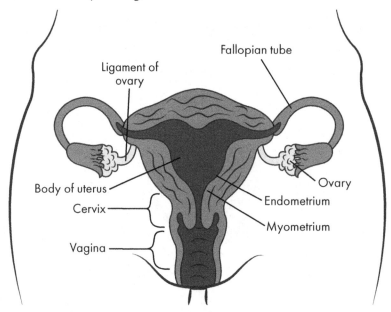

Figure 6.22. The Female Reproductive System

Fertilization occurs when the egg absorbs the sperm; it usually takes place in the fallopian tubes but may happen in the uterus itself. After fertilization the new zygote implants itself in the endometrium, where it will grow and develop over thirty-eight weeks (roughly nine months). During gestation, the developing fetus acquires nutrients and passes waste through the **placenta**. This temporary organ is attached to the wall of the uterus and is connected to the baby by the **umbilical cord**.

When the fetus is mature, powerful muscle contractions occur in the **myometrium**, the muscular layer next to the endometrium. These contractions push the fetus through an opening called the **cervix** into the vagina, from which the fetus exits the body. The placenta and umbilical cords are also expelled through the vagina shortly after birth.

The female reproductive cycle is controlled by a number of different hormones. Estrogen, produced by the ovaries, stimulates Graafian follicles, which contain immature eggs cells. The pituitary gland then releases luteinizing hormone, which causes the egg to be released into the fallopian tubes during **ovulation**. During pregnancy, estrogen and progesterone are released in high levels to help with fetal growth and to prevent further ovulation.

PATHOLOGIES OF THE REPRODUCTIVE SYSTEM

Both men and women can acquire sexually transmitted infections (STIs). These include chlamydia, gonorrhea, human papilloma virus (HPV), and genital herpes. Both **chlamydia** and **gonorrhea** are bacterial infections that have few symptoms in men, but can cause burning, itching, and discharge in women. **HPV** and **genital herpes** are both viral infections that lead to warts and open sores, respectively. HPV has also been linked to the development of cervical cancer in women.

When untreated, bacterial infections in the reproductive system in women can lead to **pelvic inflammatory disease (PIV)**. Symptoms of PIV include abdominal pain, fever, and vaginal discharge. PIV is one of the most common causes of infertility.

Endometriosis is an condition is which endometrium tissue, which usually lines the inside of the uterus, grows outside the uterus. Symptoms include pain, irregular or painful menstruation, and infertility.

Cancers of the female reproductive system include **ovarian cancer**, **cervical cancer**, and **uterine cancer**. **Prostate cancer** is a common but slow growing cancer of the male reproductive system. It is most common in older men.

The Urinary System

The **urinary system** excretes water and waste from the body and is crucial for maintaining the balance of water and salt in the blood (also called electrolyte balance). Because many organs function as part of both the reproductive and urinary systems, the two are sometimes referred to collectively as the **genitourinary system**.

The main organs of the urinary system are the **kidneys**, which perform several important functions:

+ filter waste from the blood
+ maintain the electrolyte balance in the blood
+ regulate blood volume, pressure, and pH

The kidneys also function as an endocrine organ and release several important hormones, including **renin**, which regulates blood pressure. The kidney is divided into two regions: the **renal cortex**, which is the outermost layer, and the **renal medulla**, which is the inner layer.

The functional unit of the kidney is the **nephron**, which is a series of looping tubes that filter the blood. The resulting waste includes **urea**, a byproduct of protein catabolism, and **uric acid**, a byproduct of nucleic acid metabolism. Together, these waste products are excreted from the body in **urine**.

Filtration begins in a network of capillaries called a **glomerulus**, which is located in the renal cortex of each kidney. This waste is then funneled into **collecting ducts** in the renal medulla. From the collecting ducts, urine passes through the **renal pelvis** and then through two long tubes called **ureters**. The two ureters drain into the **urinary bladder**, which holds up to one liter of liquid. Urine exits the bladder through the **urethra**. In males, the urethra goes through the penis and also carries semen. In females, the much-shorter urethra ends just above the vaginal opening.

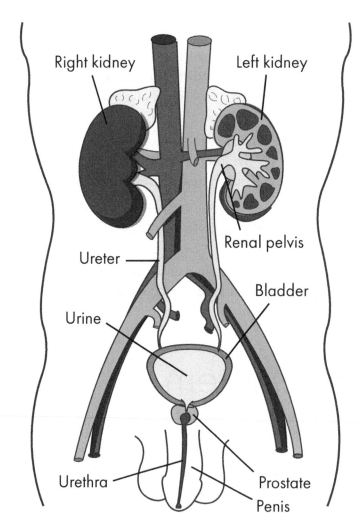

Figure 6.23. The Urinary System (Male)

PATHOLOGIES OF THE URINARY SYSTEM

Urinary tract infections (UTIs) occur when bacteria infects the kidneys, bladder, or urethra. They can occur in men or women, but are more common for women. Symptoms include burning during urination, pelvic or back pain, and an increased urge to urinate.

Chronic kidney disease, in which the kidneys do not function properly for at least three months, can be caused by a number of factors, including diabetes, autoimmune diseases, infections, and drug abuse. People with chronic kidney disease may need **dialysis**, during which a machine performs the task of the kidneys and removes waste from the blood.

Urinary system cancers include **bladder cancer** and **kidney cancer**.

The Integumentary System

The **integumentary system** refers to the skin (the largest organ in the body) and related structures, including the hair and nails. **Skin** is composed of three layers. The **epidermis** is the outermost layer of the skin. This waterproof layer contains no blood vessels and acts mainly to protect the body. Under the epidermis lies the **dermis**, which consists of dense connective tissue that allows skin to stretch and flex. The dermis is home to blood vessels, glands, and **hair follicles**. The **hypodermis** is a layer of fat below the dermis that stores energy (in the form of fat) and acts as a cushion for the body. The hypodermis is sometimes called the **subcutaneous layer**.

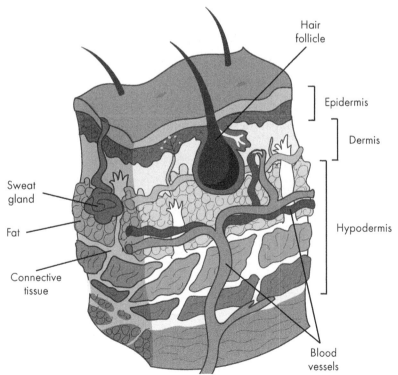

Figure 6.24. The Skin

The skin has several important roles. It acts as a barrier to protect the body from injury, the intrusion of foreign particles, and the loss of water and nutrients. It is also important for **thermoregulation**. Blood vessels near the surface of the skin can dilate, allowing for higher blood flow and the release of heat. They can also constrict to reduce the amount of blood that travels near the surface of the skin, which helps conserve heat. In addition, the skin produces vitamin D when exposed to sunlight.

Because the skin covers the whole body, it plays a vital role in allowing organisms to interact with the environment. It is home to nerve endings that sense temperature, pressure, and pain, and it also houses glands that help maintain homeostasis. **Eccrine** glands, which are located primarily in the palms of the hands and soles of the feet (and to a lesser degree in other areas of the body), release the water and salt mixture (sodium chloride, NaCl) called **sweat**. These glands help the body maintain the appropriate salt-water balance. Sweat can also contain small amounts of other substances the body needs to expel, including alcohol, lactic acid, and urea.

> **?** **Check Your Understanding:** Why would flushing—the reddening of the skin caused by dilating blood vessels—be associated with fevers?

Apocrine glands, which are located primarily in the armpit and groin, release an oily substance that contains pheromones. They are also sensitive to adrenaline and are responsible for most of the sweating that occurs due to stress, fear, anxiety, or pain. Apocrine glands are largely inactive until puberty.

PATHOLOGIES OF THE INTEGUMENTARY SYSTEM

Psoriasis is an autoimmune condition that causes inflammation in the skin, resulting in red, flaking patches on the skin. **Eczema** (atopic dermatitis) is a red, itchy rash that usually occurs in children but can occur in adults as well.

Skins cancers can be categorized as melanoma or nonmelanoma cancers. **Melanoma** cancers appear as irregular, dark patches on the skin and are more difficult to treat than non-melanoma cancers.

SEVEN: INFECTION CONTROL

The goal of infection control is to intervene in the chain of infection at the point where infection is most likely to occur in order to prevent its spread. To do this, medical assistants must understand how infections occur and are transmitted as well as the principles of proper anti-infective treatment, infection control measures, and preventive disease precautions. Using aseptic techniques and adhering to universal precautions can help control the spread of infection.

Infection Cycle and the Chain of Infection

When an organism establishes an opportunistic relationship with a host, the process is called **infection**. The process of infection starts with the transmission of organisms and ends with the development of infectious disease. There are four stages of the infection process.

+ During the **incubation period** the organism establishes a presence in the susceptible host.

+ In the **prodromal stage** the symptoms of infection begin to appear.

+ Throughout **acute illness** the organisms grow and spread quickly inside the host.

+ In the **convalescent stage** the damaged tissue begins healing and symptoms resolve.

Infections can be mild or severe, and the acuteness of an infection depends on the disease-causing potential of the infectious agent and the ability of the body to defend itself. Infections can be caused by many different **infectious agents**.

+ **Bacteria** are single-celled prokaryotic organisms that are responsible for many common infections such as strep throat, urinary tract infections, and many food-borne illnesses.

- ✦ **Viruses** are composed of a nucleic acid (DNA or RNA) wrapped in a protein capsid. They invade host cells and hijack cell machinery to reproduce. Viral infections include the common cold, influenza, and human immunodeficiency virus (HIV).

- ✦ **Protozoa** are single-celled eukaryotic organisms. Protozoan infections include giardia (an intestinal infection) and African sleeping sickness.

- ✦ **Fungi** are a group of eukaryotic organisms that include yeasts, molds, and mushrooms. Common fungal infections are athlete's foot, ringworm, and oral and vaginal yeast infections.

- ✦ Parasitic diseases are caused by **parasites** that live in or on the human body and use its resources. Common human parasites include worms (e.g., tapeworms), flukes, and ectoparasites like lice and ticks, which live on the outside of the body.

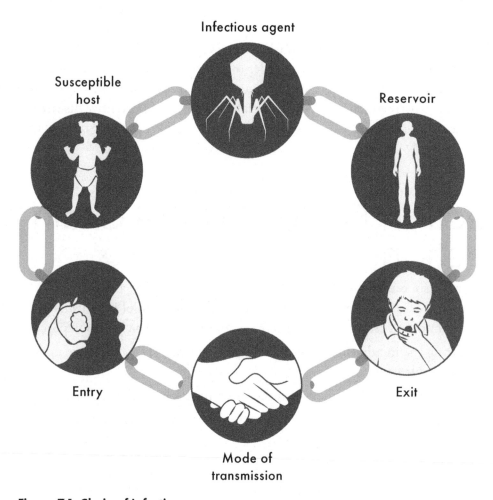

Figure 7.1. Chain of Infection

Infections travel from person to person via the **chain of infection**. The chain starts with a **causative organism** (e.g., a bacteria or virus). The organism needs a **reservoir**, or place to live. This may be biological, such as people or animals, or it may be environmental. For example, in a medical office, equipment and office surfaces may act as reservoirs. In order to spread, the infectious agent needs a way to **exit** the reservoir, such as being expelled as droplets during a sneeze.

 Helpful Hint: See chapter 6, "Anatomy and Physiology," for more information on the human body's natural barriers to infection.

For the infection chain to continue, the infectious agent needs to encounter a susceptible host—a person who can become infected. Finally, the infectious agent needs a way to **enter** the host, such as through inhalation or drinking contaminated water.

There are a variety of modes of transmission for infectious agents.

+ **Direct contact** is transmission from one infected person to another during physical contact with blood or other body fluids (e.g., transmission of herpes during sexual intercourse).

+ **Indirect contact** is transmission of the disease through a nonbiological reservoir (e.g., drinking water contaminated with giardia).

+ **Droplets** are infectious agents trapped in moisture that are expelled when an infected person sneezes or coughs. They can enter the respiratory system of other people and cause infection (e.g., transmission of influenza when an infected person sneezes).

Did You Know? Infectious disease precautions are categorized based on how the disease is transmitted. For example, droplet precautions require only a surgical mask, but airborne precautions require an N-95 respirator to prevent transmission.

+ Some droplets are light enough to remain **airborne**, meaning people may inhale infectious agents from the air long after the initial cough or sneeze (e.g., measles, which can live in airborne droplets for up to two hours).

+ Some diseases are carried by organisms called **vectors** that spread the disease; the infection does not require direct physical contact between people (e.g., mosquitoes carrying malaria).

Medical Asepsis

Asepsis is the absence of infectious organisms, and **medical asepsis** is the practice of destroying infectious agents outside the body to prevent the spread of disease. An object that has had all infectious agents removed or destroyed is **sterile**.

Medical asepsis is different from **clean technique**, which also aims to minimize the spread of infectious agents, but does not require sterilization. Wearing gloves is an example of clean technique; the gloves are not sterile, but they provide a barrier that prevents the spread of infection from patient to provider.

The most important tool used for medical asepsis is handwashing. **Aseptic handwashing** is a specific technique intended to remove all infectious agents from the hands and wrists. Aseptic handwashing should be performed whenever the medical assistant is going to interact with a sterile field (e.g., when applying a sterile dressing).

Medical asepsis also includes the removal of infectious agents from equipment and other surfaces. This process has three general levels.

+ **Cleaning** removes dirt and some infectious agents.

+ **Disinfection** kills all pathogens except bacterial spores. Most surfaces in healthcare settings are disinfected using liquid chemical agents such as alcohol or chlorine bleach.

+ **Sterilization** kills all infectious agents, including bacterial spores. Medical equipment is sterilized using heat (e.g., autoclave) or chemicals (e.g., ethylene oxide).

Disinfectants are regulated by the EPA, and medical offices must use EPA-approved disinfectants. The EPA maintains a list of disinfectants that are approved for specific infectious agents. These products have registration numbers that should be checked by the staff members who purchase cleaning supplies.

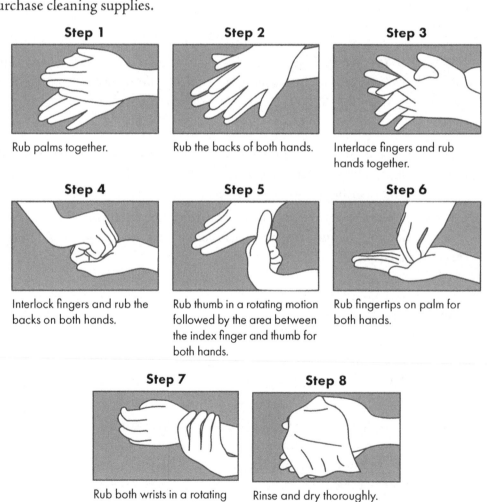

Step 1
Rub palms together.

Step 2
Rub the backs of both hands.

Step 3
Interlace fingers and rub hands together.

Step 4
Interlock fingers and rub the backs on both hands.

Step 5
Rub thumb in a rotating motion followed by the area between the index finger and thumb for both hands.

Step 6
Rub fingertips on palm for both hands.

Step 7
Rub both wrists in a rotating motion.

Step 8
Rinse and dry thoroughly.

Figure 7.2. Aseptic Handwashing Technique

Surgical Asepsis

Surgical asepsis is the practice of removing all infectious pathogens from all equipment involved in invasive procedures. Medical assistants may be asked to help sterilize equipment and may also be required to do a surgical scrub if participating in an invasive procedure.

Sterilization is the process of destroying living organisms. Chemical sterilization is also known as cold sterilization, and is used for heat-sensitive equipment, such as endoscopes. The equipment is soaked in closed containers with strong chemical agents.

Two types of heat are also used in sterilization: dry and steam. **Dry heat** is used for sterilizing instruments that corrode easily and requires one hour of heat at 320°F (160°C). The use of steam heat in an **autoclave** is the most common method used in medical offices. The steam achieves high temperatures, usually 250°F – 254°F (121°C – 123°C), under pressure. Instruments must be wrapped in special packaging for autoclaving. The time required in the autoclave varies from twenty to forty minutes, depending on how tightly the items are wrapped.

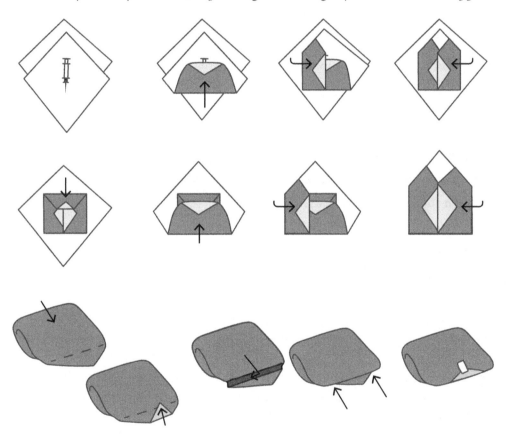

Figure 7.3. How to Wrap an Instrument for the Autoclave

Items must be wrapped following specific procedures before being autoclaved.

1. Position open wrap on a flat surface in a diamond shape with one of the points toward the body.

2. Place cleaned and dried instruments in the center of the wrap.

3. Fold the corner closest to the body over the instrument and fold the point back down to create a tab.

4. Fold the first side corner toward the center, covering the instrument. Fold the extra material back to form a tab.

5. Repeat step 4 with the second side corner.

6. Fold the last corner toward center, completely covering the instrument.

7. Fasten the packet with sterilization tape.

Before surgical procedures, all health care team members must do a **surgical scrub**.

1. Remove all jewelry.

2. Wash hands, wrists, and forearms at foot- or knee-controlled faucet.

3. Cleanse for 10 minutes.

4. Hold hands upward while rinsing.

5. Dry with a sterile towel.

6. Apply sterile gloves.

The **sterile field** is a pathogen-free area that contains the sterile instruments, solutions, and other items that will be used in the procedure. This also includes the hands and anterior neck-to-waist region of the physician and assistants.

In the sterile field, specific guidelines must be followed.

+ Check for sterile indicators and dates on all items before opening them and putting them in the sterile field.

+ Examine each item for breaks in packaging or for moisture.

+ Open the packages per instructions.

+ Maintain a border of one inch between non-sterile and sterile areas.

+ Do not reach over the sterile field.

+ Do not cough, talk, or sneeze over the sterile field.

Personal Protective Equipment

In addition to handwashing, equipment can be used to prevent the spread of infection. **Personal protective equipment (PPE)** is any item necessary for the prevention of microorganism transmission. PPE includes gloves, gowns, goggles, eye shields, and masks. Gloves and gowns help prevent the spread of pathogens from patients or equipment to other patients or equipment. The CDC recommends that health care workers remove fluid-resistant gowns before leaving a patient's room and before performing hand hygiene. Masks, goggles, and face shields should be used by health care workers when there is a likelihood of blood or body fluid splashes. All of these PPE devices protect the mucous membranes of the mouth, nose, and eyes from infected particles.

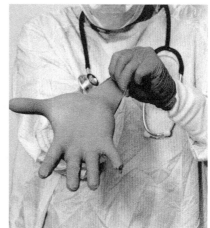

Figure 7.4. PPE

Standard Precautions and Blood-Borne Pathogen Standards

Standard precautions (also called universal precautions) are based on the assumption that all patients are infected with microorganisms, whether or not there are symptoms or a diagnosis. Standard precautions decrease the risk of transmission of microorganisms from blood and other body fluids. The standards apply to contact with blood, all body fluids, secretions, and excretions (except sweat), non-intact skin, and mucous membranes.

This set of principles is used by all health care workers who have direct or indirect contact with patients. When working with patients and specimens, the medical assistant should always follow these standard precautions.

- ✦ Assume that all patients are carrying a microorganism.
- ✦ Use PPE:
    - ✧ gloves
    - ✧ mask
    - ✧ gown
    - ✧ protective eye wear
- ✦ Practice hand hygiene:
    - ✧ Use soap and water when hands are visibly soiled.
    - ✧ Antimicrobial foam or gel may be used if hands are not visibly soiled.
- ✦ Wear gloves:
    - ✧ Gloves must be discarded between each patient.
    - ✧ Gloves may need to be discarded when soiled and a new pair applied.
    - ✧ Practice hand hygiene after removing gloves.

- Prevent needle sticks.
- Immediately place used needles in puncture-resistant containers.
- Recap needles using a mechanical device or a one-handed technique.
- Avoid splash and spray.
- Wear appropriate PPE if there is a possibility of body fluids splashing or spraying.
- Clean and disinfect surfaces after each patient.
- Use disposable barriers to protect surfaces that are hard to disinfect.

Additional precautions may be needed for patients with known infections. These precautions are based on the transmission route for the infection.

- Airborne precautions:
  - Wear N-95 respirator mask; place on before entering the room and keep on until after leaving the room.
  - Place N-95 or surgical mask on patient during transport.
  - Patient may be placed in a private room with a negative-pressure air system with the door kept closed.
- Droplet precautions:
  - Place patient in a private room; the door may remain open.
  - Wear appropriate PPE within three feet of patient.
  - Wash hands with antimicrobial soap after removing gloves and mask, before leaving the patient's room.
  - Place surgical mask on patient during transport.
- Contact precautions:
  - Place the patient in a private room; the door may remain open.
  - Wear gloves.
  - Change gloves after touching infected materials.
  - Remove gloves before leaving patient's room.
  - Wear gown; remove before leaving patient's room.
  - Use patient-dedicated equipment if possible; community equipment is to be cleaned and disinfected between patients.
  - During transport keep precautions in place and notify different areas or departments as needed.

OSHA maintains standards for universal precautions and bloodborne pathogens, and employers may face penalties if these protocols are not followed. According to the standards, employers must provide:

- all necessary PPE
- environmental control methods, including access to clean air and water and appropriate processes for waste disposal
- training on bloodborne pathogens for employees

+ an exposure control plan that explains steps to be taken by employees exposed to bloodborne pathogens

Biohazard Disposal and Regulated Waste

Regulated medical waste (RMW) (also called biohazardous waste) is any waste that is or may be contaminated with infectious materials, including blood, secretions, and excretions. Regulated medical waste must be handled carefully to prevent the possibility of an exposure incident. The disposal of RMW is governed by federal, state, and local regulations that vary by location. Some general waste disposal guidelines are given below.

+ Sharps should be disposed of in a biohazard sharps container. The term "sharps" refers to needles, lancets, blood tubes, capillary tubes, razor blades, suturing needles, hypodermic needles, and microscope slides and coverslips.

+ Blood and body fluids, such as urine, sputum, semen, amniotic fluid, and cerebrospinal fluid, can be disposed of in a drain, toilet, or utility sink. State and local regulations may limit the amount of fluid that can be disposed of into the sewage system.

+ Feces should be flushed in a toilet.

Figure 7.5. Sharps Container

+ Bandages, dressing gauzes, and gloves with small amounts of RMW can be put in regular garbage disposal cans.

+ Dirty linen should be put in a separate receptacle; if very soiled by blood, it should be put in a biohazard bag.

+ Chemicals should be stored and disposed of according to the information in the **safety data sheets (SDSs)**, which are provided by the manufacturer. The SDSs will also include a color code for potential hazards:
  ◇ red: flammable
  ◇ blue: health hazard/toxic
  ◇ yellow: reactive/oxidizing
  ◇ white: contact hazard
  ◇ green: not hazardous/suitable for general storage

 Helpful Hint: Infectious material that is not blood is referred to as "other potentially infectious material" (OPIM).

Spill kits are a collection of substances and PPE that assist in cleaning and containing infectious agents or chemical agents after a spill. Spill kits may be general purpose or they may be tailored to a specific substance, such as mercury or body fluids.

Figure 7.6. Biohazard Spill Kit

EIGHT: PATIENT INTAKE and EXAMINATION

The purpose of the patient intake and physical examination is to assess the patient's state of health and wellness and to determine the cause of the chief complaint. The medical assistant must greet the patient, obtain necessary vital signs and measurements, document the chief complaint, interview the patient, and provide the patient with a sense of support and security. The medical assistant assists the physician by:

+ preparing the exam room and necessary equipment
+ making sure the exam room is clean and free of clutter
+ preparing the patient for the exam by giving instructions
+ helping with draping/gowning
+ assisting with the exam

Patient Intake and Documentation of Care

During **intake**, the medical assistant gathers both objective data (i.e., that measured by the medical assistant) and subjective data (i.e., that reported by the patient). Objective data includes the results of the physical exam (e.g., pulse, temperature) and any laboratory screenings. The medical assistant should collect the following subjective data:

+ chief complaint: the problem or symptom that the patient describes (e.g., cough, fever, runny nose)
+ present illness: the symptoms and how long the illness has been present (e.g., fever of 101.0°F (38.3°C) for three days, dry cough for two days)
+ past medical history: medical history over a lifetime (e.g., allergies, mental illness, surgeries, medical diagnoses, hospitalizations)

- family history: medical history of biologically related family members, such as parents, grandparents, siblings, aunts, uncles, and cousins (e.g., hypertension, diabetes, cancers)
- social and occupational history: the patient's personal habits (e.g., drinking, smoking, drug use), social history, and work history
- review of systems: a list of questions used by the doctor to diagnose different medical conditions (e.g., respiratory symptoms, cardiovascular symptoms, etc.)

Helpful Hint: Subjective data is collected through a combination of intake forms and conversations with the patient.

All data gathered by the medical assistant should be included in the patient's medical record, along with a full record of the care the patient receives during the visit. This record should include intake information, diagnosis, and treatment recommendations. During intake of returning patients, the medical assistant may also verify that the patient is in compliance with previous treatment recommendations. If necessary, changes and corrections can be made to the medical record with an addendum.

Vital Signs

Vital signs monitored in the health care environment include temperature, heart and pulse rate, respiratory rate, and blood pressure. These vital signs can change with age, illness, injury, and health status. Pain is also sometimes considered a vital sign and should be addressed by the medical assistant during intake.

BODY TEMPERATURE

Body temperature can be measured with a thermometer by various routes, such as oral, axillary, forehead, or rectal. Average normal body temperature is 98.6°F (37°C) but can range from 97.8°F – 99.1°F (36.6°C – 37.3°C).

Did You Know? Infants have a higher surface-area-to-volume ratio than adults, making it harder for them to regulate their body temperature. People over sixty-five also have trouble regulating body temperature due to a decreased amount of subcutaneous fat and a decreased ability to sweat. Both populations are susceptible to hypothermia and hyperthermia.

Elevated temperature, or **fever**, is defined as a temperature higher than 100.4°F (38°C) (although this is not a universal standard—some physicians may use a different cutoff temperature). Fever is often a symptom of infection or inflammation, but can be caused by other conditions, including stress, dehydration, exercise, the environment, and thyroid disorders. **Hypothermia** (body temperature below 95°F or 35°C) can occur when the body is exposed to **cold** weather or due to medical conditions such as a thyroid disorder.

PULSE

The heart beats a certain number of times each minute, a value called the **pulse**, or heart rate. The pulse can be taken at a number of locations on the body.

+ carotid pulse, to the side of the trachea
+ radial pulse, on the thumb side of the inner wrist
+ brachial pulse, on the side of crease of the elbow

The pulse is measured as the number of times the heart beats in one minute. The radial pulse is the most common place to take a pulse, by pressing with two or three fingers and counting for a full minute (or for thirty seconds and multiplying by two).

Heart rate is also usually found on the readouts of equipment used to test cardiovascular performance, including pulse oximeters and electrocardiograms (ECGs).

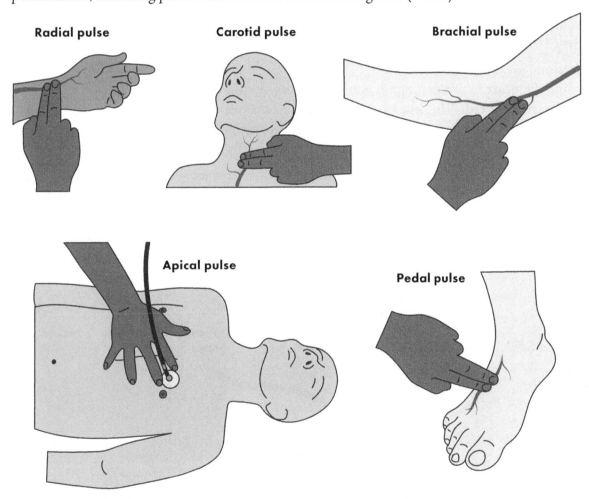

Figure 8.1. Locations for Measuring Pulse Rate

The average adult's pulse rate at rest is between sixty and one hundred beats per minute. A rapid heart rate (tachycardia) can be caused by a wide range of conditions, including infection, dehydration, shock, anemia, stress, anxiety, thyroid conditions, and heart conditions. Similarly, a slow pulse rate (bradycardia) can be caused by many factors, including certain medications (e.g., beta blockers and digoxin), fainting, and various heart conditions.

Respiratory Rate

A person's **respiratory rate (RR)** is the number of breaths taken per minute. Respiratory rate is usually found by having the patient lie on their back (although this is not required) and counting the rise and fall of their chest. For an accurate measurement, the patient should be allowed to rest before the respiratory rate is measured.

A normal adult's RR is twelve to twenty breaths per minute, although this rate can vary in adults over sixty-five. Conditions that can elevate the respiratory rate include acute respiratory distress, asthma, COPD, pneumonia, heart failure, bronchitis, and tuberculosis. Use of narcotics, drug overdose, or a diabetic coma can lower the respiratory rate.

Blood Pressure

Blood pressure (BP) is the measurement of the force of blood as it flows against the walls of the arteries, measured in mm Hg. Blood pressure is written as two numbers: systolic pressure and diastolic pressure. **Systolic pressure** is the pressure that occurs while the heart is contracting; **diastolic pressure** occurs while the heart is relaxed. A healthy blood pressure has a systolic value of 100 to 139 mm Hg and a diastolic value of 60 to 79 mm Hg.

Blood pressure can be taken manually using a blood pressure cuff and stethoscope or by using an automatic or semiautomatic blood pressure monitor. (Both the cuff and electronic monitors

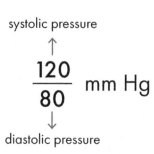

Figure 8.2. Systolic and Diastolic Blood Pressure

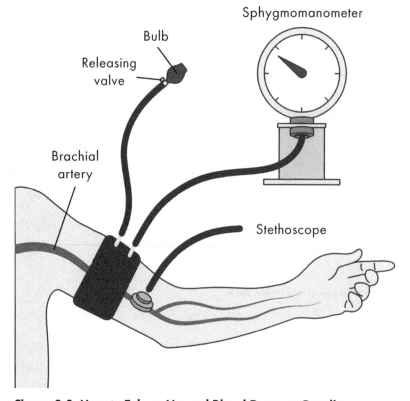

Figure 8.3. How to Take a Manual Blood Pressure Reading

are referred to as *sphygmomanometers*.) For both methods, the patient should be upright, with their feet on the floor and uncrossed, and the arm being used for the measurement should be at heart height.

To take a blood pressure manually, the medical assistant should wrap a properly sized cuff around the patient's upper arm and lightly press the stethoscope over the brachial pulse. The cuff should be inflated to 180 mm Hg; this prevents blood from flowing through the brachial artery. Releasing the valve allows air to slowly leave the cuff. When the pressure in the cuff is equal to the patient's blood pressure, the blood will rush through the artery, creating a distinctive sound called the **Korotkoff sound**. The pressure at which the first sound is heard is the systolic pressure, and the pressure at which the last sound is heard is the diastolic pressure.

To use an **automatic blood pressure monitor**, the medical assistant wraps the cuff around the patient's upper arm and turns on the monitor. It will automatically inflate, deflate, and provide a pressure reading. A **semiautomatic monitor** requires manual inflation but will automatically deflate and provide a pressure reading.

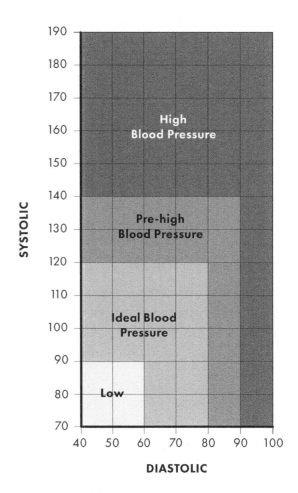

Figure 8.4. Classifying Blood Pressure

High blood pressure is called **hypertension**. Smoking, stress, exercise, eating, caffeine, certain medications, salt intake, and a full bladder can all elevate blood pressure. Prolonged hypertension can result in atherosclerosis, stroke, and heart failure. **Hypotension** (low BP) can be caused by hypothermia, shock, diuretics, and fainting. Some people, particularly those over sixty-five, may experience **orthostatic hypotension**, which occurs when standing up too quickly.

HEIGHT AND WEIGHT

The patient's height is assessed by using a fixed bar on the weight scale or wall. **Height** measurements are recorded in feet (ft) and inches (in) or in centimeters (cm). The patient's **weight** is measured using a balanced scale and recorded in pounds (lb) or kilograms (kg).

Body mass index (BMI) is a measurement of body fat that is based on a person's height and weight. To calculate the BMI, divide the weight in kilograms by the height in meters squared.

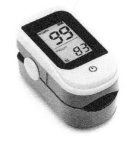

Figure 8.5. Pulse Oximeter

Table 8.1. BMI Scale	
<15	Very severely underweight
15 – 15.99	Severely underweight
16 – 18.49	Underweight
18.5 – 24.9	Normal weight
25 – 29.9	Overweight
30 – 39.9	Obese
>40	Morbidly obese

OXYGEN SATURATION AND PULSE OXIMETRY

Oxygen saturation is a measurement of the amount of oxygen in the blood. Specifically, it measures the amount of oxygen-saturated hemoglobin (the substance in red blood cells that carries oxygen) relative to unsaturated hemoglobin. Normal blood oxygen level is 94 to 100 percent. Oxygen saturation is measured using a pulse oximeter, which is usually placed on the patient's finger.

PAIN

If a patient presents with pain, the medical assistant will need to assess pain during intake. The five letters from P to T, **PQRST**, can be used as a mnemonic device.

- ✦ **Provoking**: What was happening when the pain started? What makes the pain better or worse?

- ✦ **Quality**: What does the pain feel like? Is it sharp, stabbing, dull, aching, burning, etc.?

- ✦ **Region**: Where is the pain located? Does the pain radiate or move to another area of the body?

- ✦ **Severity**: On a scale of 0 – 10 (10 being the worst pain imaginable), how bad is the pain?

- ✦ **Timing**: How long has this pain gone on? When did it start? How long does it typically last?

For pediatric patients or patients with communication barriers, the medical assistant may use a "faces" pain scale.

Figure 8.6. The Wong-Baker Faces Pain Rating Scale

Patient Examinations

Patient examination is the process of examining the body and includes listening to heart and lungs, looking in the eyes and ears, checking reflexes, assessing the abdomen, and measuring weight, height, and vital signs.

PHYSICAL EXAMINATION TECHNIQUES

Physical examination of the patient can be done using several different techniques.

- **Observation**, or inspection, is a visual review of the patient's body, looking for abnormalities, skin color and condition, and symmetry.

- **Palpation** is the use of hands and fingertips to feel for positions and sizes of organs; masses, lumps, or other abnormalities; skin moisture and temperature; and joint flexibility.

- **Percussion** involves tapping parts of the body and using the sound produced to gauge the density of structures.

- **Auscultation** is using a stethoscope on different parts of the body to listen for abnormalities.

- **Manipulation** is the passive movement of the patient's joints to assess extent of movement.

- **Mensuration** is the measurement of height and weight.

MEDICAL EXAMINATION POSITIONS

The medical assistant should position the patient appropriately for different types of exams. These positions are discussed in Table 8.2.

Table 8.2. Medical Examination Positions		
Position	**Description**	**Image**
Supine	Patient lies on their back with arms to the sides. Supine positions are used during many surgical procedures, while performing an ECG, and for obtaining orthostatic blood pressure.	
Dorsal recumbent	Patient lies on their back with knees bent and feet flat on the table. Dorsal recumbent positions are used for gynecological exams.	
Lithotomy	Patient lies on their back with buttocks on the edge of the lower end of the table, legs elevated, and feet in stirrups. Lithotomy position is used for gynecological exams, childbirth, and some surgeries.	

Sims'	Patient lies on their left side with the left leg flexed, left arm resting behind the body, right leg flexed, and right arm at the chest. Sims' position is used for taking the temperature rectally, rectal examinations, and administering enemas.	
Prone	Patient lies on their stomach. Prone position is used to examine the spine and for chiropractic procedures.	
Fowler's	Patient lies faceup with their upper body elevated at 45 to 60 degrees. Fowler's position is used in barium swallow procedures, nasopharyngeal feedings, and respiratory distress.	
Semi-Fowler's	Same as Fowler's position, except the upper body is only elevated between 30 and 45 degrees. Semi-Fowler's position is used for nasogastric feedings, X-rays, and respiratory distress.	

PEDIATRIC EXAM

The medical assistant's role in a pediatric physical exam is to obtain infants' and children's height, weight, head circumference, temperature, pulse, and respiration, and then document the measurements on the patient chart. The patient's height, weight, and head circumference are plotted on a **growth chart** to gauge whether the child is growing appropriately.

Infants should be weighed completely undressed on a pediatric scale. Head circumference can be obtained with a tape measure. Height can be measured by laying the infant on the examination table in supine position, marking the examination paper at the infant's head and feet (with legs straight), and then having a parent hold the infant while the medical assistant measures the distance between the two marks. Parents should hold fussy patients to keep them calm while the medical assistant takes the pulse and RR to ensure accurate measurements.

OBSTETRICAL-GYNECOLOGICAL EXAM

In an obstetrical-gynecological (ob-gyn) office, the medical assistant's role in the exam is to set up the exam room for procedures, obtain vitals (height, weight, blood pressure, pulse, respiration), and take patient's history. The medical assistant should be familiar with the supplies needed for specific ob-gyn procedures.

A **pelvic exam** is a visual and physical exam of the reproductive organs, including vulva, vagina, cervix, and uterus. The pelvic exam may include a Papanicolaou exam, commonly known as a **Pap smear**, during which cells are collected from the cervix to test for cervical cancer and

HPV (human papillomavirus). Both exams are performed by the physician or a nurse practitioner. The supplies for pelvic exams and Pap smears are:

- speculum
- examination gloves
- cervical spatula
- cytobrush
- liquid-based cytology container
- lubricating jelly
- examination light
- examination gown
- towelette
- plastic lab bag

The liquid-based cytology container should be filled out with patient's name, date of birth, medical record number, and date of last menstrual cycle.

The procedures carried out during a **prenatal exam** will vary with the stage of pregnancy. Either transvaginal or standard ultrasound may be used. A fetal Doppler monitor can be used to measure the fetus's heart rate, and the patient's cervix may be examined. During a **postnatal exam**, the patient's healing and mental health are assessed.

The supplies for prenatal and postnatal exams include:

- gloves
- lubricating jelly
- examination gown
- towelette
- fetal Doppler monitor

Procedures

Medical assistants may be asked to perform several basic procedures on a patient, including irrigations, dressing changes, and staple or suture removal. The steps to follow during patient procedures include:

- identifying the patient with two identifiers such as full name and date of birth
- washing hands before and after the procedures
- when performing procedures, explaining the process to the patient step by step and asking if they have any questions
- continuing to reassure the patient during procedures; this helps keep them calm and is an opportunity to gain their respect and trust
- documenting the procedure when finished, including what was done, how long it took, and how the patient responded

EYE IRRIGATION

Eye irrigation is performed when a patient's eye is irritated or damaged in an accident involving a chemical, sand, debris, or other irritant. The medical assistant should gather the necessary supplies:

- ophthalmic solution eyewash
- anesthetic eye drops
- basin
- a paper drape

The patient should lie on the exam table with the affected side down and the paper drape under their head. The medical assistant should then apply two anesthetic eye drops in the affected eye. The medical assistant then places the basin under the patient's head near the affected eye, gently opens the eyelid, and slowly drops the ophthalmic solution into the lower and upper eyelids. Then the medical assistant should have the patient move their eye up and down and from side to side. The eye should be irrigated for 15 minutes. After irrigation, the medical assistant checks the patient's visual acuity. The procedures and the patient's tolerance should be documented. The medical assistant should give the patient educational material on eye irrigation and signs and symptoms to look for.

EAR IRRIGATION

Ear irrigation is performed when a patient has excess wax (cerumen) in the ears or a child's tympanostomy tube becomes loose and is about to fall out of the ear. The supplies needed to irrigate an ear are:

+ two basins
+ warm water
+ hydrogen peroxide
+ paper drape

+ Debrox (solution to soften the earwax)
+ wax removal ear syringe

The patient should lie on the exam table in the Fowler's position, with a paper drape over the shoulder on the side of the ear to be irrigated. The medical assistant should apply two to five drops of Debrox in the ear to be irrigated. (For adults, pull the pinna of the ear up and back; for children, pull the pinna down and back.) Warm water and four to five capfuls of hydrogen peroxide are added to a basin. (The medical assistant should make sure the water is warm; cold water can give the patient a headache and dizziness.)

The medical assistant should have the patient take the other basin, hold it under the ear, and tilt their head to the side. The medical assistant should pull the warm water into the ear syringe and irrigate the ear, making sure to point the tip of the syringe toward the back of the ear canal. No more than 500 mL of water should be used. Ask the patient if they feel any pain while the ear is being irrigated. If they do, stop and inform the physician. The results of the procedure and the patient's tolerance should be documented. The medical assistant should offer the patient educational material on ear irrigation and signs and symptoms to look for.

DRESSING CHANGE

When a patient has a wound or sore, the medical assistant might have to change the dressing. There are several methods of **dressing changes**, such as wet to dry, wet to wet, and sterile dressing. The physician's order will specify which dressing method to use. The supplies needed are:

+ kling (rolled gauze)
+ tape

+ two pairs of gloves
+ scissors

- two or three pieces of four-inch-square gauze and/or nonstick Telfa pads

- normal saline

The medical assistant will put on gloves and remove the old dressing, being careful not to pull patient's skin. The area should be cleaned with normal saline and pat dry with a square of gauze. Then, the medical assistant should change their gloves and take another square of gauze or a nonstick Telfa pad and place it over the wound. The area should be wrapped with kling to secure the gauze in place. Start farthest from the heart and wrap in spirals to completely cover the gauze dressing. Tape can be used to secure the kling if necessary. The procedure and patient's tolerance should be documented. The medical assistant should give the patient educational material on dressing changes and signs and symptoms to look for.

SUTURE OR STAPLE REMOVAL

Suture or staple removal is performed on patients who have had a previous injury or surgical incision closed. Before removal of suture or staples, verify how many sutures or staples were placed and when. The supplies for a **suture removal** are:

- suture removal kit
- bandages

- gloves
- mupirocin (Bactroban) ointment

To remove sutures, the medical assistant should put on gloves, open the suture removal kit, and take out the forceps and the suture scissors. Next, grasp the knot of the suture with the forceps and use the suture scissors to cut right under the knot. The forceps can be used to pull out the suture. Repeat for the remaining sutures. Count the sutures to make sure all have been removed. Mupirocin (Bactroban) ointment should be applied to the area before covering with a bandage. The medical assistant should document the procedure, including how many sutures were removed and the patient's tolerance. The medical assistant should also give the patient educational material on suture removal and signs and symptoms to look for.

 Helpful Hint: Sutures and staples are usually removed within seven to ten days.

For **staple removal**, the medical assistant will need:

- staple removal kit
- tape, gloves
- scissors

- nonstick Telfa
- wound-closure strips

To remove staples, the medical assistant should put on gloves, open the staple removal kit, and remove the staple extractor. The medical assistant should then place the staple extractor under the staple, close the handle, and gently move the staple side to side to remove. This process should be repeated for each staple. Once all staples are removed, the medical assistant should inspect the area and count the staples to make sure they have all been removed. Cut the wound-closure strips and apply them across the incision (strips help the site heal better with less scarring). Place a nonstick Telfa pad over the incision and tape it in place. Document the procedures, including how many staples were removed and patient's tolerance. Give the patient educational material on staple removal and signs and symptoms to look for.

Patient Education

Some educational plans require little preparation and planning, such as simple medication instructions. Other plans require a multidisciplinary approach that will include physician office workers, physical therapists, and home health workers. Depending on the patient's needs, the steps of education planning are:

1. Identify the topic and purpose.
2. Assess the patient's abilities and needs.
3. Develop the plan and decide who will do what and how it will be done.
4. Implement the plan.
5. Evaluate the patient's understanding.
6. Document the education in the medical record.
7. Reevaluate the plan on follow-up.

DIABETIC TEACHING AND HOME CARE

It is important for the medical assistant to educate patients on the importance of diabetic care. This could include printing out a diabetic diet for the patient to take home, teaching the patient how to examine their feet and look for abnormalities such as calluses, sores, and discoloration and to note any numbness. The patient should be encouraged to keep a three-month follow-up with their physician for medication management and laboratory work (hemoglobin A1C, CMP, CBC, TSH, lipids, and vitamin B-12).

PATIENT MOBILITY EQUIPMENT AND ASSISTIVE DEVICES

Some patients require mobility equipment to assist in getting around, such as electric wheelchairs, walkers, scooters, lift chairs, or crutches. The medical assistant should educate the patient on safely using these devices, and provide educational material on mobility equipment and safety measures.

PRE-OP AND POST-OP CARE INSTRUCTIONS

Surgery procedures are invasive and require the patient to follow precise instructions to prevent infection. The medical assistant should instruct the patient to wash with antiseptic soap the night before and the day of surgery. They should not apply any lotions, deodorants, or perfumes the day of surgery and should not wear jewelry or watches. The medical assistant should explain what medications the patient can and cannot take the day of the procedure.

For post-op care, the patient should be educated on signs and symptoms to look for, what medications they can take, if a prescription was sent to their pharmacy, and when to follow up with the surgeon. These steps will help ensure patient compliance and reduce infection.

PATIENT-ADMINISTERED MEDICATIONS

Patients must understand the importance of taking their medications according to instructions. The medical assistant should print out a list of the patient's medications and the prescribed dosages and frequencies and describe to the patient the signs and symptoms to look for if starting new medications. The patient should repeat the instructions they were given to verify that they understand them. Education reduces overdosing and enhances patient safety.

HOME BLOOD PRESSURE MONITORING AND LIFESTYLE CONTROLS

Some patients need to monitor their blood pressure at home. They should check their blood pressure once or twice a day and document the readings in a notebook. The medical assistant should educate the patient on healthy food and drinks that can lower high blood pressure such as apples, bananas, grapes, beets, carrots, kale, and green peas and advise them to avoid salt and alcohol, which can increase high blood pressure. The patient should repeat the instructions to verify that they understand the physician's recommendations. They should be given educational materials on monitoring blood pressure to take home.

HOME ANTICOAGULATION MONITORING

The use of anticoagulants, or blood thinners, prevents blood clots in cancer patients and patients with atrial fibrillation and venous thromboembolism. Patients on anticoagulants must adhere strictly to physicians' instructions. Anticoagulant drugs include heparin, warfarin, apixaban (Eliquis), enoxaparin sodium (Lovenox), and rivaroxaban (Xarelto). Patients on anticoagulants are monitored not only by physical appearances but also by laboratory work such as an INR (international normalized ratio). The INR measures the time it takes for the blood to clot. The medical assistant should educate patients on monitoring signs and symptoms of over-anticoagulation such as bruising, nosebleeds, bleeding gums, blood in stools, and blood in vomit. Printed educational materials on anticoagulation are useful for patients to take home.

HOME CHOLESTEROL MONITORING

Patients experiencing hyperlipidemia (high cholesterol) often require medications to control or lower cholesterol, such as atorvastatin (Lipitor), rosuvastatin (Crestor), pravastatin (Pravachol), simvastatin (Zocor), and lovastatin (Altoprev). Patients on cholesterol medications must have their cholesterol checked regularly. Some side effects that can occur while taking cholesterol medications include muscle pain, headaches, abdominal pain, dizziness, and nausea. Some foods that help lower cholesterol are oats, nuts, fish, beans, and avocado. The medical assistant can print out educational material on controlling cholesterol for patients to take home.

WELLNESS AND PREVENTIVE CARE

Medical assistants must be knowledgeable about wellness and preventative care for patients. A medical assistant should be able to provide education and answer patient questions about the following topics:

+ cancer screenings: Pap smear and colonoscopy screenings to check for abnormalities of the cervix and colon

+ sexually transmitted infections (STIs): symptoms, risk factors, diagnosis, and treatment

+ hygiene: importance and step-by-step instructions for hand washing and cough etiquette

+ smoking risks and cessation: harm caused by smoking and techniques for quitting

+ osteoporosis screening/bone density scan: done in patients over fifty years of age, smokers, people with vitamin D deficiency

Medical assistants should also be able to recognize the signs of substance abuse and domestic violence. When these signs are seen, the medical office's substance abuse and domestic violence policies should be followed.

+ recognition of substance abuse: abusing illegal drugs or prescription drugs, isolation from family and friends, engaging in criminal activity, excessive drinking and changes in behavior

+ domestic violence screening and detection: bruises, excessive canceling of appointments, making excuses for the bruises, withdrawal, depression, and anxiety

Nutrition

Nutrition is the process of acquiring the energy and other resources needed for growth and development. A healthy diet includes sufficient amounts of necessary nutrients, including:

+ carbohydrates: sugars that provide an immediate source of energy

+ fats: stored energy that can be broken down and used for fuel by the body

+ proteins: molecules composed of amino acids that play an integral role in most bodily functions

+ vitamins: essential compounds that are required in small amounts

+ minerals: elements (such as calcium and phosphorus) that are essential for life

+ electrolytes: ions (such as sodium and potassium) that play an important role in maintaining the balance of water in the human body

SPECIAL DIETARY NEEDS

Medical assistants should have the knowledge to educate and care for patients with various nutritional disorders and needs. **Malnutrition** occurs when a person's diet has a deficiency of necessary nutrients. Some patients take **dietary supplements** to replenish missing nutrients. Patients with osteoporosis, for example, may take calcium supplements, and pregnant women are advised to take vitamins containing folic acid.

Patients may have special dietary needs that need to be accommodated in health care settings. Patients with allergies should be provided with meals that do not contain potentially dangerous allergens. Some other special dietary needs are listed in the table below.

Table 8.3. Special Dietary Needs

Condition	Dietary Needs
Diabetes	diet low in sugar
Cardiovascular disease or hypertension	diet low in salt and fat
Lactose sensitivity/intolerance	no dairy or dairy products
Celiac disease	no gluten (a protein found in wheat)

A high-protein diet low in fats and sugars can also help with weight control in some patients, if needed.

Some patients may also be on diets that restrict specific types of foods for reasons other than medical. **Vegans** do not eat any animal products at all. These patients are at risk for deficiencies in vitamins B-12 and D, zinc, iron, calcium, protein, and omega-3 fatty acids. **Pesco vegetarians** eat seafood and fish but no other animal or dairy products. **Lacto vegetarians** eat dairy products but no meat or eggs. Finally, **lacto-ovo vegetarians** eat dairy products and eggs, but no meat or seafood.

Therapeutic Diets

Patients may be put on therapeutic diets that are designed to help alleviate the symptoms of specific medial conditions. A **clear liquid diet** consists of fluids and some electrolytes to prevent dehydration. A clear liquid diet is often given to a malnourished patient who has not eaten for some time. Before many intestinal tests and surgeries, patients are often placed on a clear liquid diet. Allowed food items might include water, broth, clear beverages, gelatin, popsicles, hard candy, and diluted fruit juices.

A **full liquid diet** is used as a transition when going from clear liquids to altered or soft foods. Patients are often placed on a full liquid diet following surgery, or when they have difficulty swallowing, chewing, or tolerating solid foods. Foods on this diet can include ice cream, milk, pudding, custard, sherbet, strained soups, refined cooked cereals, juices, and breakfast drinks.

Mechanically altered diets are used when a patient has difficulty chewing and swallowing. Foods on this diet should be soft and moist and can include moistened bread products, cooked cereals, canned fruit, pureed soups, meat in very small pieces served with sauce or gravy, and well-cooked vegetables.

Similarly, a **soft diet** is used for patients with swallowing or chewing problems, as well as those with ulcerations of the mouth, gums, or throat. Foods that contain nuts and seeds are not allowed, and patients should be careful with raw fruits and vegetables and whole grains.

Patients with inflammation or scarring of the gastrointestinal tract or with decreased motility may be put on a **low-residue, low-fiber diet**. Foods include refined cooked cereals, white bread, cooked potatoes, refined pasta, white rice, eggs, fresh fruit without skin or seeds, and dairy products.

In contrast, a **high-fiber diet** is used for patients with constipation, obesity, diabetes, diverticulosis, and high cholesterol. Foods include whole-grain products, seeds, nuts, beans, leafy vegetables, and fruits.

EATING DISORDERS

People with **eating disorders** have abnormal or extreme behaviors and thoughts and feelings related to food and body image. Eating disorders are more common in women but occur in men as well.

An extreme desire for thinness and fear of gaining weight characterize **anorexia nervosa**. Individuals with anorexia sometimes abstain from food to such a degree that they do not maintain healthy levels of body fat and do not consume enough essential nutrients to meet requirements.

Bulimia nervosa is also associated with an individual's obsession over weight and body image, but it is characterized by an uncontrollable urge to binge followed by compensatory actions, such as purging, fasting, excessive exercise, or the use of laxatives, enemas, or diuretics to try to lose the calories consumed during the binge.

Eating disorders are as much psychiatric as they are physical, and patients who have them must be treated with sensitivity.

NINE: SPECIMENS and DIAGNOSTIC TESTING

Blood tests, urinalysis, stool samples, and cardiac testing are often necessary to determine a patient's diagnosis. Medical assistants may be responsible for performing these tests or ensuring specimens are collected properly. They are also responsible for documenting the tests they perform and providing the results to the practitioner to review in a timely manner.

Collecting and Processing Specimens

The medical assistant must be familiar with laboratory specimen collection procedures, as well as special instructions for handling and storage of several types of specimens.

BLOOD SPECIMEN: VENIPUNCTURE

Venipuncture (vein puncture), frequently referred to as a blood draw or phlebotomy, is the process of puncturing the skin to collect blood from a vein into an attached vial or tube. The process for drawing blood is described below.

1. Wash hands, then put on non-sterile gloves.
2. Confirm patient identity with TWO identifiers.
3. Label tubes with patient's first and last name, ID number, date/time of collection, and the medical assistant's initials.

   Blood is collected and stored in *evacuated tubes*. Once connected to the venipuncture needle, the vacuum in the tube pulls blood from the vein into the tube.

   Tube additives are added to the evacuated tubes for different blood tests. The additives determine which tube should be filled first to avoid damage to the blood sample or contaminating the other tubes. The colored caps of the tube correspond to the additive inside. It is important to never mix a blood sample from one tube with another tube. Below is the recommended order of draw.

Table 9.1. Blood Draw Order

Blood Draw Order	Tube Color	Description
1	color varies	blood cultures
2	light blue	sodium citrate
3	red	clot activator
4	gold	SST
5	light green	lithium heparin
6	dark green	sodium heparin
7	lavender	EDTA
8	gray	sodium fluoride
9	yellow	ACD solution

4. Select site for draw.

Blood is usually drawn from the area anterior to the elbow. The *median cubital vein* is most commonly used, but other veins, including the cephalic and basilic, may be used if the median cubital vein is not accessible. Blood may also be drawn from the veins in the back of the hand or from veins in the forearm.

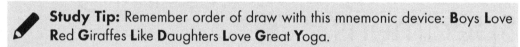

Study Tip: Remember order of draw with this mnemonic device: **B**oys **L**ove **R**ed **G**iraffes **L**ike **D**aughters **L**ove **G**reat **Y**oga.

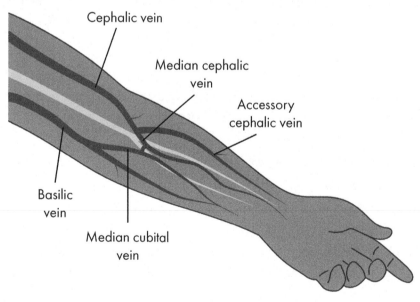

Cephalic vein
Median cephalic vein
Accessory cephalic vein
Basilic vein
Median cubital vein

Figure 9.1. Venipuncture Sites

Blood should NOT be drawn from the wrist, feet, or ankles or from sites with obvious infection or bruising. Blood draws should also not be done on the same side as a patient's mastectomy or fistula placement.

5. Apply tourniquet.

   Apply a tourniquet to the arm 2 – 4 inches ABOVE the site of the intended blood draw. This will help make veins more prominent and easier to select. Do not leave the tourniquet on for more than one to two minutes.

6. Cleanse site.

   Cleanse site with 70% isopropyl alcohol swab. Start at the intended site and then clean in concentric circles away from the center. Let skin air-dry for thirty seconds. If the area is touched after cleansing, it must be cleansed again.

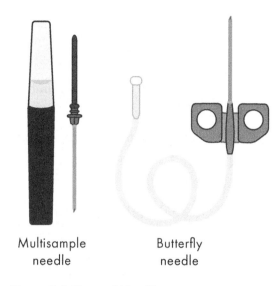

Multisample needle   Butterfly needle

Figure 9.2. Type of Needles

7. Select needle.

   Choose the appropriate needle size for the patient and type of blood draw. Needle diameter is given by its *gauge number*: smaller-diameter needles have higher gauge numbers.

   ⬦ 20-gauge multisample: large volume tubes, adults with normal-sized veins

   ⬦ 21-gauge multisample: standard venipuncture needle for patient with normal-sized veins

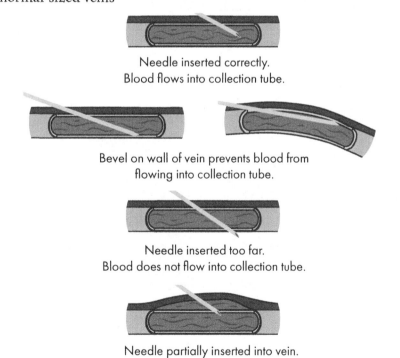

Needle inserted correctly.
Blood flows into collection tube.

Bevel on wall of vein prevents blood from flowing into collection tube.

Needle inserted too far.
Blood does not flow into collection tube.

Needle partially inserted into vein.
Blood moves into surrounding tissue, causing bruising.

Figure 9.3. Needle Placement in Vein for Venipuncture

- ✧ 22-gauge multisample syringe: older children, adults with small or "difficult" veins
- ✧ 23-gauge butterfly: infants and children, hand veins of adults
- ✧ 25-gauge butterfly: premature/neonate scalp veins

8. Anchor vein by placing thumb a few cm below site.

9. Enter skin with needle at 15 – 30-degree angle.

10. Remove tourniquet after last tube is filled and before the needle is removed.

11. Place 2 × 2 gauze over site and bandage for fifteen minutes to one hour.

BLOOD SPECIMEN: DERMAL PUNCTURE

A *capillary sample* or *dermal puncture* is done to draw a small amount of blood from the capillaries by cutting or puncturing the skin. They are used when only a few drops of blood are needed, such as an *infant heel stick* or point-of-care glucose testing on adult fingertips (sometimes called a finger stick). The process of acquiring a capillary sample is described below.

1. Wash hands, then put on non-sterile gloves.

2. Confirm patient identity with TWO identifiers.

3. Label specimen containers.

4. Select site.

   Infant heel sticks are done on the outer sides of the infant's heel. Old puncture sites should not be reused. Adult finger sticks are usually done on the medial or lateral side of the middle or ring finger. The medical assistant should never perform a finger stick on the nail or middle of the finger pad. As with venipuncture, areas with infection or bruising should be avoided.

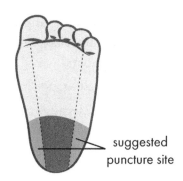

suggested puncture site

Figure 9.4. Location of Infant Heel Stick

5. Select lancet.

   The skin is punctured using a small needle called a *lancet*. The length of lancets ranges from 0.85 mm (used for infant heel sticks) to 2.2 mm.

6. Warm site with appropriate warming device if needed to increase blood flow.

7. Clean site in the same manner as used for venipuncture.

8. Puncture skin while pressing firmly on the finger and then discard lancet in sharps container.

Figure 9.5. Lancet for Adult Finger Stick

9. Wipe away first drop of blood with gauze to prevent contamination.

10. Fill tubes or other collection devices in order of draw.

    The medical assistant should hold the punctured finger or heel over a collection container and gently massage to encourage blood flow. If the blood is not sufficient, the medical assistant should take advantage of gravity by pointing the site down and applying a small amount of pressure above the site.

11. Place gauze and pressure over puncture site.

12. Apply bandage after rechecking site.

URINE SPECIMEN

Urine is assessed for various reasons and can be tested in the medical office or sent to off-site laboratories. Analysis of urine occurs by physical, chemical, and microscopic means. The urine is assessed for color, clarity, pH, specific gravity, glucose, ketones, nitrites, white blood cells, and red blood cells. A typical urine specimen should include 30–50 mL of urine collected in a dry, clean container. Medical assistants should be familiar with the different types of urine specimens:

+ A *random specimen* is collected at any time of day but is not the first or last voided.

+ A *clean catch midstream specimen* is obtained in a sterile container after the patient self-cleanses with an antiseptic towelette.

+ A *two-hour postprandial specimen* is collected two hours after a meal and is used for diabetic screening.

+ A *twenty-four-hour specimen* measures various components, such as creatinine, protein, urea, and calcium. It is collected at the patient's home in a 3,000-ml container that is kept on ice or refrigerated.

+ *Pediatric urine specimens* for infants and young children are collected using an adhesive container.

FECAL SPECIMEN

A *stool (or feces) specimen* is collected to evaluate for conditions affecting the digestive tract, including infection, parasites, cancer, bleeding, and nutrient absorption deficiency. Fecal specimens are usually collected by the patient and returned to the provider. The medical assistant should be prepared to explain to the patient how to collect the sample.

Instructions for the patient:

+ Collect stool in dry, clean container provided by the physician's office.

+ The stool should not come in contact with water, urine, or toilet paper.

+ Samples should come from three different bowel movements.

+ Patients should stop taking NSAIDs, aspirin, or steroids one week before sample collection.

+ Patients should stop taking vitamin C and iron three days before sample collection.

+ A high-fiber diet can help stimulate a bowel movement.
+ Stool samples should not be collected from patients who are menstruating, who have actively bleeding hemorrhoids, or who have a urinary tract infection.

SPUTUM SPECIMEN

Sputum is the thick mucus produced by the lungs when an infection or inflammatory process is present. It is collected by having a patient deeply cough to produce sputum into a designated sterile container. This mucus is examined by the lab to identify bacteria. If bacteria are detected, the sputum can be cultured to find which antibiotic will best treat the infection.

Instructions for the patient:
+ Do not use antibacterial mouthwash before giving the sample.
+ Drink lots of water before providing the sample.
+ If done at home, sputum samples should be collected first thing in the morning.

SWABS

A *swab* is a small amount of absorbent material on a long, thin stick. Swabs are used to collect biological material for testing and cultures from several different locations. They are sterile products, and when taking a swab, the medical assistant should ensure that swabs are not contaminated.

+ The *throat swab* is done to check the back of the throat or pharynx for bacterial infections such as strep throat.
+ A *genital swab* is used to test for sexually transmitted infections.
+ A *wound culture swab* uses a designated swab to evaluate draining, infected wounds or surgical wounds for bacteria.
+ *Nasopharyngeal swabs* test for the flu and RSV (an infant respiratory infection).

The steps for collecting a swab are:
1. Wash hands and put on gloves.
2. Open package and remove sterile swab.
3. Moisten swab using sterile sodium chloride as needed.
4. Gently pass swab over area for collection.
5. Place swab into collection tube and close.
6. Label sample.
7. Discard gloves and swab packaging.

LABELING, STORING, AND TRACKING SPECIMENS

The collection, testing, and transportation of specimens should always be carefully documented. All specimens should be properly labeled with the time of collection and TWO patient identifiers. Patient identifiers include:

+ patient's full name (last, first) or medical record number
+ date of birth
+ matching specimen barcode label

After collection, specimens should be appropriately preserved. For example, urine samples should be refrigerated after collection and may need to be packed with frozen gel packs for pickup by outside laboratories.

Some specimens require "fixation" using a *fixative*. The most commonly used chemical fixative is *formaldehyde*, which is usually combined with water to form a solution called formalin.

Formaldehyde stops a specimen from decaying, keeping it as close to its original state as possible. Generally, formaldehyde is used to preserve tissue samples that are being sent to histology for diagnosis, such as a core biopsy of a cyst or an organ. Formaldehyde can be toxic if it is inhaled or comes into contact with skin. It is also very flammable. It is important to be cautious around it.

To preserve as much of the tissue sample as possible, fixation should be done immediately after the tissue is obtained.

To preserve a specimen in formaldehyde:

1. Make sure the area is well ventilated.
2. Put on protective equipment including a face shield, an apron or lab coat, and gloves. If the solution is less than 10% formaldehyde, use regular exam gloves as protection. If the concentration is greater than 10%, medium- or heavy-weight gloves made from a waterproof material such as rubber are needed.
3. Cover the workstation with a waterproof barrier.
4. The formalin solution should be added to the container (unless a prefilled container is used) in an amount that is at least fifteen times the volume of the tissue sample to be preserved. The container should be large enough to accommodate the fixative solution and the tissue sample, with an allowance for the initial swelling of the tissue sample that will occur during fixation.

> **Did You Know?** The formalin fixative permeates a specimen very slowly, so the smaller and thinner the specimen, the easier it is to ensure the sample is preserved before the cells' breakdown. Cold will slow down the rate of perfusion. Heat can speed up the perfusion of the formalin, but it will also speed up the decay process in the tissue sample.

5. Place the tissue sample in the container.
6. Close the container, making sure the lid is on tight enough to prevent leakage.
7. Label the container with the patient's name and date of birth and date and time of sample collection.
8. Store the sample at room temperature away from any fire or heat source to be sent to the lab.

SOURCES OF CONTAMINATION

The medical assistant should be aware of possible sources of contamination that may compromise biological specimens. These sources should be avoided or mitigated to avoid false laboratory results or retesting. Possible sources of contamination are listed in the following table.

Table 9.2. Possible Sources of Specimen Contamination

Source	Example
Environment	Airborne contaminants
	Exposure to light or extreme temperatures
Container	Non-sterile container
	Noncompatible container that leaches into sample
Collection tools	Contaminated swabs or other collection devices
Health care providers	Improper hand hygiene
	Not cleaning area prior to collecting specimen

EXAMINING SPECIMENS

In a physician's office laboratory, a certified medical assistant may do simple one-step tests. These tests are referred to as waived tests because a regulating agency determines them to be low-complexity tests. Medical assistants are also responsible for monitoring the equipment in the lab to make sure they are producing accurate results.

One of the lab procedures a medical assistant may be responsible for is *inoculating* a culture. This is when a bacteria or other microorganism is introduced into or onto a culture media, such as wiping a swab of bacteria onto a petri dish. The petri dish is then labeled and stored in an incubator to wait for the results of the test. A medical assistant monitors the temperature readings and inspects the petri dishes inside the incubator for any signs of bacterial growth. *Incubators* must maintain a steady temperature and humidity level in order to grow the microbiological cultures introduced to the sterile petri dishes.

A *centrifuge* is a machine used to spin specimen tubes quickly to separate liquids with different weights, most commonly to separate blood cells from plasma cells. After spinning a blood sample in a centrifuge for ten to fifteen minutes, the plasma in the sample should rise to the top of the tube, and the red blood cells should be drawn down to the bottom of the tube. It is important to ensure that the centrifuge is properly balanced before the test is run, or the machine may be damaged.

Microscopes allow for examination of objects that are too small to see with the naked eye. A medical assistant may be responsible for preparing a specimen the provider will examine using the microscope. Preparation involves creating a *microbiologic slide*, the vehicle used for holding a specimen so it can be examined under a microscope. Usually, the specimens that are evaluated in a physician's office lab require quick action not possible with an outside lab. The specimen may also need to be evaluated quickly because it will become too compromised to be accurate if there is a delay.

For a *wet mount*, the specimen is placed onto a drop of water on a microscopic slide and then topped with a coverslip. Wet mounts allow the provider to examine bacteria that normally move or live in a liquid environment. For example, for a vaginal wet mount test, the provider examines vaginal discharge for infections that cause vaginitis.

LABORATORY QUALITY CONTROL AND ASSURANCE

Quality control processes exist to identify, reduce, and correct laboratory errors. These standardized procedures help prevent inaccurate results or the need for specimen recollection. *Testing protocols* outline specific steps on how to safely perform each test. *Testing records* and *performance logs* document daily work. All quality control activities should be documented in quality control logs.

Daily equipment maintenance is an important quality control measure.

+ *Calibration* involves maintenance of an instrument so that it provides results within an acceptable range.

+ Daily control testing should be performed before patient care every day to confirm the equipment is working correctly.

+ Monitor temperature controls: certain specimen collections and chemicals must be kept at specific temperatures to ensure accuracy. There is usually a temperature log for each storage environment in the quality control records.

+ Reagent storage: reagents are stored according to manufacturer's instructions.

LABORATORY PANELS AND PERFORMING TESTS

Common laboratory panels and tests are described in the table below.

Table 9.3. Laboratory Panels and Tests

Test Category	Testing For	Purpose and Results
Urinalysis	Physical	How the urine looks to the naked eye. Is it cloudy or clear? What color is it (dark yellow, light yellow, red, purple, or cola-colored)?
	Chemical	The **dipstick** portion of urinalysis. There are several small squares of different chemicals on the testing strip that change color when certain substances are present. These tests are red blood cell count (RBC), glucose, pH, ketones, bilirubin, and specific gravity.
	Microscopic	Examines urine under a **microscope** for presence of blood cells, urinary tract cells, bacteria, crystals, parasites, and tumor cells.
	Culture	Tests for **growth of bacteria** in a urine sample. Can help diagnose a urinary tract infection and test for type of antibiotics to treat the infection.

Table 9.3. Laboratory Panels and Tests (continued)

Test Category	Testing For	Purpose and Results
Hematology Panel	Hematocrit	**Ratio** of **red cell** volume to **whole blood** volume. Normal values: 45 – 52% in men and 37 – 48% in women
	Hemoglobin	Checks how much hemoglobin is in the patient's blood. Normal value: 13.5 – 17.5 g/dL in men and 12 – 15.5 g/dL in women
	Erythrocyte sedimentation rate (ESR)	Measures level of inflammation in the blood. This can be elevated because of infection, cancer, connective tissue disease, and inflammation. Normal values: 0 – 22 mm/hr for men and 0 – 29 mm/hr for women
	Automated cell counts	This process counts the number of white blood cells (WBC), red blood cells (RBC), and platelets in the patient's blood.
Hematology Panel (continued)	Red blood cell (RBC)	Measures RBC count. Normal values: 4.5 – 6.2 million cells per μL (adult male) and 4.0 – 5.5 million cells per μL (adult female)
	White blood cell (WBC)	Measures WBC count. WBCs are part of the **immune system**. If there is an infection or inflammation, this number can go up. Normal value: 4 – 11 thousand per μl
	Platelet	Measures the amount of platelets in the blood. Platelets help with blood clotting. Normal value: 150,000 – 450,000 per μl
	Coagulation testing/INR	PT and PTT check how quickly blood clots or how "thin" it is. INR is calculated by comparing the patient's PT level to a standardized number. INR normal value: for someone not on a blood thinner, ideal value is 0.8 – 1.1 for someone on a blood thinner (such as **warfarin**), the goal is 2 – 3
Metabolic	Glucose	Measures glucose or **blood sugar level**. Normal value: 70 – 120 mg/dL (this can vary if the patient is fasting or has just eaten)
	Kidney function tests	**BUN** (blood urea nitrogen) and **Cr** (creatinine) are markers of kidney function. Normal range 5 – 20 mg/dl Creatinine is a waste product after muscle activity. Healthy kidneys filter this out. If kidneys are not working well, this number may rise. Normal Cr range: 0.6 – 1.1 mg/dL in women, 0.7 – 1.3 mg/dL in men

Test Category	Testing For	Purpose and Results
Metabolic (continued)	Liver function tests (LFTs)	Measures the function of the liver. These tests include **bilirubin levels**, **ALT**, **AST**, **ALP**, and **albumin** levels. If the liver is damaged or diseased: ALT, AST, ALP, and bilirubin rise, and albumin decreases. Normal values: ✦ ALT: 7 – 56 U/L ✦ AST: 10 – 40 U/L ✦ ALP: 44 – 147 IU/L ✦ Bilirubin: 0.1 – 1.2 mg/dL ✦ Albumin: 3.5 – 5.5 g/dL
	Lipid profile	Calculates the amount of **triglycerides (blood fat)** and **cholesterol**. ✦ Normal values: LDL: < 100 mg/dL ✦ HDL: > 60 mg/dL ✦ Triglycerides: < 150 mg/dL ✦ Total cholesterol (good HDL + bad LDL): < 200 mg/dL, high is above 240 mg/dL This test should be a **fasting test**.
	Hemoglobin A1c	Measures **average blood sugar level** for the past two to three months by checking the percent of hemoglobin that are coated in sugar. Normal levels of nondiabetics: < 5.7% > 6.5 indicates diabetes
Immunology	Mononucleosis test (Mono spot test)	Blood test checks for **Epstein–Barr virus antibodies**. Normal range: negative
	Rapid Group A **Streptococcus** test	Throat swab culture that checks for presence of **Group A** **Streptococcus** bacteria (which causes **strep throat**). Normal range: negative
	C-reactive protein (CRP)	Another blood test for **inflammation** (similar to ESR). Elevated in inflammation, infection, sepsis, and heart disease. Normal range: < 10 mg/L
	hCG pregnancy test	This can be a blood or urine test to check for pregnancy. hCG is a **hormone produced by the placenta**. Normal range: Urine: positive or negative hCG **QUAL**itative: positive or negative hCG **QUANT**itative: > 25 mIU/mL is considered positive for pregnancy; this number will increase during the pregnancy

Table 9.3. Laboratory Panels and Tests (continued)

Test Category	Testing For	Purpose and Results
Immunology (continued)	H. pylori	Detects a **stomach ulcer–causing bacteria in the stomach** called *Helicobacter pylori* (*H. pylori* for short). It can be tested by: **Blood antibody test**—checks for antibodies to *H. pylori* (positive from active or prior infection). **Urea breath test**—the patient breathes into a bag after taking a special medication; if *H. pylori* is present, the device will detect certain carbon molecules. **Stool antigen test**. **Stomach biopsy**—sample of stomach lining during endoscopy.
	Influenza	Uses **nasopharynx swab** to test for the **flu** virus. Normal range: negative
Fecal occult blood (FOB)/Guaiac testing		Tests for the presence of **blood in the stool**, even blood that cannot be seen by the naked eye. Normal ranges: negative (no blood in stool)

Cardiovascular Tests

ELECTROCARDIOGRAPHY (ECG)

An *electrocardiogram (ECG)* is a noninvasive diagnostic tool that records the heart's electrical activity. This diagnostic test can help determine a patient's cardiac rhythm and rate. It can also help diagnose electrolyte imbalances, heart attacks, and other damage to the heart. The readout from the ECG, often called an *ECG strip*, is a continuous waveform whose shape corresponds to each stage in the cardiac cycle. A normal heart rhythm and rate is called *normal sinus rhythm*.

P wave: right and left atrial contraction and depolarization

+ *QRS complex*: contraction of the ventricles
+ *T wave*: relaxation of the ventricles and repolarization

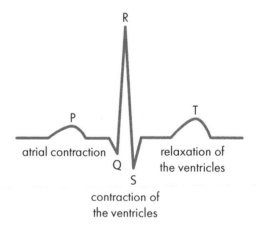

Figure 9.6. Waveforms and Intervals on an ECG

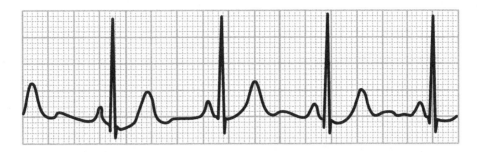

Figure 9.7. ECG: Normal Sinus Rhythm

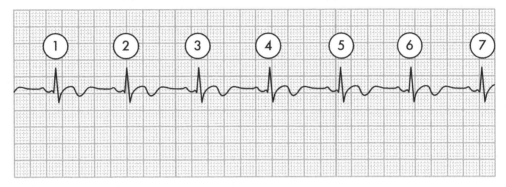

Figure 9.8. Counting Heart Rate on an ECG

The patient's heart rate can also be measured on the ECG. When calculating the heart rate from an ECG rhythm strip, count the number of QRS complexes present on the six-second strip and multiply by ten.

In the six-second strip shown in Figure 9.8, there are seven QRS complexes. The patient's heart rate is, therefore, 70 (7 × 10 = 70) bpm. (Each small box in the figure represents 0.04 seconds; each large box (five small boxes) represents 0.2 seconds.)

A *12-Lead ECG* is performed by placing ten electrodes in specific locations on the patient's chest, arms, and legs. In order for the leads to stick to the skin, the patient's skin has to be clean and dry. If there is excess chest hair, it is sometimes necessary to shave the area to keep the lead on the skin. Patients, especially those with breasts,

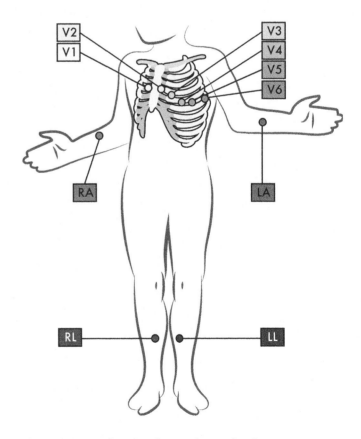

Figure 9.9. Twelve-Lead ECG Electrode Placement Diagram

should be offered a cover for the chest once electrode lead placement is done. The patient should be reclined or supine and instructed to not talk or move during the procedure.

Table 9.4. Twelve-Lead ECG Electrode Placement

Electrode	Placement
V1	fourth intercostal space to the right of the sternum
V2	fourth intercostal space to the left of the sternum
V3	midway between V2 and V4
V4	fifth intercostal space at the midclavicular line
V5	anterior axillary line at the same level as V4
V6	midaxillary line at the same level as V4 and V5
RA	between right shoulder and right wrist
LA	between left shoulder and left wrist
RL	above right ankle and below the torso
LL	above left ankle and below the torso

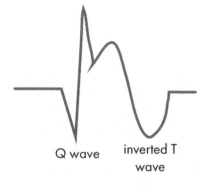

Q wave   inverted T wave

Figure 9.10. Q Wave and T Wave Inversion After Myocardial Infarction

Medical assistants do not interpret ECG strips or diagnose patients. However, they should be able to identify abnormal ECG strips and communicate to the provider what is abnormal about the strip. When reading an ECG strip, the medical assistant should look for abnormalities in heart rate or rhythm (the shape of the waves).

+ The normal number of heart beats per minute is 60 – 100. A slow heart rate (bradycardia) is < 60 bpm. A rapid heart rate (tachycardia) is > 100 bpm.

+ A *regular* rhythm has a constant rate. An *irregular* rhythm has a variable rate.

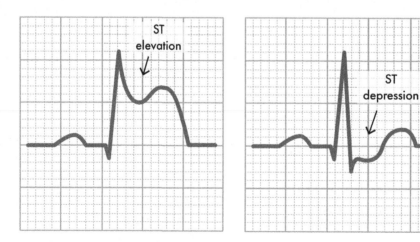

Figure 9.11. ST Elevation and ST Depression

+ The most significant finding of an ECG is the presence of *ST elevation* or *ST depression*. These rhythms are indicators of myocardial infarctions, a life-threatening blockage in the coronary arteries that requires immediate treatment.
+ Other indicators of myocardial infarction include the presence of a Q wave and a T wave inversion. (Normal T waves are upright.)

ECG strips for common dysrhythmias are shown below, along with descriptions of their important features.

Normal, regular cardiac rhythm (60 – 100 bpm)

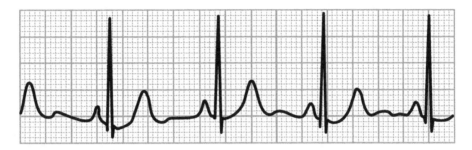

Figure 9.12. Normal Sinus Rhythm

Regular rhythm with a rate less than 60 bpm

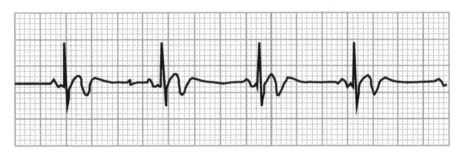

Figure 9.13. Sinus Bradycardia

Regular rhythm with a rate more than 100 bpm

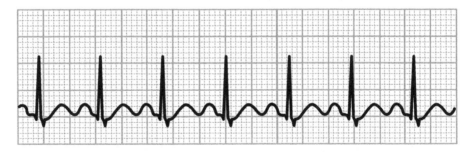

Figure 9.14. Sinus Tachycardia

An irregular rhythm with erratic or absent P waves

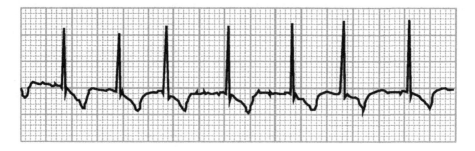

Figure 9.15. Atrial Fibrillation

Regular or irregular rhythm with no P waves; looks like sawtooth waves

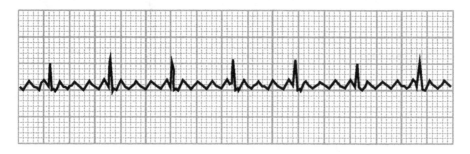

Figure 9.16. Atrial Flutter

Regular rhythm with a rate of *150 – 250 bpm*; P and T waves merge

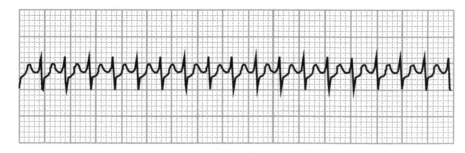

Figure 9.17. Supraventricular Tachycardia (SVT)

Irregular rhythm with abnormal P waves; has a normal rate

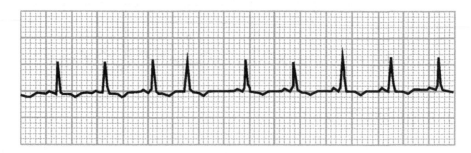

Figure 9.18. Premature Atrial Contractions (PAC)

Regular rhythm with occasional wide, weirdly shaped QRS complexes

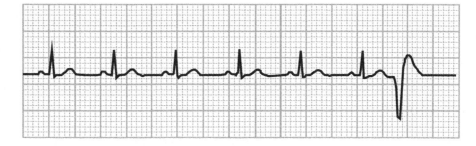

Figure 9.19. Premature Ventricular Contractions (PVC)

Regular rhythm with a rate of 100 – 250 bpm; no P wave and wide QRS

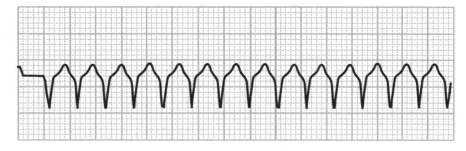

Figure 9.20. Ventricular Tachycardia

Irregular rhythm and no measurable rate; looks like a *wavy line*

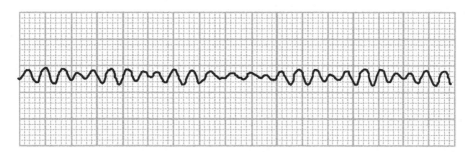

Figure 9.21. Ventricular Fibrillation

No heart rate or rhythm

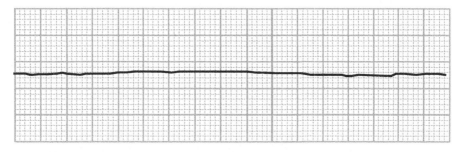

Figure 9.22. Asystole

Artifacts are ECG changes that are from interference or external factors rather than cardiac activity. They have several causes. *Internal* or *patient-based causes* include patient movement, muscle tremor, seizures, and breathing (often called a wandering baseline). *External causes* are interference from other electrical devices, cable and electrode malfunction (insufficient gel, incorrect or loose lead placement).

HOLTER MONITORS

A *Holter monitor* is a wearable device that allows for a longer length of cardiac rhythm analysis (from twenty-four hours to a few weeks). The device provides a continuous monitor of the patient's electrical activity—the patient does not have to press a button to activate this recording. This device can help detect dysrhythmias that may be occurring while the patient is not at the hospital. After the test is complete, the physician will review the readout from the monitor to determine if treatment is needed.

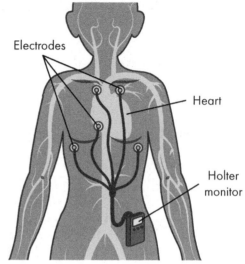

Figure 9.23. Holter Monitor

CARDIAC STRESS TEST

A *cardiac stress test* is used to observe how the heart reacts to stress. It allows the provider to check for signs of discomfort or pain during the test that can be correlated with the ECG. There are two types of stress tests: exercise and chemical.

+ On an *exercise stress test*, the patient is placed on a treadmill while wearing ECG leads.

+ With a *chemical stress test*, the patient (who may not be healthy enough to be tested on a treadmill) will receive a medication through their IV to make their heart work harder. This patient is also monitored with an ECG during the test.

In a normal healthy heart, the heart should be able to handle the "stress" without showing any changes on an ECG that suggest injury or ischemia. In an unhealthy heart, a positive stress test will show ECG changes that suggest injury or ischemia to the heart muscle.

Vision Tests
COLOR

Some people can have color vision deficiencies or *color blindness* that make it difficult to detect difference in color. The most common form is red-green color blindness, but people can also have blue-yellow color blindness or

Figure 9.24. Color Blindness Test

E

1	20/200

F P

2	20/100

T O Z

3	20/70

L P E D

4	20/50

P E C F D

5	20/40

E D F C Z P

6	20/30

F E L O P Z D

7	20/25

D E F P O T E C

8	20/20

L E F O D P C T

9

F D P L T C E O

10

P E Z O L C F T D

11

Figure 9.25. Snellen Eye Chart

complete color blindness (meaning they cannot see color). In a color blindness test, patients are asked to identify numbers and shapes made of dots that are surrounded by dots of another color. Patients who cannot differentiate between the two colors will not be able to see the number or shape.

ACUITY AND DISTANCE

The *Snellen test* evaluates *visual acuity*, or how clear your vision is at a distance. The patient covers one eye and reads from the Snellen eye chart from the top to the bottom. The lowest row that the patient can read correctly is their vision in that eye. Repeat the test with their other eye and then with both eyes uncovered.

Results are recorded as a fraction, such as 20/20 or 20/60. A visual acuity of 20/80 means that the patient can read at a distance of 20 feet what a person with normal vision can read at 80 feet. An acuity of 20/40 vision is required to drive. A person with 20/200 vision is legally blind.

An *E chart* also checks visual acuity similarly to the Snellen test. It is used for young children, patients who cannot read, or patients who do not use the Latin alphabet.

> 🔍 **Helpful Hint:** Eyesight is recorded as OU (both eyes), OD (right eye), OS (left eye). You can remember this by: y**OU** look with **BOTH** eyes; the **RIGHT** meds will not **OD**; the only one **LEFT** is **OS**.

A *Jaeger card* measures visual acuity at a normal reading distance, *fourteen inches from the eyes*. The patient keeps both eyes open and reads the smallest sentence they can without squinting.

OCULAR PRESSURE (TONOMETRY)

Ocular pressure is the measure of pressure inside the patient's eye. After numbing eye drops are applied, a tonometer is gently touched to the surface of the eye to check the ocular pressure. Elevated pressure can lead to glaucoma, eventually leading to loss of vision.

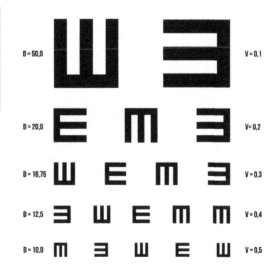

Figure 9.26. E Chart

VISUAL FIELD TESTS

Visual field tests check for peripheral vision loss and blind spots in each eye. The patient will cover one eye and look straight ahead with the other eye while answering questions about different images or light sources.

Audiometric (Hearing) Tests

PURE TONE AUDIOMETRY

Pure tone audiometry measures the patient's hearing threshold (the quietest sound they can hear). Patients wear headphones, and a beep or tone is played into one ear at a time at varying volumes. The patient is asked to raise their hand when they hear the tone. It can only be used in adults and children old enough to understand directions and cooperate.

SPEECH AND WORD RECOGNITION

Speech and word recognition tests measure how well a patient can listen to and repeat words. An example of a speech recognition test is called the *speech reception threshold (SRT)*. This test can only be performed on older children and adults who can talk. It helps to measure the extent of a patient's hearing loss. Similar to the pure tone audiometry test, the patient is given headphones to listen with. However, instead of tones, in the SRT the patient is asked to listen to and repeat words that are being said at differing volumes.

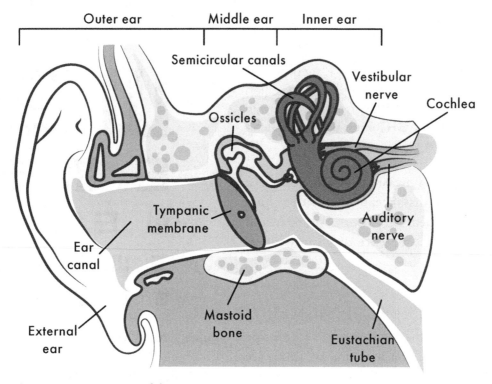

Figure 9.27. Anatomy of the Ear

Tympanometry

Tympanometry tests for abnormalities in the middle ear behind the tympanic membrane (eardrum). During tympanometry, a tube is placed in the outer ear that changes the air pressure in the ear. A tone is then played into the ear, and the movement of the eardrum is recorded on a tympanogram. An abnormal response of the eardrum under different pressures can indicate infection, ruptured tympanic membranes, malfunctioning eustachian tubes, or other issues.

Allergy Tests
Scratch Test

An allergy skin test allows providers to check for many different allergies at once. The tests are usually done on the forearms for adults and on the back for children, although high-volume tests may be done on an adult patient's back. For both locations, the area should be thoroughly cleaned and then labeled with numbers or the names of the potential allergens to be applied.

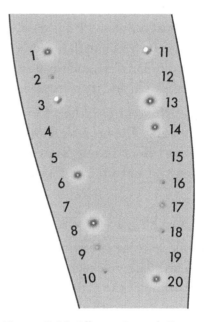

In a *scratch test*, a small amount of allergen is applied to the surface of the skin and pricked with a lancet. In *intradermal skin testing*, a small amount of the allergen is injected just under the surface of the skin.

The site is then observed for fifteen minutes to look for signs of a reaction, which includes a raised red bump and swelling around the scratch or injection site. medical assistants who assist with allergy tests should look for signs of anaphylaxis, including difficulty breathing and a rapid heart rate, which would indicate that emergency treatment is needed.

Figure 9.28. Allergy Scratch Test on Forearm

 Helpful Hint: Patients should be instructed to stop taking antihistamine medications ten days before an allergy test.

Respiratory Tests
Pulmonary Function Tests (PFT)

Pulmonary function tests (PFT) measure how well the lungs work. Measurements taken during a PFT may include:

+ tidal volume (VT): amount of air inhaled or exhaled during normal breathing
+ minute volume (MV): amount of air exhaled per minute

- vital capacity (VC): amount of air exhaled after taking a large inhalation
- functional residual capacity (FRC): amount of air left in lungs after a normal exhale
- residual volume: amount of air left in the lungs after a large exhalation
- total lung capacity: amount of air in the lungs when full
- forced vital capacity (FVC): amount of air exhaled quickly after taking a large inhalation
- peak expiratory flow rate (PEFR): the fastest rate that air can be exhaled from the lungs

SPIROMETRY

The most common PFT is *spirometry*. During the test, the patient's nose is clipped, and they are asked to breathe into the spirometer mouthpiece to obtain the values described above. There may be additional tests, such as post-bronchodilator spirometry. This involves the patient inhaling a medication and then repeating spirometry to see if their values improve.

Before the test, the patient should be instructed to avoid smoking, exercise, caffeine, and overeating. The provider should instruct patients when and how to use their breathing medications before the test. The patient should wear loose-fitting clothing: tight clothes may be too restrictive and affect test results.

PEAK FLOW RATE

While spirometer testing is done at a clinic or hospital, a *peak flow measurement* can be done at home daily to check how well a patient's asthma is being controlled. This test may detect narrowing of the patient's airways even before they begin to have symptoms of wheezing or shortness of breath and can alert a patient on when they should seek medical attention.

A *peak flow meter (PFM)* is a handheld device that measures *peak expiratory flow rate (PEFR)*. The patient blows into the mouthpiece of the device and will need to record at least three separate readings each time. With these readings, patients will be able to tell if they are in a green, yellow, or red zone.

- Green: 80 – 100% of the patient's highest peak flow. The patient's current asthma treatment is working, no new medications or activity restrictions are needed.
- Yellow: 50 – 80% of the patient's peak flow. This means the patient's airways are narrowing some and can result in mild cough, shortness of breath, fatigue, trouble with exercise or sleeping.
- Red: < 50% of the patient's peak flow. This means severe narrowing of the patient's airways, and emergent medical attention is needed.

Tuberculosis Tests and Purified Protein Derivative (PPD) Skin Tests

A *purified protein derivative (PPD)* skin test is used to detect tuberculosis. The test requires two office visits. On the first visit, the provider will inject a small amount of PPD under the top layer of skin. Two to three days later, the patient should return to the office to have the area observed for a reaction. If the patient tests positive for tuberculosis, the area will appear red and swollen.

TEN: PHARMACOLOGY

Pharmacology is the science of drugs and their effects on the human body. The agencies that regulate drugs and drug administration in the United States are the Food and Drug Administration (FDA), which regulates drugs accepted for use in the US, as well as food additives, supplements, medical devices, and cosmetics, and the Drug Enforcement Agency (DEA), which is a law enforcement agency that has oversight of controlled substances.

Prescribing information about available drugs, including dosage and side effects, is compiled in the *Physicians' Desk Reference*, also known as the *PDR*. This information is available online and is integrated into many health record systems.

Classes of Drugs

Drugs are grouped into **classes** based on their chemical structures and the conditions they treat. The major drug classes, their general purpose, and examples of each are given in the table below.

Table 10.1. Drug Classes

Drug Class	Purpose	Example(s) generic name (brand name)
antibiotics	inhibit growth of or kill bacteria	penicillin; amoxicillin; ciprofloxacin
anticoagulants (blood thinners)	prevent blood clots	rivaroxaban (Xarelto); warfarin (Coumadin)
anticonvulsants	prevent seizures	carbamazepine (Tegretol); topiramate (Topamax)
antidepressants	treat depression and mood disorders	fluoxetine (Prozac); sertraline (Zoloft); bupropion (Wellbutrin, Zyban)
antihistamines	treat allergies	diphenhydramine (Benadryl)

Table 10.1. Drug Classes (continued)

Drug Class	Purpose	Example(s) generic name (brand name)
antipsychotics	manage psychosis	aripiprazole (Abilify); lithium carbonate
antivirals	inhibit growth of or kill viruses	docosanol (Abreva); oseltamivir (Tamiflu)
barbiturates	depress the central nervous system	amobarbital (Amytal Sodium); butabarbital (Butisol Sodium); phenobarbital (Nembutal)
benzodiazepines	reduce anxiety and relax muscles	alprazolam (Xanax); clonazepam (Klonopin); lorazepam (Ativan); diazepam (Valium)
beta blockers	reduce blood pressure and improve blood flow	acebutolol (Sectral); atenolol (Tenormin); metoprolol (Lopressor); propranolol (Inderal)
calcium channel blockers	relax and widen blood vessels	amlodipine (Norvasc); felodipine (Plendil); diltiazem (Cardizem); nifedipine (Procardia)
corticosteroids	reduce inflammation	dexamethasone (Decadron); prednisone (Sterapred)
diuretics	increase the output of urine	furosemide (Lasix); valsartan (Diovan)
histamine-2 blockers	reduce stomach acid	famotidine (Pepcid); ranitidine (Zantac)
hypnotics	reduce anxiety and induce sleep	eszopiclone (Lunesta); zolpidem (Ambien)
immunosuppressants	suppress the immune system	adalimumab (Humira); methotrexate (Trexall)
local anesthetics	block sensation in a small area	lidocaine (Xylocaine, Lidoderm); benzo-caine
neuromuscular blockers	paralyze skeletal muscles	pancuronium (Pavulon); rocuronium (Zemuron)
nonsteroidal anti-inflammatory drugs (NSAIDs)	reduce pain and inflamma-tion	ibuprofen (Motrin, Advil); naproxen (Aleve, Naprosyn)
opioid pain relievers	block pain signals in brain	oxycodone (Percocet, OxyContin); morphine (Astramorph, Duramorph)
proton pump inhibitors	reduce stomach acid	esomeprazole (Nexium); lansoprazole (Prevacid); omeprazole (Prilosec)

Common Medications

The medical assistant exam will cover many commonly prescribed medications. A list of the fifty most common drugs prescribed in the US is next, along with their intended use.

Table 10.2. Fifty Most Prescribed Medications

Ranking	Medication	Common Brand Names	Drug Class (Indications)
1	lisinopril	Prinivil, Zestril	ACE inhibitor (hypertension, heart failure)
2	atorvastatin	Lipitor	HMG-CoA reductase inhibitor (high cholesterol)
3	levothyroxine	Levoxyl, Synthroid, Tirosint, Unithroid	synthetic thyroxine (hypothyroidism)
4	metformin hydrochloride	Fortamet, Glucophage	biguanide (type 2 diabetes)
5	amlodipine	Amvaz, Norvasc	calcium channel blocker (hypertension, angina)
6	metoprolol	Toprol-XL, Lopressor	beta blocker (hypertension, angina)
7	omeprazole	Prilosec	proton pump inhibitor (heartburn, GERD)
8	simvastatin	Flolipid, Zocor	HMG-CoA reductase inhibitor (high cholesterol)
9	losartan potassium	Cozaar	ARB (hypertension)
10	albuterol	Ventolin HFA, Proventil HFA, Combivent Respimat, DuoNeb	bronchodilator (asthma, COPD)
11	gabapentin	Gralise, Neurontin	anti-epileptic agent (seizures, nerve pain)
12	hydrochlorothiazide	Microzide	diuretic (hypertension, heart failure, edema)
13	acetaminophen and hydrocodone	Norco, Vicodin, Lortab	opioid (pain)
14	sertraline hydrochloride	Zoloft	selective serotonin reuptake inhibitor (mood disorders)
15	fluticasone	Flonase, Flovent	corticosteroid (allergies, asthma, COPD)
16	montelukast	Singulair	bronchodilator (asthma, COPD)
17	furosemide	Lasix	diuretic (heart failure, hypertension)
18	amoxicillin	Amoxil, Moxatag, Larotid	antibiotic (bacterial infection)
19	pantoprazole sodium	Protonix	proton pump inhibitor (heartburn, GERD)
20	escitalopram oxalate	Lexapro	serotonin reuptake inhibitor (mood disorders)
21	alprazolam	Xanax	benzodiazepine (anxiety)
22	prednisone	Sterapred	glucocorticoid (inflammation, autoimmune conditions)

Table 10.2. Fifty Most Prescribed Medications (continued)

Ranking	Medication	Common Brand Names	Drug Class (Indications)
23	bupropion	Wellbutrin, Zyban	antidepressant (mood disorders, smoking cessation)
24	pravastatin sodium	Pravachol	HMG-CoA reductase inhibitor (high cholesterol)
25	acetaminophen	Tylenol	analgesic (pain)
26	citalopram	Celexa	selective serotonin reuptake inhibitor (mood disorders)
27	amphetamine; dextroamphetamine	Adderall	stimulant (ADHD)
28	ibuprofen	Advil, Motrin	NSAID (pain)
29	carvedilol	Coreg	beta blocker (hypertension, angina)
30	trazodone hydrochloride	Desyrel	serotonin reuptake inhibitor (mood disorders)
31	fluoxetine hydrochloride	Prozac	selective serotonin reuptake inhibitor (mood disorders)
32	tramadol hydrochloride	Ultram	opioid (pain)
33	insulin glargine	Lantus	insulin (diabetes mellitus)
34	clonazepam	Klonopin	benzodiazepine (anxiety, seizures)
35	tamsulosin hydrochloride	Flomax	alpha blocker (benign prostatic hyperplasia)
36	atenolol	Tenormin	beta blocker (hypertension, angina)
37	potassium	N/A	supplement (low potassium)
38	meloxicam	Mobic	NSAID (arthritis)
39	rosuvastatin	Crestor	HMG-CoA reductase inhibitor (high cholesterol)
40	clopidogrel bisulfate	Plavix	platelet aggregation inhibitor (high risk of MI or stroke)
41	propranolol hydrochloride	Inderal, Hemangeol	beta blocker (hypertension, angina, dysrhythmias)
42	aspirin	Bayer	analgesic, anti-inflammatory, platelet aggregation inhibitor (pain, fever, MI)

Ranking	Medication	Common Brand Names	Drug Class (Indications)
43	cyclobenzaprine	Flexeril	antispasmodic (muscle spasms and pain)
44	hydrochlorothiazide and lisinopril	Zestoretic	diuretic and ACE inhibitor (hypertension)
45	glipizide	Glucotrol	sulfonylurea (type 2 diabetes)
46	duloxetine	Cymbalta	serotonin-norepinephrine reuptake inhibitor (mood disorders)
47	methylphenidate	Ritalin	CNS stimulant (ADHD)
48	ranitidine	Zantac	histamine-2 (H2) blocker (heartburn, GERD)
49	venlafaxine	Effexor	serotonin-norepinephrine reuptake inhibitor (mood disorders)
50	zolpidem tartrate	Ambien	hypnotic (sleep disorders)

Adverse Reactions

Adverse drug reaction is a broad term used to describe unwanted, uncomfortable, or dangerous effects resulting from taking a specific medication. Most adverse drug reactions are dose related, but they can also be allergic or idiosyncratic (unexpected responses that are neither dose related nor allergic responses). Adverse drug reactions are one of the leading causes of morbidity and mortality in health care. They can be classified by severity as follows:

+ mild (e.g., drowsiness)
+ moderate (e.g., hypertension)
+ severe (e.g., abnormal heart rhythm)
+ lethal (e.g., liver failure)

> **Helpful Hint:** A patient may continue taking a medication even if it has negative side effects. Some adverse reactions (e.g., dry mouth, diarrhea) subside with time, and sometimes the benefits of the drug outweigh the uncomfortable side effects. The patient should always check with the provider before discontinuing a medication.

Allergic reactions may cause itching, rash, airway edema with difficulty breathing, or a drop in blood pressure. Severe allergic reactions can cause anaphylaxis, which is a life-threatening condition requiring emergent care. An idiosyncratic reaction can cause almost any sign or symptom, and they usually cannot be predicted.

Adverse drug reactions are classified into six types.

Table 10.3. Types of Adverse Drug Reactions

Type	Description	Example
A augmented	predictable reactions arising from the pharmacological effects of the drug; dependent on dose	diarrhea due to antibiotics; hypoglycemia due to insulin
B bizarre	unpredictable reactions; independent of dose	hypersensitivity (anaphylaxis) due to penicillin
C chronic	reactions caused by the cumulative dose (the dose taken over a long period of time)	osteoporosis with oral steroids
D delayed	reactions that occur after the drug is no longer being taken	teratogenic effects with anticonvulsants
E end of use	reactions caused by withdrawal from a drug	withdrawal syndrome with benzodiazepines
F failure	unexpected failure of the drug to work; often caused by dose or drug interactions	resistance to antimicrobials

Storage of Drugs

In the medical office, medications must be stored and secured in accordance with all applicable laws. **Medication storage cabinets** and **medication supply rooms** must be kept locked. Most medications should be stored in a cool, dry place away from heat, light, and humidity. Pills and capsules in particular are easily damaged by heat and moisture.

It is important to instruct the patient to follow any storage instructions, such as refrigeration requirements, that are on the prescription label. Patients should also be reminded to store medications out of the reach of children or pets to prevent accidental ingestion of the medication.

Did You Know? Patients can safely get rid of expired, unwanted, or unused medicines through a drug take-back program. The DEA sponsors National Prescription Drug Take Back Day in communities nationwide. Some pharmacies also have mail-back programs and disposal kiosks for unused medicines.

The **expiration date** on medications, including nonprescription medications, should be noted to ensure that the drug is still safe and effective. It is also important to note when medications have been opened. Some medications lose effectiveness soon after they are opened; for example, some liquid antibiotics are only good for ten days once they have been mixed.

Preparing and Administering Medications

MEDICATION PACKAGING

Medications can be packaged in a variety of ways depending on the medication form, intended use, shelf stability, and more. Some common forms of medication packaging are discussed below.

A **multidose vial** contains more than one dose of a liquid medication intended for injection. These vials usually include preservatives that prevent the growth of bacteria. The vial should be dated when opened, and discarded within twenty-eight days (unless instructions on the vial state otherwise).

When possible, multidose vials should be used only for a single patient. When that is not possible (e.g., influenza vaccines), they should be stored in medication preparation areas. Multidose vials should be discarded if they are used in the patient treatment area to avoid contamination.

Figure 10.1. Multidose Vial

An **ampule** is a sealed container, usually made of glass, containing a sterile medication or powder to be made up in solution to be used for injection. The ampule must be broken at the neck in order to reconstitute or administer the medication. Because they must be broken for use, ampules are single use only.

Figure 10.2. Ampule

Figure 10.3. Reconstituting Powdered Medication

Unit dose packaging offers convenience and safety by supplying individual doses of medications in individual packets. The medication comes packaged in nonreusable containers and patients get the exact dose they need. The packaging can take many forms, including blister cards, strips, pouches, sticks, vials, and prefilled syringes.

> 🔍 **Helpful Hint:** When drawing up a medication from an ampule, the medical assistant should have a filter needle available to ensure that no glass shards are mixed with the medication.

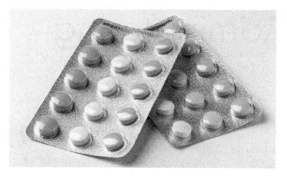

Figure 10.4. Unit Dose Packages

Prefilled cartridge needles contain accurate, premeasured doses of a medication. Since the medication is already prepared in the syringe, the chances of dosing and medication errors are reduced, as is the risk of microbial contamination. Some of these medications are prepared using a needle-free design or cartridge system, eliminating the potential for any needle-stick injuries.

Some medications must be stored in **powdered form** because they rapidly lose their effectiveness once they are mixed into a solution. These powdered medications are often supplied in vials to which a liquid (the diluent) will be added to **reconstitute** the medication before it can be administered.

When reconstituting injectable medications, the medical assistant must determine both the type and amount of diluent to be used. Sterile water and 0.9% NaCl are commonly used, but some medications require a special diluent.

DRUG DOSAGE

Some common units of measurements are:

+ microgram (mcg)
+ milligram (mg)
+ gram (gm or g)
+ kilogram (kg)
+ pound (lb)

+ liter (L)
+ milliliter (mL)
+ teaspoon (tsp)
+ tablespoon (tbsp)
+ ounce (oz)

Quick dosage calculations conversions are also listed below:

+ 1 mg = 1,000 mcg
+ 1 gm (g) = 1,000 mg
+ 1 L = 1,000 mL
+ 1 mL = 1 cc
+ 5 mL = 1 tsp

+ 15 mL = 3 tsp = 1 tbsp
+ 30 mL = 2 tbsp = 1 oz
+ 8 oz = 1 cup
+ 1 kg = 1,000 gm (g)
+ 1 kg = 2.2 lb

Table 10.4. Converting Between Units

Into Metric				Out of Metric		
If you know	**Multiply by**	**To get**		**If you know**	**Multiply by**	**To get**
Mass (Weight)						
ounces	28	grams		grams	0.035	ounces
pounds	0.45	kilograms		kilograms	2.2	pounds
Volume						
teaspoons	5	milliliters (cc)		milliliters (cc)	0.03	fluid ounces
tablespoons	15	milliliters (cc)		liters	2.1	pints
fluid ounces	30	milliliters (cc)		liters	1.06	quarts
cups	0.24	liters		liters	0.26	gallons
pints	0.47	liters				
quarts	0.95	liters				
gallons	3.8	liters				

Methods of Calculation

Any of the following methods can be used for performing drug calculations. The medical assistant should try each method and then practice the one that works best. For any of the methods, it is important to remember to convert the units of measurement to one system.

Helpful Hint: Vehicle (V) is the unit that "carries" the dose on hand. For example, a 150 mg tablet has a V of 1 because one tablet "carries" the 150 mg dose. A 200 mg/5 mL mixture has a vehicle of 5 because the 5 mL "carry" the dose of 200 mg.

Each of the three methods described below use the same variables:

+ D = desired dose or dose ordered
+ H = dose on hand or dose on container
+ V = vehicle (form and amount)
+ x = amount to give

METHOD ONE: BASIC FORMULA

Amount to give $= \frac{D}{H} \times V$

EXAMPLES

1. Order: Tagamet 600 mg

    Drug available: 300 mg tablet

    D = 600 mg

    H = 300 mg

    V = 1

    Amount to give = $\frac{D}{H} \times V$

    $= \frac{600}{300} \times 1 =$ **2 tablets**

2. Order: Dilantin 50 mg

    Drug available: 125 mg/5 mL

    D = 50 mg

    H = 125 mg

    V = 5

    Amount to give = $\frac{D}{H} \times V = \frac{50}{125} \times 5 = \frac{250}{125} =$ **2 mL**

METHOD TWO: RATIO AND PROPORTION

For this method, the known and desired quantities are written as a proportion in the form $H : V :: D : x$. The amount to give is found by multiplying the means and the extremes.

Known Quantities						Desired Quantities	
H	:	V	::	D	:	x	
			means				
			extremes				

$Hx = DV \rightarrow x = \frac{DV}{H}$

EXAMPLES

3. Order: Tagamet 600 mg

    Drug available: 300 mg tablet

    D = 600 mg

    H = 300 mg

    V = 1

    H : V :: D : x

    300 : 1 :: 600 : x

    (1)(600) = (300)(x)

    600 = 300x

    $x = \frac{600}{300} =$ **2 tablets**

4.   Order: Dilantin 50 mg

Drug available: 125 mg/5 mL

D = 50 mg

H = 125 mg

V = 5

H : V :: D : x

125 : 5 :: 50 : x

(5)(50) = (125)(x)

250 = 125x

$x = \frac{250}{125}$ = **2 mL**

METHOD THREE: FRACTIONAL EQUATION

In this method, the known and desired quantities are written as a proportion in the form
$\frac{H}{V} = \frac{D}{x}$. To find the amount to give, cross multiply and solve for x.

$\frac{H}{V} = \frac{D}{x}$ ✗ $Hx = DV$

$x = \frac{DV}{H}$

EXAMPLES

5.   Order: Tagamet 600 mg

Drug available: 300 mg tablet

D = 600 mg

H = 300 mg

V = 1

$\frac{300}{1} = \frac{D}{x}$ ✗ $300x = 600 \times 1$

$x = \frac{600 \times 1}{300}$

$x = \frac{600}{300}$ = **2 tablets**

6.   Order: Dilantin 50 mg

Drug available: 125 mg/5 mL

D = 50 mg

H = 125 mg

V = 5

$\frac{125}{5} = \frac{50}{x}$ ✗ $125x = 50 \times 5$

$x = \frac{50 \times 5}{125}$

$x = \frac{250}{125}$ = **2 mL**

Routes of Administration

The following routes are used to administer medications:

+ buccal: placed between the cheek and gum via spray, gel, or tablet
+ inhalation: inhaled into the respiratory system via mist, spray, or mask
+ intradermal (ID): injected into the dermal skin layer at a 15-degree angle via a 25-to-27-gauge needle
+ intramuscular (IM): injected into the muscle at a 90-degree angle via an 18-to-23-gauge needle
+ intravenous (IV): injected into a vein via an 18-to-22-gauge needle
+ ophthalmic: placed in the eye via ointment or drops
+ oral: taken by mouth and swallowed via capsule, tablet, liquid, gel, or solution
+ otic: placed in the ear via drops
+ parenteral: any injected medication (SC, IM, ID, or IV)
+ rectal: placed in the rectum via applicator (cream or suppository)
+ subcutaneous (SC): injected into the subcutaneous tissue at a 45-to-90-degree angle via a 22-to-25-gauge needle
+ sublingual: placed under the tongue via gel or tablets
+ topical: placed on the skin via patch, ointment, cream, liquid, or spray
+ transdermal: placed on the skin via patch
+ urethral: placed in the urethra and bladder via catheter
+ vaginal: placed in the vagina via applicator (cream or suppository)
+ Z-track: a specific IM injection method used to prevent the medication from irritating the subcutaneous tissue. The skin at the injection site is pulled to one side before injection. After injection, the skin is released, and the medication cannot seep into the subcutaneous layers.

Six Rights of Medication Administration

The "six rights of medication administration" should be followed every time a patient is given any medication to prevent errors.

1. **Right patient**: The medical assistant must check the name on the provider's order and verify the patient's first and last names.

2. **Right drug**: The medical assistant must check the drug label for expiration date and name three separate times: when taking the drug container out, after placing the medication in the dispenser (syringe or medication cup), and before returning the container to the storage or disposing of it.

3. **Right route**: The medical assistant must check the provider's order for correct route.

4. **Right dose**: The medical assistant must check the provider's order for the right dose.

5. **Right time**: The medical assistant must check the provider's order for the right time to give the medication.

6. **Right documentation**: The medical assistant must record the medication administration in the patient's record, noting date, time, drug, route, dose, site, results, tolerance, patient education, and signature of medical assistant with title.

Prescriptions
E-Prescribing

E-prescribing refers to the provider's ability to electronically send an accurate, legible prescription directly to the pharmacy. Health care providers can view a patient's medication history, create and refill prescriptions, connect to a pharmacy, and integrate the prescription with the patient's electronic medical record. An e-prescribing system will also inform the provider about generic alternatives as well as provide warnings for potential allergic reactions or medication interactions.

> **?** **Check Your Understanding:** E-prescribing has been shown to significantly reduce medication errors. How do you think e-prescribing has contributed to this reduction in errors?

Controlled Substance Guidelines

The **Drug Enforcement Agency (DEA)** is the law enforcement agency responsible for enforcing controlled substances laws as well as recommending and supporting programs to reduce the availability of illegal controlled substances. The DEA is tasked with maintaining the list of who is authorized to manufacture (drug companies), order, handle, prescribe (physicians, physician assistants, nurse practitioners, and some pharmacists), dispense (pharmacy), or store controlled substances. These organizations and individuals are responsible for maintaining a log that accurately reflects their inventory at any given time (usually at the end of a shift or the end of the day).

Medical assistants can only administer controlled substances under a physician's direct order and supervision (unless there is a state law prohibiting medical assistants from administering controlled substances).

> **?** **Check Your Understanding:** Schedule II prescriptions cannot be refilled, and a patient can only receive a 30-day supply with each prescription (for a maximum of 90 days total). Why do you think these restrictions are in place?

The **Controlled Substances Act (CSA)** is the federal drug policy under which certain stimulants, anabolic steroids, narcotics, depressants, hallucinogens, and other chemicals are regulated. There are five **schedules** (I – V) that are used to classify drugs according to their potential for abuse, likelihood of causing dependence, accepted medical application, and safety. See chapter 2 for more information on the CSA.

Medication Recordkeeping

Certain information must be documented and maintained for every prescription that is written. The provider will maintain these records within the patient's electronic health record and the pharmacy will maintain the records for the prescriptions when they are filled. The documentation should include the following information:

+ patient's full name and address

+ patient's date of birth

+ the date the prescription was written

+ the name, strength, dosage form, and quantity of the drug dispensed

+ any refill instructions from the prescriber

+ the prescriber's name, address, and DEA number (where required)

+ the complete directions for use of the drug (e.g., when to take it, how to take it, where to store it, foods that should be avoided, etc.)

Immunizations

CHILDHOOD IMMUNIZATIONS

The childhood immunization schedule is recommended by public health officials for immunity against childhood diseases. Immunizations are only given to healthy infants and children, so the medical assistant should be sure that the patient does not have a fever or any active illness. If the patient is sick, the appointment should be rescheduled. The patient's health history should not show any allergies or past convulsions due to immunizations. The parent should be advised on the benefits and risks of all immunizations prior to administration and be given a **vaccine information statement (VIS)**. These forms are produced by the CDC and provide important information about vaccine safety and benefits.

Most immunizations are given in a series. When more than one dose is required for immunity, the shot sequence is referred to as a primary series. The primary series requires a booster for the series to be complete and effective. Below are the most common vaccines and the diseases they prevent.

+ **DTaP** (Diphtheria, Tetanus, and Pertussis):
  ◇ **Diphtheria** is an acute infectious disease caused by *Corynebacterium diphtheriae*, which is a gram-positive club-shaped bacillus. Symptoms of diphtheria include headache, fever, sore throat, and malaise.

- ♦ **Tetanus** is caused by *Clostridium tetani*. Symptoms include stiff jaw, fever, and weakness.
- ♦ **Pertussis**, also known as whooping cough, is an acute infectious disease caused by the gram-negative bacillus *Bordetella pertussis*. Symptoms include fever, dry cough, and sneezing.

+ **Hib: Haemophilus influenzae type b disease** is caused by a nonmotile, gram-negative parasitic bacterium. Symptoms include sore throat, fever, cough, and muscle aches.

+ **MMR** (Measles, Mumps, Rubella):
  - ♦ **Measles**, also called rubeola, is spread by direct contact, indirect contact, or droplet infection. Lasting around ten days, it causes a red skin rash, runny nose, cough, and sore throat.
  - ♦ **Mumps** is caused by an infectious organism that attacks the parotid and salivary glands, and is transmitted by direct contact or droplet infection.
  - ♦ **Rubella**, also known as the German measles, is caused by a virus that leads to an upper respiratory infection. Other symptoms are fever, joint pain, and a fine red rash.

+ **HBV** (Hepatitis B Virus): **Hepatitis B** is a highly contagious form of viral hepatitis, caused by the hepatitis B virus (HBV). It is transmitted by contact with contaminated saliva, semen, or blood. Symptoms include nausea, vomiting, fever, jaundice, and dark urine.

+ **VZV** (Varicella-Zoster Virus): Better known as chicken pox, **varicella** is a highly contagious viral illness that is spread by direct contact and droplet infection. Symptoms include an itchy rash, fever, headache, and general malaise.

+ **IPV** (Inactivated Polio Virus): **Polio** is a serious disease that can lead to infantile paralysis (poliomyelitis). Symptoms include headache, nausea, vomiting, and rash. The vaccine contains inactivated polio virus (IPV).

ADULT IMMUNIZATIONS

While fewer in number, adult vaccines are also an important part of patient care. In addition, health care workers themselves need to get certain vaccines to help protect the vulnerable populations they interact with. Important adult immunizations and vaccines are listed below.

+ **Influenza vaccine:** Influenza viruses are associated with approximately 36,000 deaths each year in the US alone. The composition of the influenza vaccine changes from year to year based on predictions of which strains will be most prominent. Clinical researchers found that aging adults who receive this vaccine have less severe influenza illness and fewer complications, and the mortality rate is reduced.

+ **Pneumococcal vaccine:** Pneumococcal infections cause around 40,000 deaths every year in the US. The pneumococcal vaccine provides immunity to the *Streptococcus pneumoniae* organism. All adults over the age of 65 years should receive this vaccine, as should those who are considered high risk. The injection is given intramuscularly in the deltoid muscle.

+ **Herpes zoster vaccine:** The herpes zoster virus vaccine can prevent shingles for people over the age of 60. This injection reduces the occurrence of shingles, and for those who do develop shingles, it lessens illness severity.

+ **Tetanus vaccine:** Most aging adults are not aware that they need to be immunized against *Clostridium tetani*, the bacteria that lead to tetanus. The tetanus vaccine is recommended every ten years for adults and is usually available as tetanus-diphtheria toxoid (Td), given intramuscularly.

VACCINE RECORDKEEPING AND STORAGE

Before administering any vaccines, it is important to give the patient (or parent/legal guardian) copies of all pertinent vaccine information statements and make sure they understand the risks and benefits of the vaccine(s). The vaccination administration record should be completed after administration of the vaccine(s). The forms vary by state, but in general, all of the following information will be included on the vaccination administration record:

+ type of vaccine given

+ date the vaccine was given

+ funding source of the vaccine given: F (federal), S (state), or P (private)

+ route and site of administration on the patient

+ lot number and manufacturer of the vaccine

+ date on the VIS and the date it was given to the patient (or parent/legal guardian)

+ signature (or initials) and title of the person who administered the vaccine

Patients (or their parents/legal guardians) often request vaccination records to fulfill requirements for attending school or playing sports. These records might also be requested by other agencies (e.g., health departments) in the event of a recall or problem with the vaccine. It is important that these records remain up to date, accurate, and complete.

Proper vaccine storage and handling is essential for ensuring that vaccines maintain their potency and effectiveness. Different vaccines require different storage temperatures, but most must be either refrigerated or frozen. Many vaccines also need to be protected from exposure to light. Medical assistants must be familiar with and adhere to all recommendations for the proper storage of vaccines.

Table 10.5. Vaccine Storage

Store in Refrigerator: 36°F to 46°F (2°C to 8°C)	Store in Freezer: −58°F to 5°F (−50°C to −15°C)	Protect from Light:
+ 9vHPV + diphtheria toxoid, tetanus toxoid, and pertussis (DT, DTaP, DTaP-HepB-IPV, DTap-IPV, DTap-IPV/Hib, Tdap, Td) + HepA + HepB + HepA-HepB + Hib + influenza (LAIV, IIV, RIV) + meningococcal (MenACWY-D, MenACWY-CRM, MenB-4C, MenB-FHbp) + MMR + pneumococcal (PCV13 and PPSV23) + rotavirus (RV1 and RVS) + RZV	+ MMR + MMRV + VAR + ZVL	+ Afluria + Bexsero + FLUAD + Fluarix + Flublok + Flucelvax + FluLaval + Flumist + Gardasil 9 + Hiberix + IPOL + M-M-R II + Menveo + ProQuad + Rotarix + RotaTeq + Shingrix + Varivax + Zostavax

Did You Know? The transport and storage of vaccines at the appropriate temperature is referred to as the **cold chain**. Most organizations require formal training for cold chain management.

ELEVEN: EMERGENCY MANAGEMENT

A medical emergency is an unexpected life-threatening event. It can occur at any time, so it is important to be prepared and understand what to do. A medical assistant's role is to stay calm and follow the office's emergency management policy and protocol. The more prepared the medical assistant is for an emergency, the better the outcome will be for the patient. Knowing how to recognize common emergency situations and what to do can help ensure that the patient remains safe and the event does not escalate.

Some key points for the medical assistant to remember during an emergency are:

+ Secure the scene and do not panic.

+ Relocate nearby visitors and patients.

+ Work with other members of the health team to ensure that all necessary equipment is available.

+ Know the location of the crash cart.

+ Maintain cardiopulmonary resuscitation (CPR) certification and follow training.

+ Do not attempt any intervention without the proper training.

+ Be observant; the medical assistant may need to provide information about the event.

+ Remember to complete all applicable documentation regarding the emergency.

Assessment and Screening

In an emergency, the medical assistant may be the one delegated to perform the initial assessment of the patient. If the patient is actively presenting with an emergency, the initial assessment should be brief and focused on responsiveness, circulation, airway, and breathing. Unconscious patients should be aroused through speech and touch. If they remain unresponsive, the medical assistant should assess circulation. If the patient is pulseless, the medical assistant should follow CPR protocols. If the patient appears stable, a standard assessment should be performed.

Patients presenting with life-threatening symptoms will be **triaged** to determine their acuity (the level of care they will need). In most states, medical assistants are NOT allowed to triage patients, as it requires exercising clinical judgment. However, it is helpful for the medical assistant to understand how the process works in order to assist providers as needed.

> **Did You Know?** It is important that the medical assistant does not attempt to diagnose or independently treat any issues. If the medical assistant believes a patient has symptoms requiring urgent assessment or treatment, the appropriate medical provider should be notified immediately.

When patients are triaged, the provider will assess the severity of their symptoms and determine how long they can wait for care. If multiple patients require attention, the triage process will also determine who should be seen first. Each office will have its own triage protocols, which are often color-coded, as explained below.

Standard (green): Standard patients are stable and should be seen by the provider within the normal time frame.

Urgent (yellow): Urgent patients should be assessed by the provider as soon as possible to determine a treatment plan.

+ low-pulse oximetry even with unlabored breathing
+ high or low blood pressure
+ infection symptoms lasting longer than a week despite treatment (in the very young and very old)
+ significant medical history and new symptoms

Very Urgent (orange): The provider should be notified immediately. Very urgent patients should be assessed by the provider, who will determine if transfer to a higher level of care is needed.

+ labored breathing, wheezing
+ mental fogginess, confusion, difficulty speaking
+ acute changes after an injury
+ signs of infection after procedure
+ acute, unrelieved pain

Immediate (red): Patients with life-threatening symptoms need immediate care. 911 should be called and the patient prepared for transfer to emergency department.

+ airway compromise
+ agonal breaths (gasping, labored breaths) or stridor (wheezing sounds)
+ chest pain
+ uncontrolled bleeding
+ signs of shock
+ responsive to painful stimuli or voice only
+ unresponsive

During and after an emergency, the medical assistant should document the event and provide information to emergency medical services (EMS). EMS will expect a chronological timeline of the events and what interventions or treatments were given. Medical assistants should be prepared to give the following information:

+ patient's name, age, and pertinent medical history
+ the concern or chief complaint
+ current vital signs
+ what was done to treat the concern
+ patient's current condition
+ patient's allergies

Response to Emergencies
ANAPHYLACTIC SHOCK

Anaphylactic shock (or anaphylaxis) is a life-threatening, severe allergic reaction that causes widening of blood vessels and constriction of airways in the lungs. The most common causes of anaphylactic shock are food allergens, medications, and insect venom. Symptoms of anaphylactic shock include:

+ respiratory distress (can be severe)
+ swelling (edema) in face, lips, or tongue
+ skin pallor or flushing
+ low blood pressure
+ weakness
+ dizziness or fainting
+ vomiting or diarrhea
+ altered mental status
+ anxiety or confusion

 Did You Know? Many patients with allergies carry an EpiPen, which provides a premeasured dose of epinephrine for injection.

Patients receiving medications in the office may experience anaphylactic shock, so medical assistants should be familiar with its symptoms. Anaphylactic shock is treated with an epinephrine injection. The provider may choose to transfer the patient to an emergency department for further observation or if treatment is ineffective.

ASTHMATIC ATTACK

Asthma, an obstructive disease of the lungs, is characterized by long-term inflammation and constriction of the bronchial airways. Patients with asthma often experience exacerbations (called acute asthmatic attacks) triggered by lung irritants, exercise, stress, or allergies. Symptoms of an acute asthmatic attack include:

+ wheezing
+ frequent cough (productive or nonproductive)
+ shortness of breath
+ tightness in the chest
+ severe exacerbations marked by:
+ rapid breathing (tachypnea)
+ audible wheezing
+ anxiety
+ low oxygen levels

Treatment for an acute asthmatic attack aims to widen the airways of the lungs. Patients are given a bronchodilator such as albuterol or ipratropium through a mask or mouthpiece. They may also receive a corticosteroid. Patients should be monitored for dizziness and rapid heart rate following treatment.

Patients who do not respond to treatment are in **status asthmaticus**, a severe condition characterized by unmanageable asthma exacerbations with limited or no pauses between the exacerbations. These patients will require immediate transfer to an emergency department.

BLEEDING

There are three types of bleeding: arterial, venous, and capillary.

Arterial bleeding occurs when an artery is damaged. Because arteries carry high volumes of blood at high pressure, arterial bleeding can be life-threatening and requires immediate intervention to prevent low blood pressure and other issues related to decrease in blood volume.

Arterial blood is bright red and "spurts" due to the pressure of the heart pumping. The blood is often moving too quickly for clotting to occur.

Venous bleeding occurs when a vein is damaged. Veins carry high volumes of blood, but they do not supply the same pressure as arteries, so although venous bleeding may be heavy, it is slower than arterial bleeding. The blood is also darker in color because it is deoxygenated.

Capillary bleeding occurs when the small blood vessels that create the network between veins and arteries are damaged. Capillary bleeding is often seen in wound beds or with skin abrasions. Bleeding from the capillaries is usually controlled easily.

The treatment for all types of bleeding is to apply direct pressure to the site.

1. Maintain standard precautions, including wearing gloves.
2. Place the patient in a prone position.
3. Apply pressure using sterile gauze. Pressure may be applied for up to twenty minutes depending on the type of bleed.
4. If the bleed is arterial, pressure may be applied above the site of bleeding (only if directed by the provider).
5. Continue to evaluate for symptoms of shock.
6. Assist with cleaning and dressing the wound once the bleeding has stopped.

 Helpful Hint: Do not remove blood-soaked dressings, as this will interrupt the clotting process. Instead add gauze as necessary.

BONE FRACTURES

A **fracture** is any break in a bone. Fractures can be open or closed. **Open fractures** include a break in the skin; the skin is intact with a **closed fracture**. Fractures are diagnosed via X-ray.

Further classifications of fractures are made based on the configuration of the fracture.

- Non-displaced: Broken area of the bone remains in alignment; this is the optimal condition for reduction (setting) and healing.
- Displaced: Broken areas of bone are not aligned. Displacement may require manual or surgical reduction including hardware for fixation.
- Transverse: A horizontal break in a straight line across the bone that occurs from a force perpendicular to the break.
- Oblique: A diagonal break that occurs from a force higher or lower than the break.
- Spiral: A twisting break around the circumference of the bone that is common in sports injuries.
- Comminuted: The break is fragmented into three or more pieces. This is more common in people over sixty-five and those with brittle bones.
- Compression: The break is crushed or compressed, creating a wide, flattened appearance. Compression frequently occurs with crush injuries.
- Segmental: Two or more areas of the bone are fractured, creating a segmented area of "floating" bone.

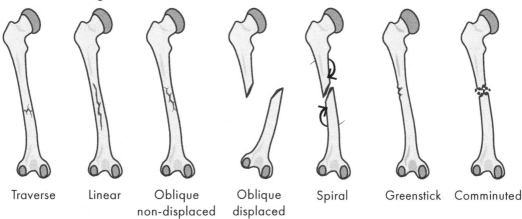

Traverse   Linear   Oblique non-displaced   Oblique displaced   Spiral   Greenstick   Comminuted

Figure 11.1 Types of Fractures

If the patient has a suspected fracture, the medical assistant should immobilize the area. If it is an open fracture, any bleeding should be controlled. The medical assistant should keep the fractured area elevated if possible and prepare the patient for further diagnostic evaluation or transfer. It is important to monitor for symptoms of shock, especially with an open fracture.

Burns

Burns are trauma to the skin or underlying tissue caused by heat, radiation, electricity, or chemical exposure.

- **First-degree burns** involve superficial epidermal damage. The skin is red and painful to the touch.
- **Second-degree burns** involve the epidermis and dermal layers of the skin. They can also be called partial-thickness burns. Usually there is blistering of the skin and significant pain.

+ **Third-degree burns** involve the entire dermis and underlying tissues. They are also called full-thickness burns. Third-degree burns appear blackened or white, and the patient may feel little or no pain due to nerve damage.

First-degree burns usually resolve on their own. Medical assistants should treat first-degree burns by cooling the area with a cold compress or running the burn under cold water. If needed, a dry nonstick dressing can be used.

When treating second- and third-degree burns, it is important that the medical assistant does not break any blisters, remove loose tissue on the burn, or remove material adhering to the burn. These actions can lead to infection and further damage. A sterile towel should be applied to the site, as well as sterile water or sterile normal saline. In the office setting, patients should be transferred to a higher level of care for further treatment and monitored for shock while awaiting transfer.

CARDIAC AND RESPIRATORY ARREST

Cardiopulmonary (cardiac) arrest occurs when the heart stops beating, which causes blood flow to stop. The patient will have no pulse and either will not be breathing or will display labored breathing (agonal gasps). Immediate **cardiopulmonary resuscitation (CPR)** should be started for any patient in arrest.

Respiratory arrest occurs when breathing stops or is no longer effective at meeting the body's oxygen needs. Respiratory arrest often occurs with cardiac arrest but can occur alone as well. It will eventually lead to cardiac arrest.

Both cardiac and respiratory arrest are life-threatening conditions that require immediate treatment to preserve life and tissue function. The medical assistant should follow these steps:

1. Get help and contact 911.
2. Assess the patient and check for pulse (for no longer than five seconds). If the patient has a pulse, perform rescue breathing. If the patient has no pulse, begin performing CPR.

Rescue breathing:

+ Use the head-tilt/chin-lift method to assess the airway.
+ Ensure the patient's airway is clear.
+ If an obstruction is visible, attempt to clear it. However, be careful to not obstruct the airway by pushing the object in deeper.
+ Provide breaths at a rate of ten to twelve breaths a minute.
+ If a pulse oximeter is available, attach it to the patient to monitor oxygenation and pulse.

CPR:

+ Perform chest compressions at a rate of thirty compressions to two breaths for a single rescuer, with a goal of one hundred compressions a minute.
+ Compressions should be two inches in depth.

+ Allow full chest recoil.
+ Use the head-tilt/chin-lift method to assess the airway after the first thirty compressions.
+ Use the automated external defibrillator (AED) as necessary.
+ Prepare for transfer to a higher level of care.

Cerebrovascular Accident (CVA)

A **cerebrovascular accident (CVA)**, or stroke, occurs when the blood supply to the brain is disrupted due to damage in the brain's blood vessels. A **hemorrhagic stroke** occurs when a vessel ruptures in the brain. The blood that accumulates damages brain tissue and causes neurological impairment. An **ischemic stroke** occurs when arteries in the brain are blocked, leading to ischemia (reduced blood flow) and damage to brain tissue. The lack of blood flow can be caused by a thrombosis (blood clot) or an embolus (other materials, such as fat).

During a cerebrovascular event or stroke it is important to remember that response time is critical—the longer the CVA is untreated, the more damage will be done to the brain. Knowing the signs and symptoms of an event and treating it as soon as possible can improve patient outcomes. The medical assistant should be able to recognize the symptoms of a stroke and communicate this to the provider.

Medical assistants should use the acronym **FAST** from the American Stroke Association to evaluate symptoms.

+ **F**ace drooping—Ask the patient to smile. Are there signs of asymmetry?
+ **A**rm weakness—Does the patient have any weakness in their arms?
+ **S**peech difficulty—Is their speech slurred or garbled?
+ **T**ime to call 911—If the answer to any of these questions is yes, the medical assistant should call 911, remembering to note the symptoms and time of onset.

Patients may present with confusion, vision changes, severe headache, dizziness, mobility issues, breathing or swallowing issues, and speech changes.

Cold Exposure

Cold exposure occurs when a person is exposed to cold temperatures for an extended period of time. Exposure to cold can lead to different outcomes based on the exposed area and the severity of the cold.

Frostbite is injury to the dermis and underlying tissue due to cold. The exposure to cold leads to cellular damage, impairment of the vascular system, and an inflammatory response. Frostbite most commonly affects fingers and toes. Skin may appear red, blue, or black, depending on the level of tissue damage.

Areas affected by frostbite should be assessed and gently rewarmed. The medical assistant should check skin tissue for sensation and note whether the skin that was exposed is hard, white, or black. The area should be gently rewarmed as instructed by the provider. Warming is usually done with lukewarm water between 98°F and 105°F. Medical assistants should always ensure that any cold-exposed tissue is clean and use only clean sterile dressings to bandage blistered or broken skin.

Chilblains are inflammatory responses that occur in the skin and small blood vessels as a result of repeated exposure to cold but not freezing temperatures. They are most commonly seen in women, underweight patients, and patients with Raynaud's disease. Chilblains are treated by gently warming the affected area with heating pads.

Hypothermia occurs when core body temperature drops below 95°F (35°C), causing a reduction in metabolic rate and respiratory, cardiac, and neurological functions. When body temperature drops below 86°F (30°C), the body is unable to maintain its core temperature. Symptoms of hypothermia include:

+ shivering
+ confusion
+ speech changes
+ extreme fatigue
+ slow heart rate
+ labored breathing

Patients with hypothermia should be insulated to prevent further heat loss and transferred to an emergency department.

CONCUSSION

A **concussion** is a short-lived and reversible change in mental status following trauma to the head. The change can last from several minutes to any time up to six hours. Patients may temporarily lose consciousness, but often they do not. Symptoms resulting from short-term injury are temporary and resolve within a few weeks. Common concussion symptoms include:

+ headache or pressure
+ mental fogginess
+ fatigue
+ speech changes
+ dizziness
+ tinnitus
+ nausea and/or vomiting

Sometimes symptoms may be delayed and do not present for several days. Patients with concussions are usually advised to rest, avoid strenuous physical activity, and avoid activities that require concentration. Multiple concussions can cause progressive damage, including permanent injury. People who engage in contact sports are at a greater risk for concussion and should refrain from playing until all symptoms are resolved and the provider has cleared them.

HYPERGLYCEMIA

Hyperglycemia (high blood sugar) occurs when serum glucose concentrations are elevated in response to a decrease in available insulin or to insulin resistance. The condition is most often associated with diabetes mellitus but can also be caused by medications (such as corticosteroids and amphetamines), infection, sepsis, and endocrine disorders.

Diabetic ketoacidosis (DKA) is a hyperglycemic state characterized by an insulin deficiency that stimulates the breakdown of adipose tissues (fat). This process results in the blood becoming too acidic. DKA develops quickly (less than twenty-four hours) and is most common in people with type 1 diabetes. It can also be caused by uncontrolled blood sugar from missed medication or from illness. Uncontrolled DKA can lead to coma and requires immediate treatment.

Symptoms of DKA include:

- dehydration and extreme thirst
- elevated blood glucose (blood sugar) levels
    - hyperglycemia: > 200 mg/dL
    - DKA: usually 350 – 800 mg/dL
- frequent urination
- ketones in the urine

- fruity breath
- extreme fatigue
- dry or flushed skin
- nausea and vomiting
- abdominal pain
- breathing difficulty
- confusion

 Did You Know? DKA may be the first sign of diabetes in an individual with undiagnosed diabetes.

Hyperglycemic patients require IV insulin and fluid and electrolyte replacement. The patient will most likely be transferred to a higher level of care.

FOREIGN BODY OBSTRUCTION

Choking is caused by a foreign body obstructing the airway. Unaddressed choking will lead to loss of consciousness and cardiac arrest. If a patient begins choking, the medical assistant should alert the nearest provider and attempt to dislodge the obstruction until a provider is available. Never perform a blind sweep, as this may lodge the object farther in the airway.

 Did You Know? Choking is the most common cause of respiratory distress in pediatric patients.

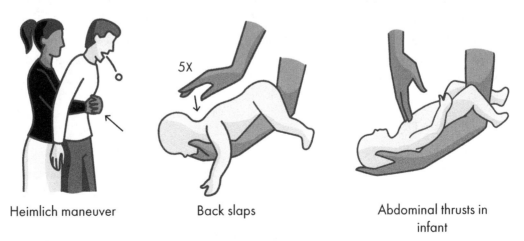

Heimlich maneuver

Back slaps

Abdominal thrusts in infant

Figure 11.2. Dislodging Foreign Bodies in Airway

If the patient is conscious, the Heimlich maneuver or abdominal thrusts should be used to dislodge the object. The medical assistant should perform five thrusts by applying pressure between the rib cage and navel. Between abdominal thrusts, the patient's consciousness should be quickly assessed. The medical assistant should perform abdominal thrusts until the object is dislodged or the patient becomes unconscious. If the patient should become unconscious, they should be lowered to the ground, and the medical assistant should continue abdominal thrusts until the patient is pulseless and requires CPR. For an infant with an obstructed airway, the medical assistant should switch between five back slaps and five abdominal thrusts.

HEAT EXPOSURE

Heat exposure occurs when the body is exposed to high temperatures for an extended period of time. Like exposure to cold, exposure to heat can present with varying symptoms based on the degree of exposure.

Heat cramps occur when physical exertion leads to a profuse loss of fluids and sodium through sweating. When fluids are replaced but sodium is not, the resulting electrolyte imbalance causes muscle cramps.

Heat exhaustion occurs when the body is exposed to high temperatures, leading to dehydration. It is not a result of the body's inability to regulate or maintain body temperature.

Heatstroke occurs when the body is unable to reduce excess heat, leading to an increased core temperature over 104°F (40°C). The resulting inflammatory process can cause multiple organ failure that, if not treated, leads to death. **Classic heatstroke** occurs as a result of prolonged exposure to high temperatures with no air-conditioning or access to fluids. **Exertional heatstroke** occurs when exercising in extreme heat.

General symptoms of heat exposure include:

+ sweating
+ rapid heartbeat
+ fainting

+ headache
+ cramping
+ nausea and vomiting

The medical assistant should rehydrate patients with heat exposure emergencies and assess their body temperature as the provider directs. Patients with heat stroke should be cooled using compresses applied to the neck, armpit, and groin. They may also need supplemental oxygen and cardiac monitoring. The provider will determine if the patient with heat exposure should be transferred to a higher level of care.

HYPERVENTILATION

Hyperventilation occurs when the patient's breathing becomes rapid and the body expels more carbon dioxide than it produces. Hyperventilation is often caused by anxiety or stress but can also be caused by cardiovascular or respiratory disorders. Hyperventilation accompanied by chest pain should be considered an acute emergency, and 911 should be contacted.

When hyperventilation is caused by anxiety, the medical assistant should help the patient relax to slow their breathing. The medical assistant should reassure the patient and assist them with the following:

+ Have them attempt pursed lip breathing.
+ Have them breathe using their belly.
+ Have them breathe through their hands.
+ Have them intermittently attempt to hold their breath for 10–15 seconds.

INSECT AND ANIMAL BITES

Most **insect bites** are more of an annoyance than an emergency. However, some bites require further evaluation and treatment. Bites may be toxic (e.g., brown recluse spider), and some insects carry disease (e.g., ticks). In some cases, an insect bite may cause an allergic reaction, including anaphylaxis. Before treatment, it is important to attempt to identify the source of the bite by having the patient describe the insect. The medical assistant should ask the patient when the bite occurred and if they are experiencing symptoms such as fatigue, confusion, rash, or swelling.

Insect bites are commonly managed by cleaning the site to prevent infection and managing symptoms. Patients with tick bites may need to be monitored for infection such as Lyme disease or Rocky Mountain spotted fever. The type of bite and the patient reaction will determine if a higher level of care is required.

When a patient presents with an **animal bite**, the medical assistant should first control any bleeding. Next, the wound site should be cleaned. Deep bites may need suturing, antibiotics, and a tetanus shot based on the patient history. The medical assistant should apply a sterile dressing and triple antibiotic cream as the provider orders. If the bite is from a wild animal the patient may need anti-rabies treatment based on the provider's assessment.

INSULIN SHOCK

Insulin shock occurs when hypoglycemia (low blood sugar) is left untreated. This can occur when diabetic patients miss a meal, take the incorrect amount of insulin, or do not increase their carbohydrate intake during vigorous exercise. Since hypoglycemia can rapidly progress to insulin shock, symptoms should be addressed immediately.

Symptoms of insulin shock include:

+ dizziness
+ tremors
+ sweating
+ mood change
+ rapid pulse
+ headache

+ confusion
+ fainting
+ poor muscle coordination
+ muscle tremors
+ seizures
+ coma

The medical assistant should obtain a baseline blood sugar and, if the patient is conscious, provide glucose followed by a complex carbohydrate. The patient's blood sugar should be rechecked after twenty minutes. If the patient is not responsive to treatment, the medical assistant should contact 911 and prepare for transport to a higher level of care. Unconscious patients are administered glucagon per the provider's orders and prepared for transport to a higher level of care.

Joint Dislocations, Sprains, and Strains

Sprains and strains are common musculoskeletal injuries that share similar signs and symptoms. **Sprains** involve the tearing or stretching of ligaments, whereas **strains** involve the tearing or stretching of muscle or tendons. Symptoms of sprains and strains include pain, swelling, and reduced range of motion.

A **dislocation** is when the bone shifts from its natural position. Patients with dislocations may present with swelling, skin redness, and pain. It is possible to see the misplaced joint with a joint dislocation.

Musculoskeletal injuries cannot be diagnosed with a visual exam, so the medical assistant should always assume a fracture is possible until it has been ruled out. To prevent further injury, the area should be immobilized with a **splint**. The provider will determine what type of splint is required. Ice should be applied to the affected area to prevent or decrease swelling.

Poisoning

Poisoning—ingestion of a toxic substance—is considered a medical emergency. If possible, the medical assistant should determine what was ingested and then consult poison control regarding treatment. It is also important to obtain and document the time the incident occurred, presenting symptoms, age and weight of the patient, and a set of vital signs. The poison control center will advise on treatment, and the provider will instruct on provision. The medical assistant should not induce vomiting unless instructed by poison control and the provider. The patient may need to be transported to a higher level of care.

Seizures

A **seizure** is caused by abnormal electrical discharges in the cortical gray matter of the brain; the discharges interrupt normal brain function. **Epilepsy** is a condition characterized by recurrent seizures.

There are many types of seizures. **Convulsive seizures** include rapid, uncontrolled contraction and relaxation of muscles. In an **absence seizure**, the patient loses consciousness but does not have uncontrolled muscle contractions. **Status epilepticus** occurs when a seizure lasts longer than five minutes or when seizures occur repeatedly without a period of recovered consciousness between them.

Tonic-clonic seizures (a type of convulsive seizure) start with a tonic (contracted) state in which the patient stiffens and loses consciousness; this phase usually lasts less than one minute. The tonic phase is followed by the clonic phase, in which the patient's muscles rapidly contract and relax. The clonic phase can last up to several minutes.

New-onset seizures in patients with no prior seizure history are treated as an emergency, and 911 should be contacted so the patient can be transferred to a higher level of care.

During a seizure, the medical assistant should act to secure the safety of the patient:

- Remove any objects that might cause injury.
- Loosen tight clothing.
- Never restrain a seizing patient.
- Do not place anything in the patient's mouth.
- If needed, place the patient in the recovery position (on their side).
- Monitor the patient's airway.
- Post-seizure patients are usually lethargic; allow recovery time.
- Ensure that the physician is aware of the situation.
- Follow provider's decision on transfer to a higher level of care.

SHOCK

Shock occurs when the cardiovascular system is compromised.

Cardiogenic shock occurs when the heart can no longer pump effectively, reducing blood flow and available oxygen throughout the body. This type of shock is most commonly seen in individuals having a heart attack.

Hypovolemic shock (decrease in blood volume) occurs when rapid fluid loss decreases circulating blood volume and cardiac output, resulting in inadequate blood flow to tissues.

Septic shock is the result of a massive inflammatory response to systemic infection. It can lead to multi-organ failure and death.

Signs and symptoms of cardiogenic, hypovolemic, and septic shock are similar and may include:

- hypotension (low blood pressure)
- rapid heart rate
- difficulty breathing
- cool, clammy skin
- low urine output

Neurogenic shock is a form of shock caused by injury or trauma to the spinal cord. Neurogenic shock disrupts the functioning of the automatic nervous system, producing massive vasodilation (widening of blood vessels). Signs and symptoms include:

- rapid onset of low blood pressure
- slow heart rate
- hypothermia

All types of shock are considered life-threatening conditions that require immediate care. In the medical office, the medical assistant should expect to help the provider address the patient's symptoms and prepare the patient for transfer to an emergency department.

SYNCOPE

Syncope (fainting) is temporary partial or full loss of consciousness caused by decreased circulation of blood to the brain. Often syncope is in response to temperature changes, low blood pressure, fear or surprise, or low blood sugar. Symptoms that may precede an episode include flushing, dizziness, sweating, weakness, and paleness.

If the patient presents with syncopal symptoms, the medical assistant should make sure they are not in danger of falling by having them sit or lie down. The provider will conduct a full examination, document vital signs following the episode, and possibly order an ECG. The provider will determine if the patient should be transferred to a higher level of care.

Vertigo

Vertigo is a sensation of spinning or dizziness. As with syncopal patients, vertigo patients should be helped so as to prevent injury. Medical assistants can provide reassurance and monitor the patient to prevent them from falling.

Wounds

Patients may present to the medical office with different types of wounds, which are categorized based on the type and severity of the injury.

+ **abrasion**—scrape on the skin surface
+ **laceration**—deep cut or skin tear
+ **puncture**—hole, usually caused by a sharp, slim object
+ **avulsion**—partial or complete tearing of the skin that may look flap-like

The goal of wound management is to facilitate healing and prevent infection. Minor wounds can usually be easily treated. Wounds should be cleaned and irrigated as necessary. The medical assistant should check the patient's medical record; a tetanus shot may be needed if they are not up to date. For deep or heavily bleeding wounds, the medical assistant should prepare to assist with suturing.

Office Emergency Readiness

Emergency Equipment

It is important that an office have a crash cart or area where emergency equipment is easily accessible. Medical assistants should be familiar with the location of emergency equipment and how it is used. The medical assistant may be asked to retrieve or use supplies from the crash cart. The table below provides a list of common medical equipment that may be needed in an emergency.

Table 11.1. Common Emergency Medical Equipment

Equipment	Use
automated external defibrillator (AED)	restarts normal cardiac rhythm in patients with specific dysrhythmias
portable oxygen tank	provides oxygen to patients with low oxygen saturation
suction equipment	clears airways
endotracheal tubes	opens airways and provides mechanical ventilation

Equipment	Use
cardiopulmonary resuscitation mask	covers patient's mouth during CPR
bag valve mask (this may have an oxygen hookup)	provides ventilation during cardiac or respiratory arrest
emergency medications	epinephrine: anaphylactic shock and cardiac arrest atropine: slow heart rate (bradycardia) sodium bicarb: high acid levels in blood and some types of overdoses activated charcoal: some poisonings ipecac: to induce vomiting aspirin: for patients experiencing symptoms of acute coronary symptoms
IV supplies	for administration of fluids and medications
dressings	for controlling bleeding and dressing wounds
personal protective equipment including gowns, gloves, surgical masks, and N-95 respirators	to prevent spread of infections

EMERGENCY RESPONSE PLAN

The office should have an established emergency response plan that details the medical assistant's role and responsibilities. Staff should review how to respond to a medical emergency at least quarterly. Common emergency procedures and appropriate responses should be detailed. Emergency plans will vary by office, but in general the medical assistant should expect to

+ alert providers to emergencies.
+ provide immediate assistance as directed by the provider.
+ help direct other office personnel.

During an emergency it is important to communicate clearly and work as a team. Important telephone numbers (e.g. poison control and the nearest hospital) should be clearly posted. All staff should be trained in CPR, and a list of everyone with CPR and first aid training should be available.

In the event that the office needs to be evacuated, medical assistants should be familiar with the approved exit routes. Many offices have an evacuation map posted. Medical assistants should understand their role in evacuating patients and be prepared to provide calm, clear directions. The most important thing to remember when responding to an emergency is to remain calm.

TWELVE: Practice Test

Read the question and then choose the most correct answer.

1. Which condition includes shock, disbelief, experiencing loss, and reintegration?

   A) defense mechanisms

   B) crisis resolution

   C) stages of grief

   D) mental illness

   E) coping mechanisms

2. A salutation in a written letter is the:

   A) major point.

   B) content.

   C) closing.

   D) format.

   E) greeting.

3. Which of the following describes patient cycle time?

   A) the length of time the average patient spends in the medical office

   B) the average length of time the physician spends with each patient

   C) the average length of time each patient waits to be seen

   D) an estimated amount of time the patient will need for their visit

   E) the average length of time the physician has between patients

4. Which of the following terms describes the position of the palm relative to the elbow?

   A) distal

   B) posterior

   C) superior

   D) medial

   E) dorsal

5. A patient is scheduled for a colposcopy. The medical assistant should assist the patient into which position?

   A) Sims' position

   B) supine position, with the head of the bed elevated 15 degrees

   C) left-side-lying position, knees to chest

   D) lithotomy position

   E) Fowler's position

6. When measuring a patient for crutches, the top of the crutches should be how far below a standing patient's armpits?

   A) 0 inches

   B) 1 – 2 inches

   C) 2 – 5 inches

   D) 5 – 10 inches

   E) > 10 inches

7. The medical assistant is speaking with a patient who has been ordered to wear a Holter monitor. Which statement by the patient indicates a need for further patient education?

   A) "I can wear the monitor while I shower."

   B) "I should keep the monitor on when I sleep."

   C) "I should avoid metal detectors and electric razors while wearing the monitor."

   D) "I should keep a log of any chest pain, shortness of breath, or skipped beats while wearing the monitor."

   E) "I will return the Holter monitor to my physician's office when the forty-eight-hour monitoring period ends."

8. The dipstick portion of a urinalysis tests for all of the following EXCEPT:

   A) pH.

   B) RBC.

   C) parasites.

   D) glucose.

   E) ketones.

9. Which of the following statements is NOT true of eating disorders?

   A) Patients with anorexia nervosa may compensate for binges by using laxatives or diuretics.

   B) Patients with bulimia may have erosion of the tooth enamel.

   C) Bingeing and purging can occur in both anorexia nervosa and bulimia.

   D) Extreme exercising and calorie restriction are common with anorexia nervosa.

   E) Patients may develop eating disorders because of issues of power and control.

10. Which of the following is a disease or dysfunction of one or more peripheral nerves, typically causing numbness and weakness?

    A) sarcoma

    B) neuropathy

    C) meningitis

    D) pertussis

    E) tuberculosis

11. Which body part is affected by a right tibia fracture?

    A) upper arm

    B) lower arm

    C) upper leg

    D) lower leg

    E) head

12. To prevent birth defects of the brain and spine, pregnant women should take a prenatal vitamin containing:

    A) folic acid.

    B) vitamin K.

    C) hemoglobin.

    D) calcium.

    E) vitamin D.

13. The medical assistant is submitting prescription refill requests to a pharmacy. One of the medication orders is illegible. Which of the following actions should the medical assistant take?

    A) ask another medical assistant to verify the order

    B) ask the prescribing physician for clarification

    C) scan the order to the pharmacy and let the pharmacy staff decipher it

    D) figure it out based on the patient's diagnosis and home medications

    E) call the patient to confirm the prescription details

14. Which of the following medications is used to prevent seizures?

   A) oxycodone hydrochloride (OxyContin)

   B) levothyroxine sodium (Synthroid)

   C) prednisone (Sterapred)

   D) pregabalin (Lyrica)

   E) aripiprazole (Abilify)

15. A patient shows signs of anaphylaxis after being administered ciprofloxacin. What should the medical assistant do first?

   A) induce vomiting

   B) obtain the patient's vital signs

   C) complete an incident report

   D) notify the health care provider

   E) begin rescue breathing and chest compressions

16. Leukocytosis means which of the following?

   A) abnormally shaped platelets

   B) abnormally shaped white blood cells

   C) decreased red blood cells

   D) elevated white blood cells

   E) abnormal change in plasma volume

17. When removing sutures, where should the suture be cut?

   A) on the opposite side of the knot

   B) immediately under the knot

   C) on the knot

   D) inside the wound

   E) the medical assistant should decide for each patient

18. Which of the following is a standardized coding system that is used primarily to identify products, supplies, and services not included in the CPT code list, such as ambulance charges and prosthetic devices?

   A) ICD-10-CM codes

   B) CPT modifier codes

   C) HCPCS modifier codes

   D) HCPCS level II codes

   E) supplemental service codes

19. Which of the following precautions would the medical assistant expect to be in place for a patient with influenza?

   A) contact precautions

   B) droplet precautions

   C) airborne precautions

   D) contact and airborne precautions

   E) protective environment

20. Which of the following signs are seen in a patient with cardiogenic shock?

   A) hypertension; slow, labored breathing

   B) decreased urine output; warm, pink skin

   C) increased urine output; cool, clammy skin

   D) hypotension; weak pulse; cool, clammy skin

   E) hyperventilation; warm, pink skin

21. A patient is having a tonic-clonic seizure. What should the medical assistant do first?

   A) call 911

   B) restrain the patient

   C) turn the patient on their side

   D) take the patient's vital signs

   E) provide a safe environment

22. Which of the following is the very brief, preferably quoted statement of the patient that is entered into the medical record giving the purpose of the office visit or hospitalization?

A) summary of origin

B) main objective

C) chief complaint

D) personal statement

E) reason summary

23. When changing a patient's dressing, a medical assistant should do which of the following?

A) remove old gloves after removing the old dressing and put on clean gloves before placing a new dressing

B) place wet gauze at the base of all wounds

C) scrub all wound bases vigorously

D) express out any drainage from the wound

E) place dry gauze at the base of all wounds

24. Which of the following patients should be seen immediately by the provider?

A) a forty-five-year-old female on oral contraceptives with unusually heavy menstrual bleeding

B) a twenty-four-year-old with a dog bite to the leg from the family dog who is current on rabies shots

C) an irritable four-month-old with a petechial rash and temperature of 103.4°F

D) a sixteen-year-old football player with a twisted ankle who has no deformity and a pedal pulse

E) a forty-year-old male with a headache and no serious medical history

25. Which of the following BEST describes bias?

A) speaking loudly to ensure that you are heard

B) showing an unfair preference or dislike of a group of people

C) being passive, withdrawn, and quiet when communicating

D) being aggressive and outraged when communicating with an angry patient

E) positive stereotyping

26. Which of the following conditions is characterized by a low number of platelets?

A) glycolysis

B) thrombocytopenia

C) thrombocytosis

D) leukocytosis

E) anemia

27. The medical assistant has just administered an IM injection to a patient. How should the nurse dispose of the needle?

A) re-cap the needle and discard it in the nearest puncture-resistant container

B) break the needle and discard it in the nearest puncture-resistant container

C) discard the needle in a puncture-resistant container in the central medication area

D) discard the needle in a puncture-resistant container in the patient's room

E) re-cap the needle and discard it in a trash can

28. The medical assistant should anticipate that the health care provider will order which of the following vaccinations for a six-month-old patient at a wellness check?

   A) DTaP and MMR

   B) Hib and varicella

   C) influenza and DTaP

   D) hepatitis A and MMR

   E) hepatitis B and DTaP

29. Which of the following shows where the V1 lead should be placed?

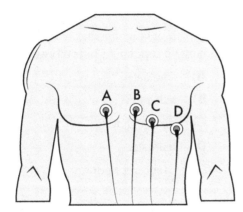

   A) site A

   B) site B

   C) site C

   D) site D

   E) site E

30. In medical coding, what do ICD codes represent?

   A) category codes

   B) diagnosis codes

   C) procedure codes

   D) organizational codes

   E) filing codes

31. According to the scale, an infant weighs 4.3 kg. What is the infant's weight in pounds?

   A) 1.95 lbs.

   B) 5.2 lbs.

   C) 8.6 lbs.

   D) 9.46 lbs.

   E) 68.8 lbs.

32. The eating disorder anorexia nervosa is defined as:

   A) binge eating at least twice a week for three months.

   B) taking excessive actions to compensate for caloric intake, such as purging.

   C) not consuming enough essential nutrients to maintain healthy body fat levels.

   D) using laxatives to compensate for excessive calorie intake.

   E) an uncontrollable urge to binge eat.

33. Which of the following statements about a choking patient is INCORRECT?

   A) The Heimlich should be performed on conscious patients who are unable to speak.

   B) A blind sweep of the airway should be done to clear the foreign body.

   C) The Heimlich should be performed with five abdominal thrusts between the rib cage and navel.

   D) Infants should receive an alternating five back slaps and five abdominal thrusts.

   E) Unaddressed choking can lead to cardiac arrest.

34. Which of the following describes a lithotripsy?

    A) surgical removal of the gallbladder

    B) surgical removal of a kidney stone or gallstone

    C) incision of the abdomen

    D) procedure to crush a stone

    E) procedure to examine the bladder

35. If a correction to the medical chart is necessary, what should the provider do?

    A) cross out the incorrect information

    B) create a completely new chart

    C) erase the incorrect information

    D) add an addendum with a time and date stamp to the bottom of the chart

    E) leave the chart alone

36. Which of the following is a two-character suffix attached to a category I CPT code that provides supplemental information?

    A) modifier

    B) ICD-10-CM code

    C) supplemental service code

    D) HCPCS level II code

    E) experimental service code

37. Which element allows hemoglobin to carry oxygen?

    A) iron

    B) calcium

    C) magnesium

    D) phosphorus

    E) ascorbic acid

38. An autoclave sterilizes equipment using which of the following techniques?

    A) using a dry heat for one hour at 320°F

    B) soaking the equipment in closed containers of a strong disinfectant chemical

    C) applying a steam heat under pressure at high temperatures between 250 – 254°F

    D) rinsing equipment with hot soap and water for ten minutes

    E) wrapping equipment in sterile cloth to prevent contamination

39. Which of the following would NOT elevate a patient's blood pressure?

    A) smoking

    B) salt intake

    C) alcohol intake

    D) diuretics

    E) pseudoephedrine

40. How many hours after administration of a Mantoux tuberculin skin test should a patient return to the medical office to have the results determined?

    A) two to four hours

    B) twelve to twenty-four hours

    C) twenty-four to forty-eight hours

    D) forty-eight to seventy-two hours

    E) seventy-two to eighty-four hours

41. Which of the following tests checks for abnormalities in the middle ear by placing a tube into the outer ear that changes the pressure?

    A) tympanometry

    B) speech recognition

    C) pulmonary function test

    D) pure tone audiometry

    E) chemical stress test

42. A urea breath test is done to test for which of the following infectious agents?

A) presence of Helicobacter pylori

B) strep throat

C) Influenza A

D) pneumonia

E) Epstein–Barr virus

43. A typical multidose vial should be discarded within how many days of opening?

A) five

B) ten

C) twenty

D) twenty-eight

E) thirty

44. Hypotension; a weak, rapid pulse; pale skin; and diaphoresis are signs of:

A) shock.

B) bladder infection.

C) strep throat.

D) cerebrovascular accident.

E) anxiety.

45. Which of the following is a state-required health professional credential for a specific occupation?

A) certificate

B) diploma

C) degree

D) license

E) continuing education credit

46. In which of the following positions should an infant be placed to measure length?

A) standing

B) supine

C) sitting

D) prone

E) reclined in a car seat

47. Which type of file is labeled by date and organized in a way that the medical assistant knows what actions should be taken on future dates?

A) reminder file

B) tickler file

C) follow-up file

D) future-action file

E) to-do file

48. Which of the following insurance programs covers people sixty-five or older, younger people with disabilities, and people with end-stage renal disease?

A) managed care organization

B) preferred provider organization

C) commercial insurance

D) Medicaid

E) Medicare

49. Which of the following organs is NOT correctly matched with its main function?

A) large intestine: nutrient absorption and waste collection

B) small intestine: nutrient absorption

C) pancreas: produces digestive enzymes (lipase and amylase)

D) stomach: creates an acidic food bolus, known as chyme

E) liver: bile production to break down fat

50. Which of the following precautions must a health care worker take when checking the blood pressure of a patient who is HIV-positive?

A) wear gloves

B) wear a gown

C) wash hands

D) use contact precautions

E) use droplet precautions

51. A patient who has osteoporosis should take which of the following supplements?

A) calcium

B) iron

C) iodine

D) vitamin C

E) vitamin K

52. When recording visual acuity, the left eye is recorded as:

A) OU.

B) OD.

C) OS.

D) OL.

E) OR.

53. In the waiting room, the medical assistant notices a woman clutching her throat. The woman is unable to speak. The medical assistant asks the woman if she is choking, and the woman indicates yes. Which of the following should the medical assistant do first?

A) establish an airway by tilting the chin back

B) administer five quick chest compressions

C) administer two rescue breaths

D) perform the Heimlich maneuver

E) have someone call 911

54. A nephrologist is a specialist who treats the:

A) nervous system.

B) brain and spinal cord.

C) kidneys.

D) liver.

E) lymphatic system.

55. A BMI greater than 40 is categorized as which of the following?

A) very underweight

B) underweight

C) overweight

D) morbidly obese

E) normal weight

56. Which of the following procedures is a surgical opening of the skull?

A) arthrotomy

B) laparotomy

C) thoracotomy

D) osteotomy

E) craniotomy

57. A phlebotomist is a medical professional who is trained to perform which of the following tasks?

A) provide hospice care

B) draw blood

C) administer medications

D) perform moderate- and high-complexity laboratory testing

E) provide home health care

58. Which portion of a SOAP note includes information the health care provider has observed or measured?

A) measures and observations

B) examination notes

C) planning notes

D) subjective notes

E) objective notes

59. Which of the following is a specified amount of money that the insured must pay before the insurance will begin to pay claims?

    A) copayment

    B) benefit

    C) network

    D) payer

    E) deductible

60. Which of the following types of tissue is found in bones, ligaments, and cartilage?

    A) nervous tissue

    B) muscular tissue

    C) epithelial tissue

    D) connective tissue

    E) membranous tissue

61. Which of the following is NOT a common parasitic infection?

    A) flukes

    B) lice

    C) ticks

    D) tapeworm

    E) ringworm

62. Which of the following patients should be seen immediately by the provider?

    A) a patient complaining of chest pain and nausea

    B) a patient with a fracture of the radius from a fall on a staircase

    C) a patient complaining of slight redness and itching at the site of a recent vaccine injection

    D) a patient presenting with a sprained ankle from a tree branch falling on him

    E) a patient complaining of a headache lasting twelve hours

63. When using a sphygmomanometer to take a manual blood pressure, where is the stethoscope most commonly placed?

    A) carotid pulse

    B) femoral pulse

    C) dorsalis pedis pulse

    D) radial pulse

    E) brachial pulse

64. Which hemoglobin A1C result would suggest that the patient's blood sugar levels and diabetes have been poorly controlled for the past several months?

    A) 0

    B) 1

    C) 2.5

    D) 5

    E) 10

65. Which symptom is a possible adverse drug effect for a twelve-year-old patient who has begun taking amphetamine and dextroamphetamine for attention-deficit/hyperactivity disorder (ADHD)?

    A) nausea

    B) seizures

    C) weight gain

    D) constipation

    E) bradycardia

66. *Lingual* means "near or next to" which of the following anatomical locations?

    A) spine

    B) tongue

    C) head

    D) gluteal muscle

    E) pelvis

67. If a patient becomes hypotensive during their exam, they should be placed in which of the following positions?

A) Trendelenburg

B) supine

C) prone

D) Fowler's

E) Sims'

68. Which of the following vessels contains deoxygenated blood?

A) pulmonary artery

B) pulmonary vein

C) aorta

D) carotid artery

E) renal artery

69. Which of the following are conscious, learned behaviors and thought processes developed in an effort to minimize anxiety, stress, and emotional discomfort?

A) coping mechanisms

B) defense mechanisms

C) Pavlovian responses

D) conscious behaviors

E) unconscious behaviors

70. Why should low couches and chairs be avoided in the reception room at an internist's office?

A) They are less visually appealing.

B) They are less comfortable.

C) It is easier for elderly or weak patients to rise from low furniture.

D) It is difficult for elderly and weak patients to rise from low furniture.

E) Higher furniture is more informal.

71. The most important element in writing an organized letter is to:

A) be thorough and give explanations at length.

B) use technical language and abbreviations, regardless of the audience.

C) quickly get to the point.

D) use bullets for each point in the letter.

E) use gender specifics for medical personnel.

72. Which health insurance group requires patients to get a referral from their primary care physician before seeing a specialist?

A) HMO

B) PPO

C) indemnity insurance

D) Medicare

E) EPO

73. A patient begins having a seizure at the primary care clinic. The health care provider should:

A) restrain the patient.

B) place a tongue blade in the patient's mouth.

C) remove any objects that can cause injury.

D) begin CPR.

E) keep the patient supine during and after seizure.

74. Which of the following blood components is responsible for fighting infection?

A) red blood cells

B) platelets

C) white blood cells

D) hemoglobin

E) plasma

75. Which of the following colors indicates a CONTACT HAZARD on a safety data sheet?

   A) red

   B) blue

   C) yellow

   D) white

   E) green

76. A patient checks into the emergency room with severe abdominal pain. She has diabetes, has recently quit smoking, and has no prior surgeries. Her mother has a history of hypertension. What is the chief complaint?

   A) diabetes

   B) no surgical history

   C) severe abdominal pain

   D) hypertension

   E) recent smoker

77. Which of the following should be done prior to eye irrigation?

   A) apply topical anesthetic drops

   B) test visual acuity

   C) record vital signs

   D) give the patient education handouts

   E) apply eye patch

78. Which color is incorrectly matched with its evacuated tube additive?

   A) light blue: sodium citrate

   B) light green: lithium heparin

   C) gray: clot activator

   D) lavender: ETA

   E) yellow: ACD solution

79. How long after a scratch test or intradermal skin test should the skin be checked for an allergic reaction?

   A) one minute

   B) five minutes

   C) fifteen minutes

   D) twelve hours

   E) twenty-four hours

80. If a nine-month-old child has received the first and second dose of the hepatitis B vaccine, what course of action will the provider recommend?

   A) no action; a third dose of the vaccine is not recommended

   B) immediately inoculate the child given the high risk of not having a third vaccine

   C) wait until the child is twelve months old to give the vaccine

   D) schedule the child for the third vaccine at the earliest convenience

   E) recommend the child receives a third dose as an adult

81. Which of the following vaccines should be stored in the freezer?

   A) MMR

   B) HPV

   C) meningococcal

   D) influenza

   E) Hib

82. Acrophobia is a fear of:

   A) insects.

   B) physicians.

   C) heights.

   D) enclosed spaces.

   E) snakes.

83. A patient is hyperventilating during a panic attack. How should the medical assistant attempt to help them?

A) have the patient recount a positive childhood memory

B) provide the patient with a glass of water

C) tell the patient to take deep breaths

D) ask the patient to identify the source of his anxiety

E) suggest the patient leave the office until they have calmed down

84. Which of the following is a partial flap-like tearing of the skin?

A) laceration

B) puncture

C) avulsion

D) abrasion

E) burn

85. When a patient rolls up their sleeve and presents their arm for a blood draw, this is an example of which type of consent?

A) informed consent

B) expressed consent

C) implied consent

D) indirect consent

E) direct consent

86. Which of the following refers to something of value owned by a company?

A) accounts receivable

B) accounts payable

C) assets

D) liabilities

E) credits

87. Health care–related surfaces and equipment should be cleaned with which disinfectant?

A) sodium hypochlorite

B) sodium hydroxide

C) diluted Lysol

D) 2:1 vinegar and distilled water solution

E) 10:1 vinegar and distilled water solution

88. Which of the following sets the rhythm for the heart?

A) Purkinje fibers

B) bundle of His

C) aortic valve

D) atrioventricular node

E) sinoatrial node

89. Which dietary change is suggested for patients with hypertension who are trying to decrease their blood pressure?

A) eating red meat daily

B) increasing potassium and calcium intake

C) increasing fluid intake

D) decreasing consumption of foods high in fat

E) decreasing sodium intake

90. Which patient position is the most common for a gynecological or pelvic exam?

A) Sims'

B) prone

C) Fowler's

D) Semi-Fowler's

E) lithotomy

91. Which of the following is the location for the V5 lead for a 12-lead ECG?

   A) in the left midaxillary line

   B) in the fifth intercostal right midclavicular line

   C) in the fourth intercostal space to the left of the sternum

   D) in the fourth intercostal space to the right of the sternum

   E) on the right ankle

92. A patient collecting a stool sample should be told to collect samples on how many days?

   A) one

   B) two

   C) three

   D) four

   E) five

93. Which of the following describes double-booking?

   A) Patients arrive without appointments and are usually seen in the order of their arrival.

   B) Each patient is given a specific time slot.

   C) Patients are scheduled for the same time slot.

   D) Patients are told to come in at the beginning of the hour and then seen in the order of their arrival.

   E) Patients with similar procedures and examinations are scheduled in a specific block of time, sometimes only on specified days.

94. Cholecystitis is which of the following?

   A) infection in the urinary bladder

   B) inflammation of the urinary bladder

   C) inflammation of the lymph nodes

   D) infection of the lymph nodes

   E) inflammation of the gallbladder

95. Which of the following medications can cause bradycardia?

   A) beta blockers

   B) insulin

   C) levothyroxine

   D) aspirin

   E) albuterol

96. Which of the following describes the proper technique for performing infant CPR?

   A) The femoral artery is checked for a pulse following each cycle of CPR.

   B) Chest compression depth should be approximately 1.5 inches, or 4 cm.

   C) A single rescuer should use three fingers on the dominant hand to do compressions.

   D) The infant should be placed facedown on the forearm with the hand supporting the head and jaw.

   E) CPR should be started as soon as the emergency response system has been activated.

97. The physician assistant has ordered acetaminophen 650 mg for a fifteen-year-old patient with a fever. How many 325-mg acetaminophen tablets should be given to the patient?

   A) one

   B) one and a half

   C) two

   D) two and a half

   E) three

98. The concrete operation phase of Piaget's theory of cognitive development occurs at which stage of life?

   A) birth to two years

   B) two to six years

   C) seven to eleven years

   D) twelve to adult

   E) adult to geriatric

99. Which of the following patients may NOT give informed consent?

A) a twelve-year-old patient with a closed fracture of the ulna

B) a seventeen-year-old patient seeking treatment for a sexually transmitted infection

C) a pregnant minor

D) an emancipated minor

E) a married minor

100. Which of the following is the MOST appropriate way to close a written communication with another professional?

A) Always,

B) Fondly,

C) Take care,

D) Yours,

E) Sincerely,

101. Which of the following laboratory tests is done to monitor patients taking warfarin?

A) CBC

B) PT/INR

C) BMP

D) BNP

E) UA

102. Which of the following is an electronic health care application that stores entered patient demographics and can perform day-to-day operations such as appointment scheduling and billing?

A) patient care application

B) patient provider software

C) electronic medical record

D) medical management system

E) electronic health record

103. Which of the following is the designated amount of money that some medical insurance plans require patients to pay at the time of service?

A) deductibles

B) copayments

C) balances

D) partial payments

E) coinsurance

104. The medical assistant has given a patient an injection and then notes that the sharps container is full. Which is the correct action by the medical assistant?

A) exchange the full container for a new one

B) place the syringe on top of the container so it will not roll off

C) force the syringe into the top of the container as well as it will fit

D) put the syringe into her pocket and dispose of it in another room

E) place the syringe in an available trash can

105. The medical assistant answers a call to the medical office and receives a bomb threat. Which of the following is NOT an appropriate action from the medical assistant?

A) assume the caller is making a real threat

B) follow facility protocol to ensure patient and staff safety

C) try to find out where the bomb is and when it will go off

D) alert the charge nurse, security, and the police department

E) evacuate patients, starting with those who are most mobile

106. Which of the following foods should a patient diagnosed with gastroesophageal reflux disease (GERD) avoid?

A) bananas

B) tomatoes

C) white bread

D) grilled salmon

E) steel-cut oatmeal

107. Which process involves externally tapping onto body structures and listening for the correlating sound to assess their density?

A) observation

B) palpation

C) percussion

D) auscultation

E) mensuration

108. An electrocardiogram (ECG) can be used to diagnose which of the following conditions?

A) diabetes

B) torn ligaments

C) cancer

D) tachycardia

E) influenza

109. Which of the following is a side effect of prednisone that should be immediately reported to the health care provider?

A) increased appetite

B) anxiety or confusion

C) strong, bounding pulses

D) weight gain of three pounds

E) nausea

110. Which of the following directional terms means "closest to the point of attachment"?

A) distal

B) proximal

C) lateral

D) medial

E) posterior

111. Which of the following is a learning process that occurs when a neutral stimulus results in learning a new behavior in response to an associated outcome?

A) resolution

B) learned responsiveness

C) displacement

D) bereavement

E) classical conditioning

112. Which of the following actions falls within the medical assistant's scope of practice?

A) obtaining a stool sample

B) prescribing medications

C) removing a patient from a ventilator

D) triaging patients in an emergency department

E) interpreting an ECG readout

113. Which of the following is the abbreviation for a charting system that lists the medical record in reverse chronological order and is divided into sections based on each health care team member's individual records?

A) SOMR

B) POMR

C) SOAP

D) MRSA

E) HOPE

114. An accurate equipment maintenance log is a legally required document:

A) for insurance purposes, and it may be subpoenaed if a patient was injured due to an equipment failure.

B) for warranty coverage to prove that regular maintenance occurred if the equipment should fail and need replacing.

C) for safety reasons in case an employee is injured while operating the equipment.

D) to prove that it has been maintained regularly for insurance replacement coverage in a case of loss.

E) for proof of office policy compliance.

115. Skeletal muscle is attached to bone by:

A) ligaments.

B) cartilage.

C) tendons.

D) nerves.

E) fascia.

116. An itemized form listing CPT and ICD-10-CM codes in which the physician will indicate the services rendered for submission to the payer is called a(n):

A) superbill.

B) provider form.

C) services form.

D) payer form.

E) insurance form.

117. A patient with slow blood clotting likely has low numbers of:

A) red blood cells.

B) plasma.

C) platelets.

D) hemoglobin.

E) white blood cells.

118. Which of the following patients is at the highest risk of developing pressure ulcers?

A) a twenty-seven-year-old patient who fractured her arm playing volleyball

B) a six-year-old patient on pelvic skin traction for muscle spasms

C) a forty-two-year-old obese patient with controlled atrial fibrillation who uses a wheelchair

D) a seventy-year-old patient with heart failure who uses a cane for ambulation in the room and hall

E) a thirty-five-year-old pregnant patient on bed rest

119. Which laboratory result will be elevated when a patient has renal failure?

A) hemoglobin

B) hematocrit

C) white blood cell

D) BUN and creatinine

E) blood glucose

120. A patient diagnosed with *C. diff* has soiled the bed, and the medical assistant is preparing to change it. Which of the following BEST describes how the soiled linens should be disposed of?

A) throw the linens in the trash can in the soiled utility room

B) leave the dirty linens in a bag in the patient's room until he is discharged

C) place the items in a red biohazard bag and place them in the soiled utility room

D) place the soiled linen in a regular dirty linen bag and place in the soiled utility room

E) rinse the soiled linens before placing them in a soiled linen bag

121. Which of the following is a common side effect of the drug levothyroxine taken for hypothyroidism?

   A) weight loss

   B) weight gain

   C) light sensitivity

   D) excessive sleepiness

   E) dehydration

122. A seventy-year-old male is found unresponsive in the hallway. What should the medical assistant do first?

   A) listen for breathing

   B) feel for a pulse

   C) assess his airway

   D) check his blood pressure

   E) check his temperature

123. The medical assistant is caring for a patient who adheres to a lacto-vegetarian diet. What is the BEST meal tray to deliver to this patient?

   A) chicken sandwich, brown rice, yogurt, and milk

   B) steamed vegetables with rice and apple slices

   C) scrambled eggs, cottage cheese, dry toast, and milk

   D) baked fish with roasted potatoes

   E) baked zucchini, spinach salad with cheese, and yogurt

124. When dealing with an angry patient, the medical assistant should:

   A) get angry and be aggressive.

   B) speak loudly to ensure that he is heard.

   C) remain calm and use a normal tone and volume of voice.

   D) get defensive.

   E) be passive, withdrawn, and quiet.

125. Which of the following refers to the procedures and level of care allowed by a health professional's certificate or license?

   A) tasks of practice

   B) scope of practice

   C) levels of practice

   D) patient practices

   E) due care

126. Which type of record is filed for a patient who has not been seen by the physician for a period of three years?

   A) active record

   B) inactive record

   C) closed record

   D) dormant record

   E) open record

127. Drug samples left by a pharmaceutical representative should be placed

   A) in the physician's office.

   B) in the exam rooms.

   C) in a locked cabinet or drawer.

   D) in a cupboard in the reception area.

   E) in a cupboard in the clinical area.

128. Which of the following is an accounts receivable report that lists unpaid customer debt in specific date ranges?

   A) age analysis

   B) diagnosis-related groups

   C) relative value units

   D) fee schedule

   E) day sheet

129. Which term describes the position of the right ear relative to the right eye?

    A) proximal

    B) distal

    C) medial

    D) lateral

    E) ventral

130. The common cold, influenza, and HIV are caused by which type of infectious agent?

    A) bacteria

    B) protozoan

    C) virus

    D) helminth

    E) fungus

131. Which vitamin is important in blood clotting?

    A) vitamin A

    B) vitamin K

    C) vitamin B

    D) vitamin C

    E) vitamin D

132. Clonazepam (Klonopin) is categorized as which type of medication?

    A) proton pump inhibitor

    B) blood thinners

    C) antibiotic

    D) antipyretic

    E) benzodiazepine

133. Agoraphobia is a fear of:

    A) spiders.

    B) crowds or public places.

    C) heights.

    D) closed-in spaces.

    E) germs.

134. A fifty-year-old construction worker presents to the ER with a forearm laceration. The blood spurts in a pulsatile rhythm from the wound when the dressing is removed. Which type of blood vessel injury is likely?

    A) arterial

    B) venous

    C) capillary

    D) aorta

    E) jugular

135. According to Drug Enforcement Agency regulations, a medical assistant can only administer a controlled substance:

    A) under a physician's direct order and supervision.

    B) whenever there is a standing protocol.

    C) if a patient requests a medication.

    D) if a patient is out of their home medications.

    E) if over-the-counter medication has not worked.

136. Which method of patient scheduling provides built-in flexibility to accommodate unforeseen situations and involves scheduling three or four patients at the top of each hour?

    A) specified time scheduling

    B) double-booking

    C) grouping procedures

    D) open office hours

    E) wave scheduling

137. An example of an expendable supply is a(n):

    A) computer.

    B) ECG machine.

    C) ink cartridge.

    D) refrigerator.

    E) exam table.

138. Money owed to a business's creditors is called:

A) accounts receivable.

B) accounts payable.

C) debits.

D) credits.

E) liabilities.

139. What is the role of monocytes in wounds?

A) They increase blood clotting.

B) They release histamines.

C) They digest pathogens.

D) They prevent inflammation.

E) They store information about previously encountered pathogens.

140. Which of the following actions does NOT require the use of standard precautions?

A) contact with blood

B) contact with urine

C) contact with sweat

D) contact with vomit

E) contact with skin

141. Which of the following symptoms, identified by a female patient, is most consistent with a myocardial infarction (MI)?

A) palpitations

B) lower extremity swelling

C) uncomfortable feeling of pressure in the chest

D) nausea

E) difficulty breathing

142. Which of the following describes an adjustment?

A) posting charges for services rendered

B) posting third-party payments

C) posting payments made by the patient

D) any changes in the patient's financial account unrelated to charges or payments

E) any changes in the patient's financial account related to either charges or payments

143. Which of the following medications is prescribed to patients at high risk for deep vein thrombosis (DVT)?

A) sildenafil citrate (Viagra)

B) celecoxib (Celebrex)

C) zolpidem (Ambien)

D) topiramate (Topamax)

E) rivaroxaban (Xarelto)

144. Which of the following patients has a second-degree burn?

A) seventeen-year-old female with sunburn on her face with no blistering present

B) three-year-old male with painful blisters on his face from pulling a pot of hot water off the stove

C) twenty-five-year-old male with charred full-thickness burns to his hands sustained during a house fire

D) forty-five-year-old female with superficial, red, painful burns without blistering on her left hand

E) sixty-year-old female who reports a deep, painless burn from prolonged exposure to household drain cleaner

145. Which injury is INCORRECTLY described?

A) A joint dislocation occurs when the bone shifts from it natural position.

B) A sprain is damage to muscles and tendons.

C) A fracture is a break or injury to a bone.

D) A strain is damage to muscles and tendons.

E) A contusion is bruising to the tissues.

146. Examples of proper telephone etiquette include:

A) being polite and professional.

B) being friendly, casual, and conversational.

C) being angry and aggressive.

D) being passive, withdrawn, and quiet.

E) speaking loudly to ensure that you are heard.

147. Which legal doctrine states that an employer can be held responsible for the actions of their employees?

A) respondeat superior

B) tort

C) advance directive

D) deposition

E) compos mentis

148. Which diet should be followed by a fifty-five-year-old male diagnosed with gout?

A) soft diet

B) diabetic diet

C) clear liquid diet

D) low-purine diet

E) high-protein diet

149. The medical assistant should carefully document any patient cancellations or no-shows in the schedule and the patient's medical record to protect the physician from potential charges related to:

A) malpractice.

B) assault and battery.

C) abandonment.

D) invasion of privacy.

E) bias.

150. Which of the following is NOT contained within a ventral cavity?

A) digestive system

B) reproductive system

C) heart and lungs

D) kidneys

E) spinal cord

151. Which of the following is an example of transmission of an infectious agent through direct contact?

A) kissing an infected person

B) inhaling droplets from a sneezing infected person

C) an infected person coughing near a susceptible host

D) eating contaminated food

E) inhaling microorganisms in the air

152. Which of the following is NOT objective patient data?

A) pulse

B) temperature

C) chief complaint

D) blood pressure

E) respiratory rate

153. Which is NOT on the clear liquid diet?

  A) broth

  B) water

  C) gelatin

  D) popsicles

  E) milk

154. Which location is a recommended blood draw site?

  A) underside of wrist

  B) antecubital fossa

  C) ankles

  D) same side of prior mastectomy

  E) feet

155. A patient starting rosuvastatin calcium (Crestor) should be warned about all of the following side effects EXCEPT:

  A) muscle pain.

  B) headaches.

  C) abdominal pain.

  D) dizziness.

  E) fever.

156. Which of the following actions should the medical assistant perform to assess the airway in an unconscious patient?

  A) head tilt and chin lift

  B) jaw thrust

  C) finger sweep

  D) wait for paramedics to assess the airway

  E) obtain a pulse oximetry reading

157. Which of the following is an order to appear in court?

  A) arbitration

  B) deposition

  C) tort

  D) mediation

  E) subpoena

158. Which of the following scheduling methods is used by urgent care facilities where patients are seen in the order of their arrival?

  A) specified time

  B) open office hours

  C) wave scheduling

  D) grouping

  E) double-booking

159. In medical coding, what does a CPT code represent?

  A) new patients

  B) diagnoses

  C) procedures

  D) symptoms

  E) abnormal laboratory results

160. Which of the following terms describes an excessive posterior curvature of the thoracic spine?

  A) kyphosis

  B) lordosis

  C) scoliosis

  D) acidosis

  E) bad posture

161. When questioning a patient through an interpreter, questions should be directed toward:

  A) the interpreter.

  B) the physician.

  C) the patient's family.

  D) other colleagues.

  E) the patient.

162. Smoking and drinking habits are recorded in which portion of the patient's medical chart?

A) social history

B) chief complaint

C) history of present illness

D) past medical history

E) past surgical history

163. At what angle should the needle enter the skin during venipuncture?

A) 5 degrees

B) 10 degrees

C) 30 degrees

D) 60 degrees

E) 90 degrees

164. Which of the following is the class of drugs used to inhibit growth of or kill bacteria?

A) antibiotics

B) antihistamines

C) calcium channel blockers

D) antidepressants

E) anticonvulsants

165. A forty-five-year-old male was playing baseball with his son. When he slid on the ground, he felt a "pop" and pain in the back of his right thigh. Since then, he has had tenderness to the posterior right thigh that is worse when walking. Which muscle did he likely injure?

A) trapezius

B) biceps

C) pectoralis

D) oblique

E) hamstring

166. Which of the following is the ratio of chest compressions to breaths during single-provider CPR on an adult?

A) 100:2

B) 15:2

C) 20:2

D) 30:2

E) 20:10

167. What is the most appropriate way for a medical assistant to handle conflict with coworkers in the medical office?

A) take the issue directly to the physician in charge

B) do not escalate the situation

C) refuse to come to work until the situation is resolved

D) take sides and defend his position

E) ask for his coworkers' opinions to resolve the conflict based on what they witnessed

168. Under CLIA, which of the following are simple, low-risk laboratory tests that may be performed by anyone who follows the manufacturer's directions?

A) low-risk testing

B) moderate-risk testing

C) high-risk testing

D) waived testing

E) simplistic testing

169. The carotid pulse can be palpated at which of the following locations on the body?

A) the anterior wrist

B) lateral to the trachea

C) below the medial biceps tendon

D) in the groin

E) on the dorsum of the foot

170. Which of the following actions is upcoding?

A) uploading diagnostic codes into a computerized billing software system

B) uploading procedure codes into a computerized billing software system

C) fraudulent billing by using a CPT code for a more expensive service than what was performed

D) mistakenly using a billing code with a higher numeric value than the one intended

E) submission of a billing code to a third-party payer

171. After cleaning the intended venipuncture site with isopropyl alcohol, how long should the skin air-dry prior to venipuncture?

A) ten seconds

B) twenty seconds

C) thirty seconds

D) one minute

E) five minutes

172. The withdrawal syndrome after stopping benzodiazepines is which type of adverse drug reaction?

A) augmented

B) bizarre

C) chronic

D) delayed

E) end of use

173. Which condition is NOT correctly paired with its recommended diet?

A) diabetes: diabetic diet

B) hyperlipidemia: low-cholesterol diet

C) hypertension: high-sodium diet

D) diarrhea: clear liquid diet

E) gallbladder disease: low-fat diet

174. A medical technologist or clinical laboratory scientist requires which of the following?

A) associate's degree (two years)

B) diploma (usually a year or less)

C) advanced degree (master's degree or higher)

D) bachelor's degree (four years)

E) on-the-job training (for at least one year)

175. Which of the following statements about personal protective equipment (PPE) is NOT correct?

A) Hands do not need to be washed before putting on gloves.

B) A face shield is worn when there is likelihood of bodily fluid splashes.

C) Fluid-resistant gowns should be removed after leaving a patient's room.

D) PPE devices protect the mucous membranes.

E) PPE devices include gloves, gowns, eye shields, and masks.

176. Which procedure code set should be used when billing Medicaid or Medicare?

A) CPT

B) modifiers

C) add-ons

D) HCPCS

E) ICD

177. Gas exchange in the lungs occurs in which of the following structures?

A) bronchi

B) pulmonary artery

C) bronchioles

D) aorta

E) alveoli

178. Which type of waste is NOT matched with its correct disposal container?

    A) capillary tubes: sharps container

    B) feces: toilet

    C) gauze with small amount of blood: regular garbage can

    D) urine: poured down the drain

    E) linen heavily soiled by blood: dirty linen receptacle

179. Which of the following describes tachypnea?

    A) twelve to twenty breaths per minute

    B) eighteen breaths per minute

    C) fewer than twelve breaths per minute

    D) more than twenty breaths per minute

    E) fewer than twenty breaths per minute

180. Which of the following urine specimens is used specifically for diabetic screening?

    A) random specimen

    B) clean catch midstream specimen

    C) two-hour postprandial urine

    D) twenty-four-hour specimen

    E) pediatric urine specimen

181. A 0.4 mg nitroglycerin sublingual tablet should be administered by which of the following methods?

    A) placed on the skin via a patch

    B) placed under the tongue and allowed to absorb

    C) placed into the eye via drops

    D) taken by mouth and swallowed

    E) injected into the subcutaneous tissue

182. A fifteen-year-old thin female presents to the clinic with extreme fatigue, increased urination most noticeably at night, and extreme thirst. Which test might be ordered by the provider in triage?

    A) hemoglobin A1C

    B) fingerstick glucose

    C) chest X-ray

    D) visual acuity

    E) abdominal ultrasound

183. Which type of white blood cells attack parasites?

    A) neutrophils

    B) eosinophils

    C) B cells

    D) T cells

    E) macrophages

184. An elderly patient has a blood pressure of 140/90 when sitting. Her blood pressure when standing is 100/60. Which term describes her condition?

    A) bradycardia

    B) orthostatic hypotension

    C) hypertension

    D) syncope

    E) tachycardia

185. Which of the following should a patient NOT do before a sputum culture?

    A) use antibacterial mouthwash

    B) use antibacterial hand soap

    C) wear restrictive clothing

    D) take an antihistamine

    E) take acetaminophen

186. Which of the following angles and needle gauges is used to inject a medication into the dermal skin layer?

 A) 45 – 90 degrees, 22 – 25 gauge

 B) 90 degrees, 18 – 23 gauge

 C) 15 degrees, 25 – 27 gauge

 D) 30 degrees, 18 gauge

 E) 45 degrees, 22 gauge

187. A large skin laceration over the site of a fractured bone can be a sign of which type of fracture?

 A) closed fracture

 B) compression fracture

 C) oblique fracture

 D) open fracture

 E) stable fracture

188. Human immunodeficiency virus (HIV) attacks which of the following cells?

 A) white blood cells

 B) red blood cells

 C) platelets

 D) B cells

 E) T cells

189. An asthmatic patient presents with cough, wheezing, and shortness of breath that has been worsening for the past few days. Which type of medication will the provider likely order?

 A) warfarin

 B) acetaminophen

 C) albuterol

 D) lorazepam

 E) famotidine

190. Pulse oximetry can be measured on a patient at all of the following locations EXCEPT:

 A) a finger.

 B) the abdomen.

 C) the great toe.

 D) an earlobe.

 E) an infant foot.

191. An RSV (respiratory syncytial virus) swab on a three-month-old is obtained using a:

 A) throat swab.

 B) nasopharyngeal swab.

 C) genital swab.

 D) wound culture swab.

 E) breath test.

192. Which of the following should be used when drawing up medication from a single-use ampule?

 A) filtered needle

 B) butterfly needle

 C) 21-gauge beveled needle

 D) 27-gauge beveled needle

 E) IV start kit

193. Which endocrine gland is NOT correctly matched to its function?

 A) adrenal: fight-or-flight response, regulation of salt and blood volume

 B) pituitary: growth, temperature regulation, reproductive function

 C) parathyroid: metabolic use, hunger and thirst

 D) ovaries: maturation of sex organs, pregnancy, lactations

 E) thyroid: metabolism, energy use

194. A Pap smear collects cells from the:

A) heart.

B) skin.

C) cervix.

D) stomach lining.

E) lung.

195. A specimen is placed onto a microscopic slide, then a drop of water is applied and covered with a coverslip. This is an example of which type of specimen collection?

A) wet mount

B) wound culture

C) nasopharyngeal swab

D) blood culture

E) urinalysis

196. 5 cc is equivalent to how many milliliters?

A) 2.5

B) 5

C) 7.5

D) 10

E) 15

197. After a Pap smear, the specimen is placed into a liquid-base cytology container. All of the following information must be on the label EXCEPT:

A) vital signs.

B) the patient's name.

C) date of birth.

D) medical record number.

E) date of last menstrual cycle.

198. How is silence an effective therapeutic response when communicating with patients?

A) It is not therapeutic; it implies that the medical assistant is not listening.

B) It encourages the patient to keep her feelings to herself.

C) It allows the patient time to think and reflect and lead the conversation.

D) It allows the medical assistant to think about other tasks she needs to perform for the patient.

E) It helps the patient feel in control of the situation and her health.

199. While assisting the surgeon with an emergency appendectomy in the operating room, the surgical assistant removed all jewelry before washing his hands and then applied a sterile gown and gloves. He carefully opened sterilized instruments and gauze onto the surgical tray. He then stepped away from the sterile field to sneeze. When the assistant turned back toward the table, he touched the sterile field with the back of his gown. Which of the following is a break in sterile technique?

A) removing jewelry prior to handwashing

B) donning sterile gown and gloves

C) inspecting instruments for sterile indicators

D) stepping away from the sterile field to sneeze

E) touching the sterile field with the back of his gown

200. Which dysrhythmia is shown in the following ECG readout?

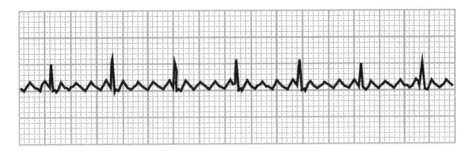

A) atrial flutter

B) atrial fibrillation

C) asystole

D) normal sinus rhythm

E) ventricular fibrillation

ANSWER KEY

1. C) is correct. Shock and disbelief, experiencing loss, and reintegration are components of the stages of grief.

2. E) is correct. In a letter, the salutation is the greeting.

3. A) is correct. Patient cycle time is the length of time that the average patient spends in the medical office, from when they enter to when they leave the office, including wait time.

4. A) is correct. The palm of the hand is distal (away from the trunk) relative to the elbow.

5. D) is correct. A colposcopy is a painless gynecological procedure, usually done after an abnormal Pap smear. Putting the patient in the lithotomy position, in which the patient is on their back with hips and knees flexed, allows the provider to access the cervix.

6. B) is correct. Crutches should hit 1 – 2 inches below a patient's armpits.

7. A) is correct. The Holter monitor should be kept dry and cannot be worn while swimming or bathing.

8. C) is correct. In the dipstick portion of a urinalysis, a dipstick placed into a urine sample tests for pH, RBC, glucose, and ketones. The microscopic portion of the urinalysis may be helpful in identifying bacteria, blood cells, parasites, and tumor cells.

9. A) is correct. Following binges with the use of laxatives or diuretics is a diagnostic criterion for bulimia. The other statements are true.

10. B) is correct. Neuropathy is a disease or dysfunction of one or more peripheral nerves, typically causing numbness and weakness.

11. D) is correct. The tibia is a lower leg bone.

12. A) is correct. Taking folic acid before and during pregnancy aids in preventing brain and spine birth defects.

13. B) is correct. The medical assistant should always get clarification from the prescribing physician.

14. D) is correct. Pregabalin (Lyrica) is prescribed to patients with epilepsy to help prevent seizures.

15. D) is correct. The first action is to notify the health care provider for further orders.

16. D) is correct. Leukocytosis is elevated white blood cells.

17. B) is correct. Sutures should be cut immediately under the knot during removal. This allows the least amount of skin surface contamination to be dragged through the inside of the wound when the suture is pulled out.

18. D) is correct. The HCPCS (Health Care Common Procedure Coding System) level II is an alphanumeric code set that primarily includes non-physician-related services such as ambulance charges and prosthetic devices.

19. B) is correct. Influenza is spread primarily by droplets. Droplet precautions focus on diseases that are spread by large droplets (greater than 5 microns) expelled into the air and by being within 3 feet of a patient.

20. D) is correct. Classic signs of cardiogenic shock include a rapid pulse that weakens; cool, clammy skin; and decreased urine output. Hypotension is another classic sign.

21. E) is correct. Safety is the top priority during seizure activity, so the medical assistant should remove any objects in the immediate area that may cause the patient harm.

22. C) is correct. A very brief, preferably quoted statement of the patient that is entered into the medical record giving the purpose of the office visit or hospitalization is called the chief complaint.

23. A) is correct. It is important to always change gloves after removing an old or dirty dressing. Before applying a new dressing, the medical assistant should change into a new set of gloves to prevent contamination.

24. C) is correct. Petechial rash and fever are signs of meningitis, which is a medical emergency, especially in an infant.

25. B) is correct. Bias is showing an unfair preference or dislike of a specific group of people.

26. B) is correct. Thrombocytopenia is a deficiency in the number of platelets.

27. D) is correct. Needles should be placed intact into the nearest puncture-resistant container.

28. E) is correct. This child is now due for the third round of the hepatitis B and DTaP vaccines.

29. A) is correct. The V1 lead should be placed at the fourth intercostal space to the right of the sternum.

30. B) is correct. ICD (International Classification of Diseases, 10th revision, Clinical Modification is the current version) codes are diagnosis codes used for billing purposes.

31. D) is correct. 1 kilogram is equal to 2.2 pounds: $4.3 \text{ kg} \times \frac{2.2 \text{ lb}}{1 \text{ kg}} = 9.46 \text{ lb}$.

32. C) is correct. People with anorexia generally avoid food to such an extreme degree that they are unable to maintain healthy body fat or necessary nutrient levels.

33. B) is correct. Never perform a blind sweep of the airway since this may cause the object to become further lodged into the airway.

34. D) is correct. Lithotripsy is a procedure to crush a stone (e.g., kidney stones).

35. D) is correct. Any corrections to the chart will need to be done with a timed and dated addendum.

36. A) is correct. A modifier is a two-character suffix attached to a category I CPT code with a hyphen. It provides supplemental information and is found in the appendix of the CPT code manual. The functionality modifier directly affects reimbursement and should be used first; the informational modifier is second.

37. A) is correct. Iron plays an important role in the ability of hemoglobin to carry oxygen. When a patient has iron deficiency anemia, their body cannot carry oxygen to the cells and tissues very well. This is why anemic patients often feel short of breath or chronically tired.

38. C) is correct. An autoclave uses a steam heat at high temperature and high pressure to sterilize equipment. The equipment is wrapped and closed with sterilized tape prior to sterilization.

39. D) is correct. Diuretic medication is used to lower a patient's blood pressure.

40. D) is correct. The Centers for Disease Control and Prevention recommends the skin test be read forty-eight to seventy-two hours after administration. Results read after seventy-two hours are not accurate, and another skin test should be conducted.

41. A) is correct. Tympanometry measures how the eardrum moves and responds to sounds under different pressures.

42. A) is correct. Helicobacter pylori (or H. pylori) is a stomach infection usually found in patients with gastric ulcers.

43. D) is correct. Typical multidose vials must be used or discarded within twenty-eight days of opening.

44. A) is correct. These are symptoms of shock. Shock can be cardiogenic (from the heart), an allergic reaction, hypovolemic (lots of vomiting or blood loss), septic (infection), or neurogenic (a brain injury).

45. D) is correct. A license is required by the state where a health care professional works for a specific occupation, whereas certification for a specific occupation is optional.

46. B) is correct. To measure length, place the infant supine on the exam table.

47. B) is correct. A date-labeled file organized so the medical assistant knows what actions should be taken on future dates is called a tickler file.

48. E) is correct. Medicare is the federal health insurance program that covers people sixty-five or older, younger people with disabilities, and people with end-stage renal disease.

49. A) is correct. The large intestine is responsible for most of the WATER absorption. The majority of nutrient absorption is performed in the small intestine.

50. C) is correct. Washing hands is sufficient, since taking a patient's blood pressure does not involve contact with blood or secretions.

51. A) is correct. Patients with osteoporosis need calcium supplements to promote bone health.

52. C) is correct. Eyesight is recorded as OU (both eyes), OD (right eye), OS (left eye). Remember: yOU look with BOTH eyes. The RIGHT meds will not OD. The only one LEFT is OS.

53. E) is correct. Based on directives from the American Red Cross, when confronted with a conscious, choking person who is unable to cough, speak, or breathe, the medical assistant should first send someone to call 911, then lean the person forward and give five back blows with the heel of their hand. If that is ineffective, the Heimlich maneuver should be performed to remove the obstruction.

54. C) is correct. A nephrologist specializes in the care and treatment of the kidneys.

55. D) is correct. A normal BMI is 18.5 – 24.9. A person with a BMI of < 15 is severely underweight, and > 40 is morbidly obese.

56. E) is correct. A surgical opening of the skull is called a craniotomy.

57. B) is correct. A phlebotomist is a medical professional trained to draw blood.

58. E) is correct. Objective notes are the portion of a SOAP note that includes information the health care provider has observed or measured.

59. E) is correct. A specified amount of money that the insured must pay before the insurance will begin to pay claims is called a deductible.

60. D) is correct. Connective tissue, such as bones, ligaments, and cartilage, supports, separates, and connects the body's organs and structures.

61. E) is correct. Ringworm is a fungal infection, not a parasitic infection.

62. A) is correct. Triage works on the principle that patients with the highest acuity have priority over patients with injuries or conditions that are not considered life-threatening. Chest pain and nausea indicate a possible myocardial infarction, which can be life-threatening and requires immediate intervention.

63. E) is correct. The stethoscope is placed over the brachial pulse (near the antecubital fossa) as the cuff is inflated and then slowly deflated.

64. E) is correct. A patient with A1C levels of > 6.5% is considered to have diabetes; patients who do not have diabetes should have an A1C of < 5.7%.

65. B) is correct. Seizures are a serious, adverse drug effect that may occur when taking dextroamphetamine. Nausea and constipation are common side effects but are not considered adverse drug effects.

66. B) is correct. Lingual means "pertaining to, near, or next to the tongue."

67. A) is correct. In Trendelenburg position, the patient is reclined with their feet higher than their head.

68. A) is correct. The pulmonary artery carries deoxygenated blood from the right ventricle into the lungs.

69. A) is correct. Coping mechanisms are conscious, learned behaviors and thought processes developed to minimize anxiety, stress, and emotional discomfort.

70. D) is correct. Low couches and chairs should be avoided in the reception room at an internist's office because it is difficult for elderly and weak patients to rise from low furniture.

71. C) is correct. The most important element in writing an organized letter is to quickly get to the point.

72. A) is correct. A Health Maintenance Organization (HMO) is a type of health insurance group that contracts, for a relatively low cost, with health care providers who act as primary care physicians and are known as "gatekeepers" because it is necessary to obtain a referral from them to see a specialist. Any health care providers seen by the patient must be a preapproved "in-network" provider.

73. C) is correct. When a patient is seizing, the medical assistant should remove any surrounding objects that could injure the patient during the seizure. The patient should not be restrained, nor should anything be put in their mouth. The medical assistant should not begin CPR unless there is no pulse or the patient is not breathing. After the seizure, the patient should be moved into the recovery position on their side.

74. C) is correct. White blood cells, or leukocytes, play an important role in fighting an infection. A patient with a dangerous blood infection such as sepsis will have a markedly elevated white blood cell count (WBC). This is called leukocytosis.

75. D) is correct. White is indicative of a contact hazard.

76. C) is correct. The chief complaint is the problem or symptom the patient describes as the reason for the visit.

77. A) is correct. Eye irrigation can be uncomfortable for a patient. It is much more tolerable if the surface of the patient's eye has been numbed with anesthetic drops.

78. C) is correct. The red tube contains clot activator. The gray tube contains sodium fluoride.

79. C) is correct. Results of the allergy test should be recorded after fifteen minutes.

80. D) is correct. The provider will recommend the child receive the third vaccine at the earliest convenience, as it should be routinely administered any time from six to nineteen months of age.

81. A) is correct. MMR, VAR, ZVL, and MMRV should be stored in the freezer (−50 to −15°C).

82. C) is correct. Acrophobia is a fear of heights.

83. C) is correct. The medical assistant can assist the patient in changing their physiologic response by directing them to take deep breaths. This directive will help the patient focus on the present moment and help to alleviate the panic.

84. C) is correct. A skin avulsion is a tearing of the most superficial skin layer.

85. C) is correct. When a patient rolls up their sleeve and offers their arm for a blood draw, this is an example of implied consent.

86. C) is correct. An asset is something that is useful or valuable to a company, such as a building or equipment.

87. A) is correct. Health care–related surfaces and equipment should be cleaned with sodium hypochlorite (bleach).

88. E) is correct. The SA node, or sinoatrial node, is the intrinsic pacemaker. It typically sets the heart rate between 60 – 100 beats per minute and is located in the right atrium.

89. E) is correct. Decreasing sodium intake is an effective way to reduce blood pressure in a patient with hypertension.

90. E) is correct. In a lithotomy position, the patient will be on their back with their feet in stirrups. This is a common position for a pelvic exam or vaginal delivery.

91. A) is correct. The V5 lead should be placed in the left midaxillary line.

92. C) is correct. Stool samples will need to be collected on three different days.

93. C) is correct. Double-booking is a scheduling method in which patients are scheduled for the same time slot. This method is considered to be ineffective but sometimes unavoidable.

94. E) is correct. Cholecystitis is inflammation of the gallbladder.

95. A) is correct. Beta blockers are known to cause a slowing in heart rate.

96. B) is correct. CPR on infants less than one year old includes a chest compression depth of approximately 1.5 in, or 4 cm.

97. C) is correct. Two tablets of 325-mg acetaminophen are equal to 650 mg of acetaminophen (650/325 = 2).

98. C) is correct. The concrete operation phase of Piaget's theory of cognitive development occurs at age seven to eleven years.

99. A) is correct. A minor with a non-emergent medical condition cannot give informed consent. Consent must be given by the patient's guardian.

100. E) is correct. Closing a written communication with another professional or a superior using "Sincerely," is most appropriate.

101. B) is correct. PT and INR are laboratory tests that evaluate how long it takes for a person's blood to clot. Patients on warfarin will have elevated PT/INR.

102. D) is correct. A medical management system is an electronic health care application that stores entered patient demographics and can perform day-to-day operations such as appointment scheduling, billing, and other administrative tasks.

103. B) is correct. Copayments are designated amounts of money that some medical insurance plans require patients to pay at the time of service.

104. A) is correct. The full container should be replaced with a new one.

105. E) is correct. The nurse should not evacuate or move patients until directed to do so by security or police; they can determine the safest area if evacuation is necessary.

106. B) is correct. The nurse should instruct the patient to eat a low-fat, high-fiber diet, avoiding acidic foods. Tomatoes are highly acidic, and consumption of tomatoes or tomato-based sauces can worsen the symptoms of GERD.

107. C) is correct. Percussion involves tapping on the outside of a structure, such as the lung or abdomen, to determine its density (solid, fluid-filled, air-filled).

108. D) is correct. Tachycardia is an abnormally fast heart rate, and electrocardiograms show the electrical activity of the heart.

109. B) is correct. Side effects of prednisone include hypokalemia (low potassium). Anxiety, confusion, and lethargy are signs of hypokalemia and should be reported.

110. B) is correct. A directional term for "closest to the point of attachment" is proximal.

111. E) is correct. A Pavlovian, or conditioned, response occurs when a neutral stimulus results in learning a new behavior in response to an associated outcome.

112. A) is correct. Obtaining a stool sample from the patient is within the scope of practice of a medical assistant.

113. A) is correct. The abbreviation for a commonly used charting system in which the medical record is in reverse chronological order and divided into sections based on each health care team member's (source) individual record is SOMR (source-oriented medical record).

114. A) is correct. An accurate equipment maintenance log is often a legally required document for insurance purposes and may be subpoenaed if a patient was injured due to an equipment failure.

115. C) is correct. The skeletal muscles and the bone are attached by the tendons.

116. A) is correct. An itemized form listing CPT and ICD-10-CM codes in which the physician will indicate the services rendered to be submitted to the payer is called a superbill (also encounter form or charge slip).

117. C) is correct. Platelets, also known as thrombocytes, play an important role in blood clotting.

118. B) is correct. The patient in pelvic traction is on bed rest wearing a traction belt around the pelvis. This patient is the most immobile of the patients listed.

119. D) is correct. The kidneys filter the blood to remove waste products such as urea and creatinine, but if they are not working properly, these materials are not removed. This causes an elevation or buildup of BUN and creatinine in the blood.

120. C) is correct. *C. diff* is highly contagious, and soiled linens require special handling. The medical assistant should place all linens in a red biohazard bag and put them in the designated area for biohazard bags in the soiled utility area.

121. A) is correct. A side effect of levothyroxine is weight loss.

122. B) is correct. Initial order of assessment: circulation (feel for a pulse) → check the airway → look and listen for breathing.

123. E) is correct. Lacto-vegetarians eat milk, cheese, and dairy but no meat, fish, poultry, or eggs.

124. C) is correct. When dealing with an angry patient the medical assistant should remain calm and use a typical tone and volume of voice.

125. B) is correct. The procedures and level of care allowed by a health professional's certificate or license is known as their scope of practice.

126. B) is correct. If a patient has not been seen by the physician for a period of three years, their medical record should be filed as an inactive record.

127. C) is correct. Drug samples left by a pharmaceutical representative should be placed in a locked cabinet or drawer.

128. A) is correct. An accounts receivable report that lists unpaid customer debt in specific date ranges and can help a billing department with collection time frames is called an age analysis or aging of accounts.

129. D) is correct. The ear is lateral to the eye because it is farther from the midline of the face or body than the eye.

130. C) is correct. Viruses are responsible for the common cold, influenza, and HIV (human immunodeficiency virus).

131. B) is correct. Vitamin K is essential in the blood-clotting process.

132. E) is correct. Clonazepam (Klonopin) is a benzodiazepine.

133. B) is correct. Agoraphobia is the fear of crowds or public places.

134. A) is correct. In an arterial bleed, bleeding is often pulsatile and spurting.

135. A) is correct. Medical assistants can only administer controlled substances under direct supervision of a physician.

136. E) is correct. The wave scheduling method provides built-in flexibility to accommodate unforeseen situations, such as patients who end up needing more time with the physician than was allocated, late-arriving patients, or no-shows. This method involves scheduling three or four patients at the top of each hour.

137. C) is correct. An example of an expendable supply is an ink cartridge.

138. B) is correct. Monies owed to a business's creditors are called accounts payable.

139. C) is correct. Monocytes use phagocytosis to "swallow" and break down pathogens.

140. C) is correct. Standard precautions are recommended whenever the nurse comes in contact with blood or body fluids that could transmit blood-borne pathogens.

141. C) is correct. An uncomfortable feeling of pressure, squeezing, fullness, or pain in the center of the chest is the predominant symptom of an MI in women.

142. D) is correct. An adjustment refers to any changes in the patient's financial account unrelated to charges or payments. The most common type of adjustment is a credit adjustment or insurance write-off, often as a professional courtesy or insurance discount.

143. E) is correct. Rivaroxaban (Xarelto) is a blood thinner that helps prevent clots and DVT.

144. B) is correct. Painful burns with blistering are seen with second-degree burns. There is no blistering with first-degree burns. Third-degree burns often have charred skin present.

145. B) is correct. A sprain involves ligament damage. A strain involves muscle and tendon damage.

146. A) is correct. Examples of proper telephone etiquette include being polite and professional.

147. A) is correct. The law stating that an employer can be held responsible for the actions of their employees is known as respondeat superior, which is Latin for "let the master respond."

148. D) is correct. Gout patients should be on a low-purine diet. When the body digests purine, it creates uric acid as a waste. If uric acid blood levels go up, patients can develop a condition called gout. Gout occurs when painful uric acid crystals build up in the joint (often the great toe).

149. C) is correct. The patient schedule is a legal document, and medical assistants should carefully document any patient cancellations or no-shows in the schedule and in the patient's medical record to protect the physician from potential charges of patient abandonment and negligence.

150. E) is correct. The dorsal cavity contains the cranial and spinal cavities, both lined by meninges. The other organs are found in the ventral cavity.

151. A) is correct. Direct contact is the transmission of infectious agents through physical contact between two people, such as kissing.

152. C) is correct. The chief complaint is an example of subjective data, or data reported by the patient.

153. E) is correct. Milk is not considered a clear liquid.

154. B) is correct. In the antecubital fossa, the median cubital vein is a common site for a lab draw.

155. E) is correct. Fever is not a common side effect of cholesterol-lowering medications.

156. A) is correct. A head tilt/chin lift is the most common way to assess an airway. If a neck injury is suspected, a jaw thrust maneuver is instead recommended.

157. E) is correct. An order to appear in court is called a subpoena.

158. B) is correct. Urgent care facilities use the open office hours scheduling method, in which patients are seen in the order of their arrival.

159. C) is correct. CPT (current procedural terminology) codes are a numeric or alphanumeric medical code set, consisting of five characters, that is used to report medical, surgical, and diagnostic procedures and services to entities such as physicians, insurance companies, and accreditation organizations.

160. A) is correct. In patients with kyphosis, the upper back curves more than normal and can look rounded, humped, or hunched.

161. E) is correct. When questioning a patient through their interpreter, whether they cannot hear or do not speak English, one should always direct questions to the patient.

162. A) is correct. Social and occupational history details patients' habits, including tobacco use, alcohol use, drug use, occupation, and who lives with the patient (parents, spouse, etc.).

163. C) is correct. The needle should enter the skin at a 30-degree angle during venipuncture.

164. A) is correct. Antibiotics stop the growth of or kill bacteria.

165. E) is correct. The hamstring muscles are in the posterior thigh.

166. D) is correct. The ratio should be thirty chest compressions followed by two breaths for each

cycle of single-provider CPR, with a goal rate of one hundred compressions/minute.

167. B) is correct. When attempting to resolve conflicts with coworkers or patients in the medical office the medical assistant should not escalate the situation.

168. D) is correct. CLIA waived tests can be performed by anyone who follows the manufacturer's directions carefully under CLIA. These tests are deemed to be simple and have a low risk for erroneous results.

169. B) is correct. The carotid pulse is palpable lateral to the trachea; both carotid pulses should not be measured at the same time.

170. C) is correct. Upcoding is a form of fraudulent billing using a CPT code for a more expensive service than what was performed.

171. C) is correct. The skin must air-dry for thirty seconds after cleansing.

172. E) is correct. Stopping a benzodiazepine (such as lorazepam) can cause an end-of-use adverse reaction or withdrawal symptoms because the body has become dependent on the medication.

173. C) is correct. Hypertensive patients should be on a LOW-sodium diet. Salt can increase blood pressure and should be avoided in the diet of a hypertensive patient when possible.

174. D) is correct. A bachelor's degree (four-year college degree) is required to work as a medical technologist or clinical laboratory scientist.

175. C) is correct. Fluid-resistant gowns should be removed BEFORE leaving the patient's room to prevent spread of infection into the hallway.

176. D) is correct. Although the HCPCS level I code set is identical to the AMA's (American Medical Association) Current Procedural Terminology (CPT) code set, technically use of the Healthcare Common Procedure Coding System (HCPCS) is required when billing Medicaid or Medicare.

177. E) is correct. Alveoli are tiny air sacs at the ends of bronchioles. Their membrane is only one cell thick and is where oxygen is brought into the blood, as carbon dioxide is diffused out.

178. E) is correct. Linen that is lightly soiled can go in the dirty linen receptacle. However, linen that is heavily soiled by blood should be placed in a biohazard bag.

179. D) is correct. The normal respiratory rate is twelve to twenty breaths per minute. Tachypnea is abnormally rapid breathing, so more than twenty breaths per minute is considered tachypnea.

180. C) is correct. A two-hour postprandial urine is collected two hours after a meal to test for glycosuria.

181. B) is correct. *Sublingual* means "under the tongue." Nitroglycerin is often given this way. Ondansetron, a medication for nausea and vomiting, is also often administered sublingually.

182. B) is correct. This patient has signs of diabetes. A fingerstick glucose will screen for an elevated blood sugar.

183. B) is correct. Eosinophils are a type of white blood cell designed to attack multicellular parasites.

184. B) is correct. Orthostatic hypotension is a rapid drop in blood pressure when a patient changes position, from supine to sitting or sitting to standing. It is often caused by dehydration.

185. A) is correct. The medical assistant should make sure a patient does not use antibacterial mouthwash before a sputum specimen.

186. C) is correct. Intradermal injections are injected at 15 degrees with a 25 – 27-gauge needle.

187. D) is correct. An open fracture occurs when the fractured bone pokes through the skin.

188. E) is correct. HIV attacks helper T cells. If T cell levels get below 200, the patient has progressed to AIDS.

189. C) is correct. Albuterol is a bronchodilator that is used for treatment of asthma attacks.

190. B) is correct. The abdomen is not a dependable location to measure pulse oximetry.

191. B) is correct. Nasopharyngeal swabs are often used to test for RSV and influenza.

192. A) is correct. A filtered needle will prevent any broken glass from mixing with the medication as it is drawn into the syringe.

193. C) is correct. The parathyroid is responsible for controlling the calcium and phosphate levels in the blood. Each person has four parathyroid glands, located on the posterior surface of the thyroid gland.

194. C) is correct. A Pap smear collects cells from the cervix to test for human papillomavirus (HPV) and cervical cancer.

195. A) is correct. This describes a wet mount preparation. It is used to examine bacteria that normally move or live in a liquid environment.

196. B) is correct. 5 cc = 5 mL.

197. A) is correct. Pap smears should be labeled with the patient's name, date of birth, medical record number, and last menstrual cycle date.

198. C) is correct. Silence allows the patient time to think and reflect and lead the conversation in the desired direction.

199. E) is correct. Only the front of the gown from the waist up and arms is considered sterile.

200. A) is correct. In atrial flutter, there are no discernible P waves, and a distinct sawtooth wave pattern is present. The atrial rate is regular, and the PR interval is not measurable.

Follow the link below to access your online study resources:

www.ascenciatestprep.com/medical-assisting-online-resources

APPENDIX: MEDICAL TERMINOLOGY

Signs and Symptoms

agonal respiration: breathing pattern characterized by labored breathing, gasping, and myoclonus

anuria (anuresis): inability to urinate or production of < 100 mL of urine a day

aphasia: impairment in ability to speak, write, and understand others

bradycardia: slow heart rate

bradypnea: slow respiration rate

clonus: rhythmic, involuntary muscular spasms

cyanosis: blueish skin

diaphoresis: excessive sweating

diplopia: double vision

dysphagia: difficulty swallowing

dyspnea: difficulty breathing

dysuria: difficult or painful urination

ecchymosis: bruising

edema: swelling caused by excess fluid

epistaxis: bleeding from the nose

erythema: redness of the skin

febrile: related to fever

hematemesis: blood in vomit

hematochezia: bright red blood in stool

hematuria: blood in urine

hemoptysis: blood in expectorate from respiratory tract

hypercapnia: high levels of CO_2 in blood

hyperpyrexia: body temperature > 106.7°F (41.5°C)

hypertension: high blood pressure

hypotension: low blood pressure

hypoxemia: low levels of oxygen in the blood

ischemia: restricted blood flow to tissue

jaundice: yellowing of the skin or sclera

jerk: a quick, sudden movement

melena: dark, sticky digested blood in the stool

nocturia: excessive urination at night

oliguria: low urine output

orthopnea: dyspnea that occurs while lying flat

orthostatic (postural) hypotension: decrease in blood pressure after standing

otalgia: ear pain

otorrhea: drainage from the ear

pallor: pale appearance

petechiae: tiny red or brown spots on the skin caused by subcutaneous bleeding

polydipsia: excessive thirst

polyphagia: excessive hunger

polyuria: abnormally high urine output

presyncope: feeling of weakness and light-headedness

rhinorrhea: drainage from the nose

stridor: high-pitched wheezing sound caused by a disruption in airflow

syncope: temporary loss of consciousness

tachycardia: fast heart rate

tachypnea: fast respiratory rate

tinnitus: perception of sounds that are not present ("ringing in the ears")

urticaria: hives

vertigo: sensation of dizziness and loss of balance

Other Medical Terms

abate: become less in amount or intensity

abduction: the movement of a limb away from the body's midline

abrasion: an area of the skin damaged by scraping or wearing away

absorb: to take in

abstain: refrain; choose to avoid or not participate

access: means of approach or admission

acoustic: related to sound or hearing

acuity: sharpness of vision or hearing; mental quickness

adhere: hold closely to an idea or course; be devoted

adverse: harmful to one's interests; unfortunate

amalgam: a mixture or blend

ambulatory: able to walk

analgesic: a drug that relieves pain

anomaly: something unusual

apnea: temporary cessation of breathing

aseptic: free from bacteria and other pathogens

attenuate: to weaken

audible: loud enough to be heard

benign: not harmful; not malignant

bias: an unfair preference or dislike

bilateral: having two sides

cannula: a thin tube inserted into the body to collect or drain fluid

cardiac: pertaining to the heart

cephalic: relating to the head

chronic: persistent or recurring over a long time period

co-morbidity: two disorders that occur at the same time

cohort: a group of people who are treated as a group

complication: something intricate, involved, or aggravating

comply: acquiesce to another's wish, command, etc.

compression: pressing together

constrict: cause to shrink, cramp, crush

contingent: depending on something not certain; conditional

contraindication: discouragement of the use of a treatment

copious: abundant and plentiful

culture: the growth of microorganisms in an artificial environment

defecate: have a bowel movement

deleterious: harmful or deadly to living things

depress: weaken; sadden

depth: deepness; distance measured downward, inward, or backward

dermal: relating to skin

deter: to prevent or discourage

deteriorating: growing worse; reducing in worth; impairing

diagnosis: analysis of a present condition

dilate: expand; make larger

dilute: weaken by a mixture of water or other liquid; reduce in strength

elevate: raise; lift up

empathy: understanding of another's feelings

endogenous: something produced within the body

enervating: causing debilitation or weakness

enhance: to improve; to increase clarity

enteral: relating to the small intestine

ephemeral: lasting only for a short period of time

exacerbate: make more bitter, angry, or violent; irritate or aggravate

excess: the state of being more or too much; a surplus or remainder

exogenous: something produced outside the body

exposure: the state of being exposed or open to external environments

external: located outside of something and/or apart from something

fatal: causing death or ruin

fatigue: weariness from physical or mental exertion

flaccid: soft; flabby

flushed: suffused with color; washed out with a copious flow of water

focal: centered in one area

gaping: to be open; to have a break in continuity

gastric: relating to the stomach

hepatic: relating to the liver

hydration: the act of meeting body fluid demands

hygiene: the science that deals with the preservation of health

imminent: very likely to happen

impaired: made worse, damaged, or weakened

incidence: frequency or range of occurrence; extent of effects

incompatible: unable to be or work together

infection: tainted with germs or disease

inflamed: condition in which the body is inflicted with heat, swelling, and redness

ingest: take into the body for digestion

initiate: set going; begin; originate

innocuous: harmless

intact: remaining uninjured, unimpaired, whole, or complete

internal: situated within something; enclosed; inside

invasive: being intrusive or encroaching upon

labile: unstable

laceration: a rough tear; an affliction

languid: tired and slow

latent: hidden; dormant; undeveloped

lethargic: not wanting to move; sluggish

longevity: having a long life

malady: a disease or disorder

malaise: a general feeling of illness or discomfort

malignant: harmful

manifestation: a demonstration or display

musculoskeletal: pertaining to muscles and the skeleton

neurologic: dealing with the nervous system

neurovascular: pertaining to the nervous system and blood vessels

nexus: a connection or series of onnections

nutrient: something affording nutrition

obverse: the opposite

occluded: shut in or out; closed; absorbed

occult: hidden

ossify: to harden

overt: plain to the view; open

palliate: to lessen symptoms without treating the underlying cause

paroxysmal: having to do with a spasm or violent outburst

pathogenic: causing disease

pathology: the science of the nature and origin of disease

posterior: located in the back or rear

potent: wielding power; strong; effective

pragmatic: concerned with practical matters and results

precaution: an act done in advance to ensure safety or benefit; prudent foresight

predispose: give a tendency or inclination to; dispose in advance

preexisting: already in place; already occurring

primary: first; earliest; most important

prognosis: a forecast

rationale: rational basis for something; justification

recur: appear again; return

regress: to return to a former state

renal: pertaining to the kidneys

resect: to remove or cut out

resilient: quick to recover

respiration: breathing

restrict: attach limitations to; restrain

retain: hold or keep in possession, use, or practice

shunt: a tube that diverts the path of a fluid in the body

soporific: a drug that induces sleep

status: relative standing; position; condition

stenosis: narrowing of a passage

sublingual: beneath the tongue

subtle: understated, not obvious

succumb: to stop resisting

superficial: shallow in character and attitude; only concerned with things on the surface

supplement: an addition to something substantially completed; to add to

suppress: restrain; abolish; repress

symmetric: similar proportion in the size or shape of something

symptom: a sign or indication of a problem or disease

syndrome: a set of symptoms that characterize a certain disease or condition

systemic: affecting the whole body

therapeutic: pertaining to the curing of disease; having remedial effect

transdermal: passing through the skin

transient: lasting for only a short time or duration

transmission: the act or result of sending something along or onward to a recipient or destination

trauma: a bodily injury or mental shock

triage: the act of sorting or categorizing conditions and diseases in preparation for treatment

unilateral: relating to only one side

vascular: pertaining to bodily ducts that convey fluid

virus: an agent of infection

vital: pertaining to life; alive; essential to existence or well-being

void: empty; evacuate

volume: the amount of space occupied by a substance

Made in the USA
Monee, IL
07 July 2020